Both Prayed to the Same God

"The Almighty has His
own purpose..."
(A. Lincoln)

[handwritten signature]

Both Prayed to the Same God

Religion and Faith in the American Civil War

Robert J. Miller

LEXINGTON BOOKS

A division of
ROWMAN & LITTLEFIELD PUBLISHERS, INC.
Lanham • Boulder • New York • Toronto • Plymouth, UK

LEXINGTON BOOKS

A division of Rowman & Littlefield Publishers, Inc.
A wholly owned subsidiary of The Rowman & Littlefield Publishing Group, Inc.
4501 Forbes Boulevard, Suite 200
Lanham, MD 20706

Estover Road
Plymouth PL6 7PY
United Kingdom

British Library Cataloguing in Publication Information Available

Library of Congress Cataloging-in-Publication Data

Miller, Robert J., 1950–
  Both prayed to the same God : religion and faith in the American Civil War / Robert J.
Miller.
    p. cm.
  Includes bibliographical references and index.
  ISBN-13: 978-0-7391-2055-2 (cloth : alk. paper)
  ISBN-10: 0-7391-2055-7 (cloth : alk. paper)
  ISBN-13: 978-0-7391-2056-9 (pbk. : alk. paper)
  ISBN-10: 0-7391-2056-5 (pbk. : alk. paper)
  1. United States—History—Civil War, 1861–1865—Religious aspects. 2. United
States—Religion—19th century. I. Title.
  E635.M55 2007
  973.7'1—dc22   2007023936

Printed in the United States of America

♾™ The paper used in this publication meets the minimum requirements of American
National Standard for Information Sciences—Permanence of Paper for Printed Library
Materials, ANSI/NISO Z39.48–1992.

Dedication

As with many "projects" in life, this book could not have been written without the support and assistance of others. There are many people to whom I want to express my deepest gratitude for helping achieve this long-awaited dream of putting *Both Prayed to the Same God* into print. It is to them that I dedicate this book.

To those who read the original manuscript and offered invaluable corrections and comments—*James McPherson, Mark Noll, Jerry Marshall, Fr. Tom Blantz* (CSC) and *Fr. Harry Grile* (C.SS.R.)

To the Holy Cross community at Corby Hall in Notre Dame, whose gracious hospitality on my January–July 2006 sabbatical provided a pleasant home and fertile place to rest, relax, research and write

To my CWRT friends *Bruce Allardice* (for his experienced editorial "nit-picking" and helpful manuscript suggestions), *Rob Girardi* (for the cover image, indexing, text additions, and invaluable insights) and *Jerry and JoEllyn Kowalski* (for a Round Table friendship that has become a true fellowship in Faith)

To my high school teacher *Fr. Ed Cosgrove C.SS.R.* (who first lit the fire of a love for American History), my *family and friends* (who patiently tolerate and support my history "addiction"), and especially *John Siefken* (Civil War aficionado who *"fought the good fight"* better than most)

To the exceptional, dedicated members of the *Civil War Round Table of Chicago* for friendship, camaraderie and support for the vision and dream of *Both Prayed to the Same God.*

To all those laboring to preserve our endangered Civil War battlefields, and those who meet faithfully to provide places where memories of the American Civil War are kept alive

To our ancestors who lived the history we only write about—the soldiers, civilians, slaves, freedmen, pastors, theologians and political leaders of mid-nineteenth-century America—and to the awesome Lord of all History who somehow *"makes everything work out for good."*

Contents

Any history of that army which omits an account
of the wonderful influence of religion upon it—
which fails to tell how the courage,
discipline and morale of the whole
was influenced by
the humble piety and evangelical piety
of many of its officers and men—
would be incomplete and unsatisfactory.

J. William Jones, *Christ in Camp*

Preface

As he waited to go into action at Vicksburg on May 19, 1863, a private in the 37th Mississippi Volunteer Infantry wrote in his diary:

> I took out my Bible and read it with peculiar interest, especially the 91st Psalm, and felt that I could claim the promise therein contained. Indeed I was both spiritually and physically strengthened, and believed I could go into battle without a dread as to consequences. Was determined to discharge my duty both to my God and my country.

The verses from the King James version of Psalm 91 that strengthened this soldier undoubtedly included this one: "*I will say of the Lord, He is my refuge and my fortress: my God; in Him will I trust.*" This soldier was far from unique. Thousands of his fellows in both the Confederate and Union armies carried Bibles and sought their comfort on the eve of battle. They trusted in God; they prayed to Him; and so did their families back home. Many soldiers, like this Mississippian, associated God with country and expressed their determination to keep faith with both.

The Civil War was not a war of religion; it did not pit one faith against another. As Abraham Lincoln said in his second inaugural address, both sides "read the same Bible, and pray to the same God." But religion permeated the war effort on the battlefield and the home front. The Second Great Awakening among Protestant denominations, and the large-scale immigration from Ireland and the German states in the antebellum decades had generated dynamic energy and growth among both Protestant and Roman Catholic denominations. Even though the United States and the Confederate states did not fight a religious war against each other, religious convictions helped fuel their determination to fight. Clergy and laity alike, in North as well as South, believed that God was on their side.

But as Lincoln noted, also in his second inaugural address, North and South could not both be right. In fact, he suggested, perhaps neither was right. "The Almighty has his own purposes," said the Union president. His main purpose in this war seemed to be the abolition of slavery. To accomplish that purpose, he sent this "mighty scourge of war" to a guilty nation—North as well as South. And if God willed that the war continue

> until all the wealth piled by the bond-man's two hundred and fifty years of unrequited toil shall be sunk, and until every drop of blood drawn with the lash, shall be paid by another drawn with the sword, as was said three thousand years ago, so still it must be said "the judgments of the Lord, are true and righteous altogether."

The four million slaves certainly believed that God was on the side of freedom in this war. In their view, God had raised up Father Abraham as a modern Moses to open their way to the Promised Land. America's enslaved population had also passed through a Great Awakening of religious conversion in the nineteenth century. Unlike white people in North and South, the black population experienced the Civil War not as punishment for the sin of slavery but as a triumphant moment of religious as well as secular liberation.

Of the thousands of books written about the American Civil War, few have focused on its crucial religious dimensions. Robert Miller has done much to remedy that deficiency in this important volume. Readers will find here the stories of believers—and even skeptics—in North and South, of Protestants and Catholics and Jews, of clergy and laypersons, of soldiers and civilians, chaplains and generals, men and women, slaves and free people, woven together in a tapestry that offers a vivid picture of the importance of religion in the Civil War.

James M. McPherson

Introduction

> "Both read the same Bible and pray to the same God, and each invokes His aid against the other ... The prayers of both could not be answered. That of neither has been answered fully. The Almighty has His own purposes."
>
> Abraham Lincoln, Second Inaugural Address

"In the beginning . . ."

It was in 1983 that my love affair with the American Civil War began. Always a history buff (a welcome hobby in my fulltime task as a Catholic priest), in the spring of 1983 I was preaching in Vicksburg, MS, and had a rare chance to take a personal guided tour of the Vicksburg battlefield. From that time on, the events and people of the Civil War era became as familiar to me as my own neighbors and family. Before long, I had read all the "classic" books, gone on battlefield tours, heard excellent Civil War talks, and walked the "sacred ground" of places like Gettysburg, Shiloh, Antietam, Manassas, Champion Hill, and Kenesaw. After joining the Chicago Civil War Round Table, I had the privilege of recently being President of this august group—which included organizing battlefield tours of the Atlanta and Vicksburg Campaigns, as well as coordinating a marvelous slate of speakers for the 2005–2006 year.

But as these years of Civil War interest rolled by, I gradually began to perceive a vacuum in what I was seeing and reading. There were books on every wartime topic and battle imaginable, but something was missing from this glut of Civil War materials. It was the spiritual element was strangely absent—in this most deadly of all American wars, there were few places or people that chronicled the human spirit's search for eternal meanings and higher purposes, for Divine inspiration and justification.

Throughout history, religion and faith have always deeply impacted the human race, and this was especially true in our unique North American heritage. Religion and faith were inextricably linked to the very foundations of the United States, and historically have remained a key underpinning for our society. Spiritual forces also kindled the fire of revival in isolated locales, brought solace to all classes and colors in times of woe, gave purpose and meaning to lost souls, offered challenges to societal attitudes, and provided the anchor of "holy ritual" (i.e., funerals, weddings, baptisms) in the tragedies and joys of life. All of this was never truer than in the tumultuous mid-nineteenth century of the United States of America.

Thus, several years ago I concluded that it was not enough to just analyze Civil War battles in stunningly obsessive detail, or walk the exact paths that attacking troops took at Gettysburg. It was not enough to study in painstaking detail new insights on some Southern general's approach at a specific 1863 battle, or argue yet again why the North won (or the South lost). True devotees of the American Civil War must look into the hearts and souls of our long-lost but unforgotten antebellum ancestors, to try and touch those *spiritual motivations* that brought them to the moral impasse of slavery, encouraged them forward into horrific battles, and sustained them in the "terrors of the night." For it is the human soul—touched by the indefinable "spark" of Divinity, containing the "fingerprint of the Sacred"—which in the end contains our greatest hopes, and encourages our most profound dreams. This is as true and real today as it was in 1861. The spiritual story of those Civil War soldiers, preachers, politicians and civilians who wrestled in their souls with the momentous challenges of their day simply begs to be told.

Oh, thou heart-searching God, we trust that thou sees we are pursuing those rights which were guaranteed to us by the solemn covenants of our fathers, and which were cemented by their blood.

Rev. Basil Manly at Confederate Convention (February 4, 1861)

A perspective on the topic

Thus, this research project on Civil War religion began, and eventually (thanks to a sabbatical at Notre Dame University) came into book form. I write from two very personal perspectives—*first,* as a lifelong student and amateur historian of Civil War history; and *second* as an ordained Catholic clergyman, trained in Church history and theology, and rooted in thirty years of pastoral ministry. As such, I approach this topic not from an academic religious or history paradigm, but rather from a "popular history" perspective of a dedicated (and passionate!) generalist. In other words, *Both Prayed to the Same God* is purposely intended to be scholarly and informative but not academic or esoteric. Extensive research has been done to clearly chronicle the essential features which comprise the religious aspect of the Civil War, yet information is presented in a way and style which will hopefully attract all types of audiences—academics, historians, popular readers, and Civil War aficionados.

It has been my privilege to draw upon the scattered works of numerous historians and religious scholars over the past decades, many of whom are mentioned in the "further reading recommendations" list of each chapter. But, *Both Prayed to the Same God* is really rather unique in the teeming field of Civil War literature. It is one of the first books whose entire focus is on a broad and widely encompassing overview of religion and faith in America's Civil War.[1] While a number of previous books touch on interesting fringes or localized aspects of the topic, most Civil War books tend to ignore religion and faith, marginalize it, or limit it to a few sentences about chaplains or soldiers' desperate prayers. There was a clear need to research the ignored material, and then make the basic issues and perspectives which make up this crucial topic available in one volume. Thus, this book has a twofold purpose—both of which reflect the motives under which this "magnificent obsession" of an idea came into birth in the first place.

Did You Know...

The American Civil War has been known by some thirty different names? These are some: War between the States, Mr. Lincoln's War, the Second American Revolution, the Great Rebellion, the War for the Union, the Brothers' War, the War to Suppress Northern Arrogance, the Yankee Invasion, the Lost Cause, and the War of Northern Aggression?

Apologia

First, the reader will find the author an unabashed *apologist* for the issue of Civil War religion. The story of the impact of religion and faith during the War simply demands to be brought out of the shadows and into the light. With churches being the dominant national influence on Americans in the mid-nineteenth century, with perhaps as many as one-half of all soldiers taking religion very seriously, with the nation's preachers and denominations leading the charge into disunity and separation—how can anyone today claim to be a "Civil War buff" and yet ignore the overwhelming role that religion had? In the mid-nineteenth century, people numerically heard more homilies than received pieces of mail in any year. Nearly every American believed in God and accepted the God's Laws and Presence as one of Life's givens. To somehow ignore the soldiers' desperate faith, the preachers' intense moralizing, the two Presidents' Days of Prayer and "conversion experiences," the church's spiritual and clerical support, the civilians' charitable work, the black spirituals about freedom—to ignore all this is to miss seeing the huge elephant standing in one's living room.

Perhaps the topic has been long ignored because of the problematic nature of religion's role in our personal, societal and national lives in recent generations. As this twenty-first century dawns, more people are conflicted about the role of religion and spirituality in their own lives (as well as in our national life) than at any other time in our history. We live now in a highly sceptical, postmodern age—where "de-construction" of past absolutes is the norm. Mistrust of all authority is presumed, a sense of Tradition and Transcendence has been lost, cynicism and pessimism about life is universal, and youth have troubles with "absolutes," boundaries and commitment to anything lasting or historical.

All this is indeed a radically different world than the 1860 Civil War era—where Tradition had enormous meaning, basic respect for institutions was implicit, boundaries were expected and generally respected, and religion and faith were accepted as foundational to all of life. Perhaps renowned historian Eugene Genovese captures best the need for a book like this in an age like this:

> In this secular, not to say cynical, age few tasks present greater difficulty than that of compelling the well educated to take religious matters serious. Yet, for all except the most recent phase of the history of a minority of the world's peoples, religion has been embedded in the core of human life, material as well as spiritual. Bishop Berkeley spoke a simple truth: "Whatever the world thinks, he hath not meditated upon God, the human mind, and the 'summum bonum' may possibly make a thriving earthworm, but will most indubitably make a sorry patriot and a sorry statesman."[2]

During Union Gen. John Foster's "march" towards Wilmington NC, a chaplain from Massachusetts talked with a wounded soldier of the 3d NY Artillery. The chaplain asked the soldier "Were you supported by divine grace?" The tough soldier replied "No, we were supported by the 9th New Jersey."

Cited in James M. McPherson, *For Cause and Comrades* (1997)

Overview

Secondly, *Both Prayed to the Same God* is intended to be an *overview* of the topic—a comprehensive summary of the central issues which frame the topic of religion and faith in the American Civil War. As an overview, this work is not intended to be chronological religious history of the War, nor an in-depth analysis of the finer shades of these issues, nor a deep delving into the theology, morality, denominational minutiae, public records, private journals or ecclesiastical histories of the time. Others have done great work here already, and hopefully more will be forthcoming in years ahead.

It is my limited goal to undertake a well-researched summary of the dominant features and central themes which make up the area of religion, faith, morality in the War between the States. These thematic overviews will be more clearly outlined in the opening chapter, but it may be helpful to the reader to immediately grasp the "idée fixe," or basic underlying themes, running throughout the entire book. These are the central premises which form the underpinning of this book—giving shape, scope, and depth to the material ahead.

(1) *The most undeveloped and ignored area of Civil War studies* is the impact that Religion and Faith had upon this conflict. It has indeed been an "elephant" hiding in the closet of Civil War research, writing, and preservation.

(2) *It was an extremely devout country that went into the Civil War.* From the very beginning of the United States, we have been "awash in a sea of faith," with religion playing an enormous role in the development of our American entire culture and life. George Marsden has said that "American history recounted without its religious history is like Moby Dick without the whale."

(3) *In the pre-war decades (1840–1850s), religious divisiveness paved the way for political division.* Religion and faith was used to rationalize the motives of both sides, support both Southern slavery and Northern abolitionism, inflame the country's increasingly inflammatory rhetoric, and encourage sectarian divisiveness.

(4) *During the War itself, the single greatest institution in maintaining morale among soldiers was faith in God.* Faith had enormous role in motivation and attitudes of a huge number of soldiers—as many as one-half of all soldiers by one estimate. During the war, chaplains labored valiantly, civilians gave millions in charitable support, and slaves clung to their "invisible institution."

(5) *After the War, religion and faith continued to play a significant role* in shaping how the conflict was remembered, empowering freedmen for new worship opportunities, and providing a framework for the great "theological" document to come out of that era.

It is my most sincere hope that the pages ahead will help validate the importance of the entire subject to the larger Civil War community, as well as assist scholars and popular readers alike to more clearly see the shape of the elephant standing before us. In working to bring this topic to a more prominent position in contemporary Civil War studies, I also would hope that this work may inspire further research, interest and study of religion and faith in the mid-nineteenth-century era. There is indeed much more to be "mined" out of this rich field of gold—the ultimate, eternal Transcendent Values which gave our nineteenth-century ancestors a purpose for living, dying and fighting in this country's most tragic era.

Our Thanksgiving Day celebration began during the Civil War. On October 3, 1863, a proclamation by Abraham Lincoln officially established this day, in no small measure due to the advocacy of Sarah Josepha Hale, a prominent writer and editor of the popular magazine *Godey's Lady's Book.*

Library of Congress Civil War Desk Reference (2002)

Notes

1. The other books dedicated to this topic in its broadest perspective are *Religion and the American Civil War*, edited by Randall Miller, Harry S. Stout, and Charles Reagan Wilson (New York: Oxford University Press, 1998); Stephen Woodworth, *While God is Marching On—The Religious Life of Civil War Soldiers* (Lawrence, Kan.: University Press of Kansas, 2001), and Gardiner Shattuck Jr., *A Shield and Hiding Place: The Religious Life of the Civil War Armies* (Macon, GA: Mercer University Press, 1987). *Religion and the American Civil War* is an excellent series of compiled essays that approach the topic in a broad-based way, and the latter two books more narrowly focus on the solder's religious life and not on the larger religious aspects of the Civil War.

2. Eugene Genovese, *Roll, Jordan, Roll—The World the Slaves Made* (New York: Vintage Books, 1976), 161.

Section One

ELEPHANT IN THE LIVING ROOM

The sort of sustained, productive attention that has been paid to religion in the colonial period, the Revolutionary era and the modern age is simply not present for the Civil War. Despite the uncontested and unrivaled centrality of the Civil War in American history, despite its importance for both the history of the South and the history of African-Americans, and despite its nearly mythic place in the popular mind . . . surprisingly little attention has been devoted to the war as a religious experience and event. Religious language and imagery were not just words and abstractions. People used them to survive and interpret the war and to build new lives after the war. Therein lies one of the principal 'truths' about religion and the Civil War and one of the principal roads worth taking in thinking about the meaning of the war.

Randall Miller, *Religion and the American Civil War* (1998)

Chapter One

THE IGNORED CIVIL WAR

> Americans were a religious people. Not only did they attend church but they also sought divine sanction for their social and political views . . . The country's most socially and politically influential leaders were either committed Christians themselves or demonstrated that they knew their politically decisive constituents to be so.
>
> Eugene Genovese, *Religion and the American Civil War* (1998)

Seeing the elephant

There is an elephant in the Civil War living room. The throngs of Civil War afficionados tromping through America's preserved battlefields rarely see it. Most avid amateur Civil War "students" never read about it. The ever-growing flood of Civil War literature mostly chooses to ignore it. Even professionals like the National Park Service, prominent historians, famous authors and glib speakers tend to gloss quickly over it. What is this "elephant" that so many disregard, despite recent surges in Civil War interest? It is the topic of *religion, faith, morality, and America's churches in the Civil War.* For decades, the Civil War community has generally tended to avoid or peripheralize some historically significant facts from that era—that for a great majority of mid-nineteenth century soldiers and citizens, religion and faith was one of the most deeply influential forces in life; and that in America's greatest conflict, religion and faith played a profoundly important and noteworthy role. That religious influence includes these elements:

- helping by rhetoric to divide the nation prior to the War
- preparing the way for secession by denominational divisiveness
- providing political and moral justification through theology and Scripture
- rationalizing the underlying motives of each respective side
- supporting sectarian divisiveness throughout War
- bolstering and maintaining civilian support for the War
- ministering to soldiers' spiritual and material wartime needs
- encouraging soldiers to go forward despite horror and death
- promoting and continuing divisiveness after the War

Few other topics have been less written about or least discussed than the role that religion and faith played in America's Civil War. In 1994 one historian estimated that some fifty thousand books and articles had been written on the War. If so, that number has surely doubled since then with an onslaught of new writings in the past decade. The gamut of Civil War-related literature books, movies, and assorted material is broad and far-reaching—from movies to historical novels, CDs to DVDs, personal biographies to war diaries, tactical/strategic analyses to books on uniforms, food, sex, medicine, and more. But somehow, this overwhelming body of work seems to have focused on everything *but* religion and faith. Consistently ignored have been books, articles, museum exhibits, presentations, symposia, and in-depth research on areas such as:

- how faith motivated mid-nineteenth-century American soldiers and society
- religion's political and social impact before, during and after the Civil War
- how denominational divisiveness presaged and provoked the secession crisis
- the vital role religion played for Lincoln, Davis and "Lost Cause" advocates

---

Ken Burns' 1990 Civil War documentary frequently quoted Elisha Hunt Rhodes (2nd RI). But nothing in the documentary gave any hint of the fact that Rhodes was a deeply religious man, attended church regularly, and journaled frequently on religious topics. "Neither his religion or that of the other soldiers seemed to matter in that series . . . The marginalized role to which religion has been relegated in modern America has made the vital faith of past generations almost invisible to students of history."

Steven E. Woodworth, *While God is Marching On* (2001)

Historian James Moorhead comments accurately that "religion in the Civil War has not so much been debated among historians as it has been ignored. Of the thousands of titles dealing with the Civil War, surprisingly few address the significant role that religion has in framing the issues of the conflict." In his introduction to *Religion and the Civil War* (a 1998 book that has helped fill the gap on this topic), Randall Miller phrases the predicament succinctly:

> The sort of sustained, productive attention that has been paid to religion in the colonial period, the Revolutionary era, and the modern age is simply not present for the Civil War. Despite the uncontested and unrivaled centrality of the Civil War in American history, despite its importance for both the history of the south and the history of African Americans, despite its nearly mythic place in the popular mind (as seen in the massive continuing interest of the Ken Burns series), surprisingly little attention has been devoted to the war as a religious experience and event. [1]

Pulitzer-winning historian James McPherson contends as well that the religious aspect of the Civil War has too long been ignored. He notes that because the American Civil War was *not* a war of religion, historians have tended to overlook the degree to which it *was* a religious war. "Union and Confederate soldiers alike were

4

heirs of the Second Great Awakening. Civil War armies were, arguably, the most religious in American history. And these convictions were not confined to the armies . . . a heightened religious consciousness infused the home fronts as well." McPherson goes on to clearly challenge future historians to study in greater depth the religious history of the Civil War. "Religion was central to the meaning of the Civil War, as the generation that experienced the war tried to understand it. Religion should also be central to our efforts to recover that meaning." [2]

God is our only refuge and our strength . . . Let us confess our many sins, and beseech him to give us a higher courage, a purer patriotism and more determined will: that he will convert the hearts of our enemies; that he will hasten the time when war, with its sorrows and sufferings, shall cease, and that he will give us a name and place among the nations of the earth.

Gen. Robert E. Lee, General Orders #83, August 13, 1863

Building on the past

Until very recently, the topic of religion and faith generally has laid on the outer periphery of Civil War studies. In the past few decades, some excellent historical work was done treating interesting "corners" on the theme of Civil War religion. In 1985 C.C. Goen wrote on the role of denominational schisms in bringing about the War, and Gardiner Shattuck in 1987 on the religious life of the opposing armies. James Silver wrote in the 1950's on the Southern churches' role in bringing on secession and promoting the War, and James Moorhead in 1976 gave the Northern perspective with the apocalyptic fervor of Yankee Protestants. In 1980 Charles Reagan Wilson published a fascinating study of the religious roots of the Lost Cause.[3] Various scattered monographs and articles detailing diverse religious aspects of the war have also been published throughout the past decades.[4]

Recent years have seen further significant contributions trickling into the field. The religious world of Civil War soldiers was detailed by Steven Woodworth, and Confederate soldiers' religious faith by Kent Dollar and John Brinsfield, Jr., with marvelous books on Civil War chaplains being published in 1998, 2003 and 2006.[5] Further "corners" of the field continue to be documented, with a recent focus on works that help recover the broader social and cultural histories surrounding the War. Studies have been done in areas such as the slaveholders' worlds, the role of religion in the antebellum period, the faith of Lincoln and his Second Inaugural, Southern ideologies and attitudes, etc.[6] Within the past two years, excellent books by Mark Noll and Harry Stout have made significant contributions to the field (as we shall see later). But taken together, there still is no comprehensive overview of the topic as a whole. As one author phrases it well, "The religious history of the Civil War has yet to be written." The book that comes closest, taking the most wide-ranging and inclusive approach towards the topic are the sixteen excellent essays collected in the 1998 book *Religion and the American Civil War.* [7]

In that book, Harry Stout and Christopher Grasso speak of interesting changes occurring in the Civil War literature of more recent vintage. "After a century of domination by political and military historians, professional and antiquarian, the war is at last recognized for the 'total' event that it was . . . entirely new histories are appearing that tell the other stories, the stories of noncombatants at war." However, the two authors go on to mention that some of these studies are not without shortcomings, noting that

> religion in these studies seems to remain an unchanged "evangelical" presence, formed in the antebellum period, surviving in the post-bellum period, and static in between. In fact, combatant and noncombatant southerners were very much caught up with religion; it not only shaped their public and private discourse but did so in dramatically different ways between 1861–1865. [We need to] bring religion onto center stage and see it as the dynamic process it was. [8]

Stout and Grasso's main point is well-made. Religion and faith should not be seen as merely a peripheral "add-on" to the reality of the War—an "Oh, by the way" tangent attached to the "real" history of battles, generals and soldiers. As both an influential institutional presence in America and an enormously meaningful personal experience, religion and faith were central to the meaning and understanding of the events of the mid-nineteenth century. Too often, however, the values and institution of religion have been seen as mere side-stage props in the main-stage military or political drama that the War years were. It is time for a change in attitude. Religion and faith must be brought out from the wings onto center stage, and seen as the dynamic, influential, motivational force it was during the War years.

Without the [Southern] clergy's active endorsement of secession and war, there could have not been a Confederate nation. Christianity represented the most powerful cultural system in the Old South. Without Christian legitimation, there could be no sense of rightness.

Harry Stout and Christopher Grasso, *Religion and the American Civil War* (1998)

The shape of the elephant

As we begin to focus upon this ubiquitous elephant in our Civil War living room, we first must become aware of the shape, size and contour of this hidden creature. The chapters ahead will present succinct overviews of a number of the crucial religious events, spiritual themes and faith-based activities which had such a dramatic impact upon the Civil War. Some are directly connected to the War's origin. Others detail crucial background material, thus helping illuminate wartime attitudes and actions. In some way, all of them relate to how the War was argued, prosecuted, fought, understood, and coped with. All of them help define the "shape of our elephant," so to speak—the key religious issues, trajectories and perspectives which need to be factored into any true and full history of our "War between the States."

What follows in the chapters ahead is not intended to be exhaustive of the topics mentioned herein, but merely suggestive and evocative. Its purpose is to stimulate reflection about the powerfully archetypal themes of God, spirituality, religion, belief, courage, and faith which run through human history in general—and our greatest American conflict in specific. Here then, in brief, are the beginning contours of this "invisible elephant" of Civil War religion and faith—a summary of the central religious issues comprising this long ignored and forgotten topic.

- *America's "first truly moral encounter."* The Great Paradox of America was the development of race-based slavery at the same time that ideals of liberty and freedom developed. This Paradox led to a moral impasse in America, and the subsequent War that followed was the bitter fruit of our first truly moral encounter as a nation. The effects remain with us today.

- *The role of religion in antebellum America.* In de Tocqueville's words, religion was "the foremost of the political institutions" of early America. No other antebellum group had as much power to regularly influence the greatest numbers of citizens as did America's clerical religious leaders. It was a deeply religious country that went to war in 1861.

- *Role of the Bible.* The Bible was America's most read and valued book, yet because of a unique "democratic way" of interpretation, at this time of conflict, it was not only unable to provide guidance, but even helped divide the country. What the Bible said about slavery caused serious theological conflicts for church and country.

- *Religious divisiveness.* As the country was dividing economically and socially, it was also growing apart religiously. The increasingly heated rhetoric over abolitionism and slavery led to the three largest religious de-

7

nominations in America splitting many years before actual fighting ever broke out. Their divisions paved the way for what was to come.

● *Religious support systems.* Religion, faith and churches provided amazing systems of support for Americans whether slave or free. Black Americans sought Exodus freedom, religious chaplains ministered in powerful ways, religious-inspired giving and charity made significant war-time contributions.

● *War-time effects of revivalism.* America had just emerged from the Second Great Awakening. As the war grew longer and deadlier, religious revival came to play an enormous role for both troops and armies. While Southern revivals perhaps lengthened the war, many prominent leaders were touched by faith during the war years.

● *Post-war influences.* Following the war, religion's impact continued. It became the moral foundation of the "Lost Cause," whose greatest proponent was a Baptist minister. The war also brought about a gradual "masculinization" of religion, a literal explosion of black church life, and saw the development of a new civil religion of national unity and patriotism.

● *The religious impact of Lincoln's faith.* Though Lincoln's religious beliefs are much discussed, he was undoubtedly a faith-filled man who acknowledged God's role in his life, and became more faith-motivated as President. His Second Inaugural Address is the most profound religious and theological document of the war.

Christianity is a national religion . . . Almost all of the American people profess to respect Christianity, and appeal to its precepts as a test of morals, and as furnishing us with the rules of life.

Moses Stuart, *Conscience and the Constitution* (1850)

Further reading recommendations

Kent T. Dollar. "Introduction." Pp. 1–12 in *Soldiers of the Cross: Confederate Soldier-Christians and the Impact of the War on their Faith*. Macon: Mercer University Press, 2005.

James M. McPherson. "Afterward." Pp. 408–412 in *Religion in the American Civil War*, edited by Randall M. Miller, Harry S. Stout, and Charles Reagan Wilson. New York: Oxford University Press, 1998.

Randall M. Miller. "Introduction." Pp. 3–18 in *Religion in the American Civil War*, edited by Randall M. Miller, Harry S. Stout, and Charles Reagan Wilson. New York: Oxford University Press, 1998.

Gardiner Shattuck Jr. *A Shield and Hiding Place: The Religious Life of the Civil War Armies*. Macon, GA: Mercer University Press, 1987.

Steven Woodworth. *While God is Marching On—The Religious World of Civil War Soldiers*. Lawrence: University Press of Kansas, 2001.

Notes

1. James Howell Moorhead, "Religion in the Civil War: The Northern Side," http://nhc.rtp.nc.us:8080/tserve/nineteen/nkeyinfo/cwnorth.htm, National Humanities Center, October 2000. Randall Miller, "Introduction," in *Religion in the American Civil War*, edited by Randall M. Miller, Harry S. Stout, and Charles Reagan Wilson, (New York: Oxford University Press, 1998), 3.

2. James M. McPherson, "Afterward," in *Religion in the American Civil War, op. cit.*, 409, 412.

3. James W. Silver, *Confederate Morale and Church Propaganda* (Tuscaloosa, AL.: The Confederate Publishing Company, 1967); James H. Moorhead, *American Apocalypse – Yankee Protestants and the Civil War, 1860–1869* (New Haven CT: Yale University Press, 1978); C.C. Goen, *Broken Churches, Broken Nation—Denominational Schisms and the Coming of the Civil War* (Macon, Ga.: Mercer University Press, 1985); Gardiner I. Shattuck, *A Shield and Hiding Place: The Religious Life of the Civil War Armies* (Macon, GA.: Mercer University Press, 1987) and Charles Reagan Wilson, *Baptized in Blood—The Religion of the Lost Cause* (Athens: University of Georgia Press, 1980).

4. Articles have appeared in a wide variety of localized and national publications sporadically through the years, dealing with topics such as revivals in the armies, the religion of such people as Stonewall Jackson, the role of the Sanitary and Christian Commissions, chaplain's work, etc. Interesting peripheral topics that have been explored are the religious concerns of southern women and southern slaveholders, and specific denominationally-slanted reflections and studies in church-affiliated journals. Two examples of entire magazines being

dedicated to the topic are the cluster of articles published in *Christian History*, No. 33 (1992) and in *Books and Culture: A Christian Review*, July/August 2003, 16–37.

5. Warren B. Armstrong (*For Courageous Fighting and Confident Dying*); John W. Brinsfield; William C. Davis; Bernard Maryniak and James I. Robertson (*Faith in the Fight - Civil War Chaplains*); Steven Woodworth (*While God is Marching On—The Religious World of Civil War Soldiers*); John Wesley Brinsfield (*The Spirit Divided—Memoirs of Civil War Chaplains, The Confederacy*); and Kent Dollar (*Soldiers of the Cross: Confederate Soldier-Christians and the Impact of the War on their Faith*).

6. John McKivigan and Mitchell Snay (*Religion and the Antebellum Debate over Slavery*); Ronald White (*Lincoln's Greatest Speech*); Samuel Hill (*The South and the North in American Religion* and *Southern Churches in Crisis Revisited*); John Daly (*When Slavery Was Called Freedom*); Eugene Genovese and Elizabeth Fox-Genovese (*Roll, Jordan, Roll—The World the Slaves Made* and The *Mind of the Master Class—History and Faith in the Southern Slaveholders' Worldview*).

7. *Religion and the American Civil War*, edited by Randall M. Miller, Harry S. Stout, and Charles R. Wilson (New York: Oxford University Press, 1998). The book is the published result of an October 1994 symposium on the topic held at Louisville Presbyterian Theological Seminary, which brought together many of the leading scholars of both American religious and civil war history. The essays were subsequently edited by Miller, Stout, and Wilson, and published by Oxford University Press.

8. Harry S. Stout and Christopher Grasso, "Civil War, Religion and Communications—The Case of Richmond," in *Religion in the American Civil War, op. cit.,* 313–4.

Chapter Two

RELIGION AND FAITH

> Those who did openly profess and live the Christian faith probably numbered somewhat under half of the total number of soldiers . . . those men [were] perhaps well over a million in number.
>
> Stephen Woodworth, "The Meaning of Life in the
> Valley of Death," *Civil War Times* (December 2003)

Is there a difference?

Before beginning our analysis of Civil War religion, we need to "set the table" with an important preliminary discussion. Our twenty-first century culture is described by many as a "secular post-modern society"—that is, as having lost many of its formal connections with the Transcendent and Traditional. Thus, when attempting to speak about the role of the Deity in people's lives, in any generation or time, the topic needs clarification. Whenever human beings attempt to "approach the Unapproachable" in Life, they do so with innate human fallibilities, deep prejudices and limited understanding. As a result, throughout history there have been endless differences of opinions, divergent spiritual responses and outright deadly disagreements about the requisite human response to the Almighty in both organized religion and personal faith. Perhaps it is the very words themselves which lie at the heart of our confusion—"*religion*" and "*faith*." Despite the implicit connectedness of both to Divinity and spirituality, the two words are not the same, and do not refer to the same things intrinsically.

If we approach the topic of Civil War religion and faith without clarifying these two unique responses to the Divine, the already confused waters of the topic become even muddier. It is my personal belief that believers in the mid-nineteenth century shared a roughly similar pattern with believers of nearly *every* generation in modern history. In every generation, there are those who could be truly called "*religious people*"—for whom organized Religion plays a significant, influential and normative part in everyday life. But there are also those better described as "*people of Faith*"—people for whom Faith in the Deity is extremely important on some level of being, but for whom organized Religion may or may not play an influential role. Finally, there are those for whom *both* descriptions could together apply—who have a deeply personal relationship with the Deity as well as a strong religious affiliation and practice. Of course, it goes without saying that both "religion" and "faith" may be possessed in differing degrees and varying levels of personal commitment.

11

> I never knew the comfort there is in religion so well as during the past month. Nothing sustains me so much in danger as to know there is one who ever watches over us.
>
> Frederick Pettit letter to his sister, June 1, 1864

Religion

Religion is best described as organized faith, namely the systematization and ritualization of spirituality and Faith. As such, we are able to measure, codify and analyze "religion" in many ways—by statistical analysis, attendance patterns, doctrine and theology, available "assets" (buildings, schools, clergy, publications) etc. When we speak of our mid-nineteenth century Civil War, there certainly is much of "religion" to be studied and analyzed—for as will be seen, in many ways it was a more traditionally "religious" environment than our present generation. We could look at the Civil War era from many varied "religious" perspectives:

- mid-nineteenth-century denominational histories
- ecclesiastical public statements and policies
- analyses of denominational size, ethnic makeup, growth patterns
- sermons, speeches, publications, diaries of ministers who were chaplains, leaders, public figures

In pages ahead, we will summarize some important religious themes and denominational "movements" from the Civil War era. Indeed, the role of organized religion during the War years has often been frequently ignored—for example, the predominant religious underpinnings of America prior to the War; the prophetic role that denominational schisms played in presaging and perhaps even provoking disunion in 1861; the "invisible institution" that black religion became during the era of slavery.[1] But the study of organized religion alone can never capture the fullness of the Divine "movements" that occur in people's lives, or indeed in societies as a whole, during times as horrific as war or tragedy. Sometimes, *faith* in God "breaks out" or flourishes quite apart from any organized *religious* context. Indeed, America's distinct religious ethos seems to be a unique combination of independence in personal attitude and action, and dependence upon one's God in professed spirituality.

Eugene Genovese has done fascinating research bolstering this point. In his studies of the worldview of the antebellum South, he maintains that southerners of "high and low class" were indeed committed Faith believers, although many never formally affiliated with any organized religious church. Genovese writes

Statistics on church membership prove little for either the South or the North. As late as 1861, in the South as in the North, no more than 10 to 20 percent of the white population belonged to a church. But evidence abounds that many of the most pious men and women refused to join a church for a wide variety of reasons: unwillingness to commit themselves to a particular theology, a deep sense of unworthiness in their Christian professions, an inability to submit fully to stern demands of church discipline, the lack of a preferred denominational church in their vicinity; and more. But these people nonetheless went to preaching on Sunday and often during the week, sometimes attending two or three services a day; and they prayed at home as well as in church. [2]

The pattern Genovese reports on in the pre-war South is not an unusual one among human beings. Countless numbers of people never formally join any religious denomination, nor do they profess any external religious affiliation, or get heavily involved in activities of organized religious groups. However, this does *not* mean there is not a strong impulse towards Faith in a Higher Power in their life, or a fervent belief in the role of the Divine. The sentiment of one Northern Civil War soldier, a corporal in the 2nd IA, aptly expresses this "impulse towards the Divine" which exists in far more hearts than will ever fill every available church pew. "I am not the Same Man, Spiritually, that I was . . . My only fear is that I am too late . . . but with God's help I will come through all right—at least I will try." [3] Therefore, we must for a moment consider the role of Faith apart from the structure, ritual and organized nature of formal "Religion."

> One Confederate chaplain commented that "Strange as it may appear to some, scores of men are converted immediately after great battles."
>
> Steven Woodworth, *While God Is Marching On* (2001)

Faith

Faith is a personal human response to the experiencing of a Higher Power or Divine Presence moving in life. It is a response usually characterized by deeper trust, reliance, assurance and belief in the Deity (however defined in one's life). The "Faith impulse" is part and parcel of humanity's innate desire to reach beyond oneself—to move outside Self to a higher and better place; to touch and embrace a Power and Presence greater than this world. Faith is the attempt to better understand the passing pains, struggles and confusions of this life, by relating them to Eternal Truths that underlie all existence. Faith thus gives meaning, purpose and destiny to one's life and actions. All of these "efforts at Faith" can occur *without* connection to any formal religion, *without* any formal denominational or theological guidance, and far *outside* church services—for they are simply part of the archetypal underpinnings of our human condition.

13

Much of the "Faith" humans experience does become "Religion"—that is, one's *personal* Faith experiences become linked through conscious choice to one or another external religious structure or denomination. But, not all Faith can be captured this way—for millions of humans never intimately connect to formal religion in any way. This type of faith cannot be easily analyzed, codified or studied—for it deals with the mysterious, immeasurable movements of the human conscience and spirit reaching out in free will and choice for some Higher Power, however that Power is conceived or defined.

In speaking of the Civil War specifically here, Randall Miller confirms this exact sentiment when he writes: "The people's actions did not necessarily follow the words and demands of the preachers and politicians . . . the people met God on their own, and His terms." [4] One Confederate soldier named V.H.A. Dawson perhaps said it best when in May 1861 he opined that he was "interested in the Christian system and, like a majority of Americans of that era, believed in the truth of the Christian system, but did not consider himself a Christian." [5]

Without a doubt, thousands of Civil War soldiers, perhaps belonging to no specific denomination or organized religion, had deeply powerful Faith experiences during their Civil War days. The simple truth is that the sudden shock, trauma, death, suffering and horrors of the events they saw *inevitably* led many soldiers to Forces bigger than self, to confront eternal Truths greater than the horrors around them. Steven Woodworth writes that "soldiers who could dismiss religion amid the rough camraderie of camp found it more difficult to do while staring death in the face." [6]

Examples of their Faith experiences abound in soldiers' journals and diaries. One such was Whitfield Stevens of the 8th GA (Bartow's Regiment), who was deeply touched after his regiment was badly mauled at Manassas. Recalling his Methodist upbringing and subsequent "backsliding," he was grateful that God had spared him. That evening he "went off by himself amid the pines, kneeled down and thanked God for sparing him." He died later in the war with the words of Scripture on his lips. [7]

James McPherson, in *For Cause and Comrades,* speaks of how the horrors of war and the comforts that Faith in God could bring have always been linked. "Wars usually intensify religious convictions. A survey of American enlisted men in World War II found that the foremost factor enabling them to keep going when the going got tough was prayer. The same was true of Civil War soldiers. There were few atheists in the rifle pits of 1861-65." [8] A Union soldier in the 114th Ohio assured his father, "I am trying to live a better man than I was at home. I see the necessity of living a Christian here where they ar[e] dropping all around you."

Abraham Lincoln

There may be no better model for the distinction between Religion and Faith than Abraham Lincoln. The unchurched son of a hardshell Baptist layman, Lincoln in his adult life was never a man of strong denominational affiliation or connection to organized Religion, but in his later life he certainly appeared to become a man of deep Faith and belief. Historians have differed about what Lincoln believed and what influenced him in terms of his faith and religion. His Springfield law partner William Herndon argued that Lincoln's use of religious ideas and language was calculated, designed to "play to the audience" and draw a responsive chord. Always a man wary of emotion, Lincoln early in life embraced reason and logic, remarking on one occasion that he was ready to join any church that would inscribe above its altar as the sole qualification for membership the Great Commandment of Love (love of God, neighbor and self).[9]

Certainly Lincoln did not worship regularly or publicly in any one denomination—although his later life tendencies led him most frequently to Presbyterian churches (both in Springfield and Washington). The preaching and writing of Rev. Phineas Gurley (New York Avenue Presbyterian Church) seems to have had a very powerful impact upon Lincoln, and has been called "the overlooked figure in the Lincoln story."[10] While in Washington as President, Lincoln became more regular in attending church, frequently sitting in Gurley's study where he could hear his church preaching. Ronald White makes the point that much of Lincoln's Second Inaugural Address' "spiritual" influence came from Gurley's preaching and subsequent correspondence with Lincoln.[11]

> I have often been driven to my knees by the realization that I had nowhere else to go.
>
> Abraham Lincoln

But, just as happened with countless soldiers, it was the Civil War itself that had the most dramatic influence upon Lincoln's religion and faith (as it did with Confederate President Jefferson Davis, an 1862 Episcopal convert). As a Commander in Chief of all military forces, and as President committed to preserving the Union at all costs, the war's emotional, psychological and spiritual impact was overwhelming. Lincoln was caught up not just in the minutiae of finding generals who could win the fight, but wrestled continually with the larger philosophical and religious questions and purposes of this great conflict. It seems clear that because of the enormous weight of the War, Lincoln's personal faith grew, and even the external practice of religion increased. Especially after the February 1862 death of his beloved son Willie, "heaven seemed to become more than a poorly defined abstraction. He needed there to be some place where his boy abided and was happy."[12]

In Ronald White's words, Lincoln found himself "pushed beyond fatalism to an encounter with and appropriation of the ideas and language of providence." White comments that "there is widespread evidence that in his presidential years, Lincoln was embracing a faith that would sustain him in times of stress and grief"; and that Lincoln's "own faith pilgrimage to a more personal God [was] accompanied by a greater practice of prayer." Despite his lack of formal education early in life, it is certain that one of Lincoln's four favorite books was the King James Bible—a book which witnesses said he read often, had memorized many passages from, and which had a "central place" in his life from his earliest days. As the war wore on, religious themes increasingly appeared in his messages, and the fast days and national holiday of Thanksgiving he proclaimed during the Civil War further indicates his willingness to rely upon all resources (even spiritual) at his disposal in the terrible conflict.[13]

Thus despite Lincoln's fatalism, reliance upon reason and skepticism about institutional religiosity, "there is widespread evidence that he was embracing a faith that would sustain him in times of stress and grief. The bulk of his reflection on the meaning of God and faith evolved in the context of the political questions and issues of the Civil War. Sometimes this was done in private . . . most often it was worked out in public addresses and comments." [14]

In conclusion, as we prepare now to review the role of Religion and Faith in the Civil War, defining the differences between them is essential to more clearly understanding the powerful role they played during the War years. In the mid-nineteenth century, there truly was an enormous and socially acceptable "impulse towards the Divine" which found powerful and personal expression in soldiers and civilians alike who wrestled with the horrors of the Civil War. This impulse towards the Divine was expressed *both* in formal organized Religion, and in spontaneous movements of personal Faith. Whether mid-nineteenth-century soldiers or civilians attended church regularly or professed formal affiliation with any organized religious denomination, still without a doubt Faith in God (particularly as expressed in the historically-conditioned sentiments of that time) played an enormous role in soldiers, politicians and civilian's lives.

If a man ever needed God's help it is in time of battle," wrote a private in the 24th GA, a sentiment echoed across the lines by a private in the 25th MS: "I felt the need of religion then if I ever did.

James M. McPherson, *For Cause & Comrades* (1997)

Further reading recommendations

Eugene Genovese. "Religion in the Collapse of the American Union." Pp. 74–88 in *Religion and the American Civil War*, edited by Randall M. Miller, Harry S. Stout, and Charles R. Wilson. New York: Oxford University Press, 1998.

Philip Shaw Paludan. "Religion and the American Civil War." Pp. 21–40 in *Religion and the American Civil War*, edited by Randall M. Miller, Harry S. Stout, and Charles R. Wilson. New York: Oxford University Press, 1998.

Ronald White. *Lincoln's Greatest Speech*. New York: Simon and Schuster, 2002.

Notes

1. C.C. Goen, *Broken Churches, Broken Nation* (Macon, GA: Mercer University Press, 1985) is the best analysis written of the highly visible and powerful role that America's churches played in the eventual schism that rent America in 1861, especially in the "popular denominations" of the Methodists, Baptists and Presbyterians. Eugene Genovese, *Roll, Jordan, Roll—The World the Slaves Made* (New York: Vintage Books, 1976) is truly foundational in its description of the religious world that Southern slaves built.

2. Eugene Genovese, "Religion in the Collapse of the American Union," in *Religion and the American Civil War*, ed. Randall Miller, Harry S. Stout, and Charles Reagan Wilson (New York: Oxford University Press, 1998), 75–76.

3. James McPherson, *For Cause and Comrades* (New York: Oxford University Press, 1987), 63–64.

4. Randall Miller, "Introduction," in *Religion and the American Civil War*, ed. Randall Miller, Harry S. Stout, and Charles Reagan Wilson (New York: Oxford University Press, 1998), 16.

5. As cited in Stephen Woodworth, *While God is Marching On—The Religious Life of Civil War Soldiers* (Lawrence: University Press of Kansas, 2001), 138.

6. Ibid., 162.

7. William Bennett, *Narrative of the Great Revival in the Southern Armies During the Late Civil War between the States of the Federal Union* (Harrisonburg, VA.: Sprinkle Publications, 1989), 133–136. One very fertile field for faith conversion was in Civil War hospitals. Hospital stays were definite motivations for soldiers to take both religion and faith seriously. Cf. Steven Woodworth, *While God is Marching On*, 189–90.

8. McPherson, *For Cause and Comrades*, 63. In his book *Soldiers of the Cross*, Kent T. Dollar briefly discusses the irreligiosity of troops early in the Civil War. He maintains that most historians accept early irreligiosity as a basic premise, averring that only as the war dragged on did soldiers really "return" to their basic religious roots. Dollar maintains that for devout Christian soldiers that was not the case. Cf. Kent T. Dollar, *Soldiers of the Cross: Confederate Soldier-Christians and the Impact of the War on their Faith* (Macon, GA: Mercer University Press, 2005), 5.

9. I am grateful to Mark Noll for his clarification of *"hardshell"* as a technical term for a strongly local, Calvinistic, anti-elite strand of believers especially prominent in the Southern backcountry and upper South. In regards to Lincoln's religion, early "preachers turned historians" emphasized that he was a religious person imbued with strong Protestant values, but the Lincoln biographers of the last half-century "have not wasted many words on Lincoln's religion", in the words of Ronald White. Later biographers such as Stephen Oates, David Donald and Kenneth Stampp "have focused on fatalism as the key category to understand Lincoln . . . both biographers and historians have depicted him as atheist, agnostic, deist, fatalist, spiritualist and Christian." Cf. Ronald White, "Lincoln's Sermon on the Mount," in *Religion in the American Civil War*, op. cit., 217–18.

10. Ronald White, *Lincoln's Greatest Speech* (New York: Simon and Schuster, 2002), 132.

11. White, *Lincoln's Greatest Speech,* 131–149.

12. After the September 1862 battle of Antietam, Lincoln wrote a fascinating document entitled *"Meditation on the Divine Will."* Though intended for his eyes only, it was (in Mark Noll's words) "the most remarkable theological commentary of the war." For an elaboration of this, cf. Mark A. Noll, *America's God* (New York: Oxford University Press, 2002), 431. The cited quote is from Philip Shaw Paludan, *A People's Contest—The Union and Civil War, 1861–1865* (New York: Harper & Row, 1988), 370.

13. White's quote is from "Lincoln's Sermon on the Mount," in *Religion and the American Civil War,* 208. The other three books that were Lincoln's favorites were *Aesop's Fables, Pilgrim's Progress,* and Shakespeare's plays. Cf. also Ronald White, *Lincoln's Greatest Speech, op. cit.,* 108–112, 129–153; James McPherson; *Abraham Lincoln and the Second American Revolution*; (New York: Oxford University Press, 1991), 95.

14. White, "Lincoln's Sermon on the Mount," 208.

Chapter Three

THE GREAT PARADOX

> Missouri senator Thomas Hart Benton compared the ubiquity of the slavery issue to ancient Egypt's plague of frogs. "You could not look upon the table but that there were frogs, you could not sit down at the banquet but there were frogs, you could not go to the bridal couch and lift the sheets but there were frogs!" It was the same way with "this black question, forever on the table, on the nuptial couch, everywhere!"
>
> C.C. Goen, *Broken Churches, Broken Nation* (1985)

America's first moral encounter

Black Americans "have no rights a white man need respect." Roger B. Taney's infamous 1857 decision in the Dred Scott case was simply the last link in the chain of a Great Paradox which since 1619 had slowly come to strangle America. It was that Great Paradox—twisted into a political compromise that birthed the Constitution and an economic reality that built a nation—which haunted America, until a terrible War brought a measured moral resolution so appalling that its toll has not yet been matched. Simply put, the rise of American liberty and equality was accompanied by the rise of black servitude. Built on Daniel Webster's ideal vision of "liberty and union, now and forever, one and inseparable," the United States was also built upon the harsh reality of inequality, oppression and race-based slavery. That two such contradictory developments took place simultaneously over our earliest formative history (the seventeenth— nineteenth centuries), and that the "American Creed" did not apply (or applied only partially) to blacks, is the *Great Paradox* of American history.[1]

The Great Paradox was actually composed of dozens of minor paradoxes. Our early insistence on freedom of the seas ("Free ships make free goods") demanded goods made to a large degree by slave labor. America's single most valuable early commodity (tobacco) was produced mainly by slave labor. Puritan and Yankee shipowners found strong economic grounds for cutting themselves in on the lucrative slave trade. Religious denominations and leaders who self-righteously preached "liberty for captives" did so from foundations made secured through the work of Negro slaves. From slave-owning founding fathers (Thomas Jefferson, George Washington, James Madison) to slave-owning founding religious leaders (Cotton Mather, George Whitfield, Catholic priests, Protestant ministers, even Quakers)—the Great Paradox involved the complicity of an entire nation in both its attitude and action. "Nowhere in Christendom was

Negro slavery more heavily institutionalized, nowhere was the disparity between ideals and actuality so stark, nowhere were the churches so implicated."[2]

The Great Paradox then became institutionalized in America's founding documents—today considered of near "sacred" significance. The U.S. Constitution, written in 1787, did not specifically mention slavery or race. Though the delegates spoke often about "blacks," "negroes," and "slaves," the words themselves were never used in the final document. The Founders were highly aware of the volatile issue confronting them—one that threatened to derail their new nation before it ever began. At the Constitutional Conventions, for example, South Carolinian representatives in particular were often on their feet demanding security for "this species of property." In the end, among other social, intellectual and racial concerns, it was fundamental economic interests which provided a stable foundation for agreement. While powers of taxation, war, commercial control, and disposition of western lands were conferred on the new government, they were *not* allowed any general authority to define property. The Founders re-affirmed the right to own property (including human property) and none of the powers conferred on Congress permitted a direct attack on such property.[3]

The Great Paradox was deepened by the fact that the five provisions of the Constitution dealing with the "peculiar institution" actually gave Southern states *more* protection for domestic slavery than they had before! The famous "three fifths clause" counted three-fifths of all slaves for purposes of representation in Congress; a slave trade clause prevented the ending of slavery before 1808; a fugitive slave clause prohibited states from emancipating fugitive slaves and mandated their return. Other clauses only further supplemented these direct protections of slavery. Despite flaring tempers and highly charged emotions, a crucial political compromise had been expediently forged between the Founding Fathers of the North and South. Rufus King observed later that these compromises (especially the three-fifths clause) was believed at the time to be a great concession, "and proved to have been the greatest which was made to secure the adoption of the constitution."[4]

Yet if America celebrated political victory in this new Constitution, they were only dancing with the devil. For behind the compromised birth pains of an American nation lay the dormant seeds of a deep moral flaw. The unwillingness (or inability) of the delegates to put the words "slave" or "slavery" into the Constitution is a revealing human insight. James Iredell (North Carolina) simply said that northern delegates had "particular scruples" on the subject and didn't want the word mentioned, and southerners were willing to do without the word. Jonathan Dayton (New Jersey) justified it by saying they wanted to avoid any "stain" on the new government. It was too late. The moral stain was already visible upon America's Constitution.

> In 1711, in pleading for Negro evangelization, Anglican Bishop William Fleetwood told masters that Christianity posed no threat to slavery. He declared that masters "are neither prohibited by the Laws of God, nor those of the Land, from keeping Christian slaves; their slaves are no more at liberty after they are Baptized than they were before . . . The Liberty of Christianity is entirely spiritual."
>
> H. Shelton Smith, *In His Image, But . . .* (1972)

The moral impasse

Most of America's Founding Fathers never denied that slavery was an evil—rather they simply concluded it was an evil they were willing to live with. Even the church leaders of the early Republic were not conscious of any extraordinary tension between equality and slavery. What both were unable to see was that resolution of the crisis surrounding the constitutionally-protected institution of race-based slavery would become the central moral issue in American history. One wonders how many of the Founders realized that, at the core, it really was n issue of *morality*—the first truly moral encounter that American politicians and churches would confront, and unfortunately one which would inexorably lead to a deadly theological, Scriptural, and political impasse.

In his award-winning book, *Religious History of the American People*, Sydney Ahlstrom speaks to the complicated moral nature of race and slavery. "The rise of abolitionism [in the 1830's] marks the beginning of the nation's central experience, its first truly moral encounter. This encounter led by steady steps to the war that brought forth a new nation not really dedicated to the proposition that all men are created equal, but nevertheless, one that could be led to put the right words in the Constitution." Congregationalist preacher Edward Beecher (son of the notable American churchman Lyman Beecher) saw slavery as an enveloping "organic sin," a moral imperfection that the South increasingly chose not to recognize, as they focused on moral failure elsewhere. Race-based slavery was a moral issue (and the Civil War a "moral" war) *not* because one side was evil and the other good, or one side more pure of motive than the other, but because it sprang from a moral and spiritual impasse on issues which mid-nineteenth century Americans could no longer compromise or avoid. [5]

Morality is concerned with issues of right and wrong, good and evil, as understood through reason, the Church and the revealed Word.[6] With the Great Paradox compromised but not resolved, the impasse of such conflicting interpretations of right and wrong could only grow worse as theologians and politicians clashed with increasing ferocity. Nowhere else in American religious history has the disparity between Constitutional *ideals* (freedom, justice, liberty for all) and *actuality* (institutionalized race-based slavery) been so starkly defined. Moral and spiritual questions with heavy implications abounded. What should the future be for the institution of slavery in a country founded on principles of "liberty and justice for all"? Do individual states or groups of states in a democratic republic have the right, ability or freedom to withdraw from a newly formed union? Is the American Creed of "life, liberty, and the pursuit of happiness" merely an oratorical ploy or meaningful hope for all citizens?

As the nineteenth century began, never in the United States was Jefferson's analogy more true—too long had America held the wolf by its ears. Sooner or later, the grip would have to be released. Other Western nations were already moving towards larger moral, humanitarian and democratic understandings of equality and freedom. In the early nineteenth century, slavery was outlawed in the French Empire (1794–1802 and 1848) and Great Britain (1833–1834). Slaves were being emancipated in many other places—Upper Canada (1793), Argentina (1813), Mexico (1829), Chile (1823) and Denmark (1848) are examples.[7]

Although America moved in a "strangely retarded way," a moral consensus of true freedom and liberty for all in America was slowly growing. In the coming moral crisis, churches, pastors, and theologians would all be involved up to their ears. At no time in our history would America's churches ever be more implicated, vocal, opinionated—or more guilty. "Honorable, ethical, God-fearing people as well as self-seeking, egotistic opportunists and status seekers were on both sides. Social, economic, political and psychological forces intensified feelings, clouded the fundamental issues, and consolidated existing fears and antipathies—but the moment of truth had to come." The "moment" came when the guns sounded in 1861. And yet, in perhaps the final gleam of the Great Paradox, the bloody post-war aftermath of that "moment of truth" continues to be America's chief moral challenge to this very day.[8]

The blood price for Constitutional resolution of the Great Paradox was especially steep for the South. Of a potential military population of about a million, roughly three-quarters of a million served in the Confederate army at some time or another—and 250,000 of them died during the Civil War.

E.B. Long, *The Civil War Day by Day* (1971)

Racism and *"Imago Dei"*

Union soldier James Hildreth used to complain that blacks had become so independent since the Emancipation Proclamation that there was nothing to do but kill them. If a black came into the camp of the 4th NY Heavy Artillery, the soldiers would cry out "Kill him!" and club the unfortunate person.[9] The attitude of Hildreth, a Northerner and Union soldier, may have been extreme, but it was not rare—and as such it reveals a final ramification of the Great Paradox and its Civil War "resolution" which continues with us to this day.

What led to the Civil War? Though not the only cause, *slavery* was the main reason—for had there been no slavery, or no consequent moral condemnation of that slavery, there would have been no war. But what led to the American institution of race-based slavery? In yet another ramification of the Great Paradox, a factor which must be considered is the *implicit racism* of our founding elders, and the racially-motivated tensions still existing to this day. The Englishmen who colonized America (and their revolutionary descendents) consciously or unconsciously believed that liberties and rights should be confined to people of a light complexion.

The ongoing racial antagonisms and mythologies of Americans were foundational in maintaining the Great Paradox throughout the mid-nineteenth century up to its deadly dénouement in Civil War. Narrow and limited racial views were then played out with sad post-war repercussions as Jim Crow slowly undid the small steps towards equality begun in Reconstruction. Even today, although racism of the traditional sort (a belief in white superiority) seems to be dying out, still what one author calls "race-structured thinking" remains a major factor in modern American society.[10] It seems that race continues to be the one "moral encounter" we still must painfully learn to deal with.

Unfortunately, as we shall see, one of our greatest tragedies was the inability of antebellum religious institutions and leaders to bring Wisdom and spiritual consensus to the worst calamity of American history. Sadly, at a time when moral issues were most pressing, the "official custodians of America's conscience" could offer little to help the nation slow down the runaway sled of the slavery issue. The decades leading up to the War sadly revolved far too often around loud rhetoric and "slavery apologetics" (either pro- or anti-), using standard Biblical proof texts for slavery and creating in the process major theological and Scriptural crises. As Harry Stout aptly remarks, "the clergy were virtually cheerleaders . . . they were the sources where moral arguments *should* have prevailed."[11]

While acknowledging the dangers of temporal "time-leaps" of judgment, my research for this book has left me with poignant sadness over one Scriptural doctrine that might have offered some Wisdom—had anyone been able or willing to hear. How sad that mid-nineteenth-century social, cultural, economic, exegetical, and political factors utterly overwhelmed a simple viewing of a basic

23

and foundational Scripture known well to all denominations—the "imago Dei" doctrine of Genesis 1:27. *"God created humanity in his image, in the image of God he created him."* This Scripture is a doctrine also echoed in Gen. 5:1, Gen. 9:6, 1 Cor. 11:7 and James 3:9. It is from this foundational Scripture that Believers of all denominations discover the Truth that all people are equal in the God's sight, and they therefore owe one another equality of respect and goodwill.

As Scripture scholars point out, this is a truly revolutionary text—for it images a God whose "creative use of power invites, evokes and permits. There is nothing here of coercive or tyrannical power, either for God or humankind." God is revealed as a generous Creator, sharing power with a variety of creatures (especially humanity), inviting them—and even trusting them. Race was never an issue for this Creator God—nor do the Biblical stories of God's Creation make distinctions between different races.[12] How truly sad it is that we Americans who "read the same Bible and pray to the same God" have not been able to embody the truths of "imago Dei." Perhaps our Great Paradox could have found resolution without the massive blood sacrifice of 1861–1865.

Nothing short of miracles such as the world has never seen can keep at bay the two great antagonistic forces . . . They must drive at each other till one of them goes to the bottom. *Events*, the master of men, have for years been silently settling the basis of the two great parties, the nucleus of one slavery, of the other freedom.

Abolitionist Theodore D. Weld to James G. Birney, 22 Jan 1842

24

Further reading recommendations

Sydney Ahlstrom. Pp. 648–697 in *A Religious History of the American People*. New Haven, CT: Yale University Press, 1972.

Charles A. Beard. "The Constitution: A Minority Document." Pp. 120–136 in *Conflict and Consensus in Early American History* (7th Edition), edited by Allen F. Davis and Harold D. Woodman. Washington, DC: Heath and Company, 1988.

Howard Jones. "Introduction." Pp. vii–xvii in *The Legacy of the Civil War*, Robert Penn Warren. Lincoln: University of Nebraska Press, 1961.

Alan J. Levine. Pp. 43–71 in *Race Relations within Western Expansion*. Westport, CT: Praeger Press, 2004.

Staughton Lynd. "The Conflict over Slavery." Pp. 137–148 in *Conflict and Consensus in Early American History* (7th Edition), edited by Allen F. Davis and Harold D. Woodman. Washington, DC: Heath and Company, 1988.

H. Shelton Smith. *In His Image, But . . . Racism in Southern Religion, 1780–1910*. Durham, NC: Duke University Press, 1972.

Notes

1. Edmund S. Morgan, "Slavery and Freedom: The American Paradox," in *Colonial America—Essays in Politics and Social Development* (4th edition), edited by Edward S. Morgan (New York: McGraw-Hill, Inc., 1993), 265. The year 1619 also saw the beginning of representative government in white America, as well as the introduction of the Southern tobacco culture and the onset of race-based slavery. Slave labor was used to some extent in every American colony. Cf. also Alan J. Levine, *Race Relations within Western Expansion* (Westport, CT: Praeger Press, 2004), 58–59.

2. Sydney E. Ahlstrom, *The Religious History of the American People* (New Haven, CT: Yale University Press, 1972), 648–654. Cf. also Nathan Irvin Huggins, *Black Odyssey—The African-American Ordeal in Slavery* (New York: Vintage Books, 1990); H. Shelton Smith, *In His Image, But . . . Racism in Southern Religion, 1780–1910* (Durham, NC: Duke University Press, 1972); *Conflict and Consensus in Early American History* (7th Edition), edited by Allen F. Davis and Harold D. Woodman (Washington, DC: Heath and Company, 1988).

3. Staughton Lynd, "The Conflict over *Slavery*," in *Conflict and Consensus in Early American History, op. cit.*, 138 and 146. Lynd's essay is excellent in demonstrating the issue of how strong a role the institution of slavery and its potential consequences played at the Constitutional Conventions. For an analysis of the strong economic motivations of the Founding Fathers, see Charles A. Beard, "The Constitution: A Minority Document," in *Conflict and Consensus in Early American History, op. cit.*, 120–36.

4. Rufus King is cited in Lynd, *op. cit.*, 138. For an excellent detailed breakdown of the five Constitutional clauses protecting slavery, see *Encyclopedia of African American History 1619-1895*, Vol. 1 (A-E), edited by Paul Finkelman (New York: Oxford University Press, 2006), 330ff. Cf. also Howard Jones, "Introduction," in Robert Penn Warren's *The Legacy of the Civil War* (Lincoln: University of Nebraska Press, 1961) for a concise summary of this entire section.

5. Ahlstrom, *op. cit.*, 635. This issue was a moral encounter because slavery is intrinsically (though not exclusively) a moral issue. The institution of slavery raised uncomfortable but vital philosophical issues: (a) the natures of people other than the white Protestant-dominated majority, (b) the equality of human beings formed by the same Creator, and (c) the limits to which American ideals and freedoms would be applied to those segregated "outside" the accepted American political and religious mainstream. Although individual soldiers would later chose to fight for their own unique personal reasons and motivations (as James McPherson notes well in *For Cause and Comrades*), there can be no doubt that the slavery issue was *the* motivating and instigating factor behind the American Civil War (as many Union soldiers would come to realize by war's end). I am grateful for Sydney Ahlstrom's insights on pp. 648–659 about the moral nature of the slavery and Civil War crises. Harry Stout has continued that stream of thought, developing it more fully in his book *Upon the Altar of the Nation—a Moral History of the Civil War* (New York: Viking/Penguin, 2006).

6. *Our Sunday Visitor's "Catholic Encyclopedia,"* edited by Rev. Peter Stravinskas (Huntington, IN: Our Sunday Visitor, 1991). "Morality" is defined here as true teaching about right and wrong, good and evil, as understood through natural reason, the teachings of the Church and the revealed Word.

7. Daniel Jackson, "Crossfire," *North and South* 9, No. 4 (August 2006): 90–91.

8. Ahlstrom, *op. cit.*, 655.

9. Reid Mitchell, *Civil War Soldiers* (New York: Penguin Books, 1988), 123.

10. In many ways, all pre-war antislavery arguments were doomed to fail because (as Mark Noll succinctly summarizes) of "whites' inability to regard African-Americans as fully human." So deeply was black inferiority fixed in the minds of white Americans of all levels and professions of society, that "a revolution in the nation's racial attitudes would have been necessary" to offer any other truly viable alternatives that might have prevented war. Cf. Mark Noll, *The Civil War as a Theological Conflict* (Chapel Hill: University of North Carolina, 2006), 73–74. I have borrowed the concept of *"race-structured thinking"* from Alan J. Levine, *Race Relations within Western Expansion, op. cit.*, 109. In his 1903 book *The Souls of Black Folks,* W.E.B. DuBois remarked perhaps prophetically that "the problem of the twentieth century is the problem of the color line." Indeed, it was only after the 1960s civil rights movement that many of the freedoms teasingly promised immediately following the Civil War were finally achieved. David Blight's work *Race and Reunion* elaborates on the theme of America's post-war racial problems, and in that excellent book he bluntly remarks that "race was deeply at the root of the war's causes and consequences." David Blight, *Race and Reunion* (Cambridge, MA: Belknap Press, 2001), 4.

11. Harry S. Stout, *Upon the Altar of the Nation—a Moral History of the Civil War, op. cit.*, xvii.

12. These quotes are from renowned Old Testament scholar Walter Brueggemann, as cited in J. Richard Middleton, *The Liberating Image—The "Imago Dei" in Genesis 1*

(Grand Rapids, MI: Brazos Press, 2005), 1. I find the definition of racism based upon this "imago Dei" concept very relevant and apt today. "Racism from the Christian standpoint is a response that violates the equalitarian principle implied in the biblical doctrine of 'imago Dei.' If a person regards another race as an inferior member of the human family and seeks to deny it an equal opportunity for growth and participation in the common life, he is a racist. Racism is a two-directional in its evil expression. On one hand it impeaches the impartiality of God and, on the other, it breeds social discord." (H. Shelton Smith, *In His Image, But . . . Racism in Southern Religion, 1780–1910*, Duke University Press, Durham, NC; 1972; 1). On this topic also, see Steven L. McKenzie, *All God's Children— A Biblical Critique of Racism* (Louisville, KY: Westminster Press, 1997). Alan J. Levine, *Race Relations within Western Expansion, op. cit.* 43–71 is excellent in his analysis of the broader issues (historical perspectives, slave mythologies, misconceptions) of American slavery vis-à-vis other cultures and time periods.

Section Two

A DEVOUT COUNTRY HEADS TO WAR

The importance of religion for American society in 1860 lay partly in its wide dispersion. Even more, it resided in its overwhelming presence when compared with other institutions of government, culture, education, and the media that have grown so fast in American society since the close of the Civil War. As a promoter of values, as a generator of print, as a source of popular music and popular artistic endeavor, and as a comforter (and agitator) of internal life, organized religion [in 1860 America] was rivaled in its impact only by the workings of the market, and those workings were everywhere interwoven with religious concerns.

Mark A. Noll, *The Civil War as a Theological Crisis* (2006)

Chapter Four

THE FOREMOST POLITICAL INSTITUTION IN THE COUNTRY

> Upon my arrival in the United States, the religious aspect of the country was the first thing that struck my attention . . . Religion in America takes no direct part in the government of society, but nevertheless it must be regarded as the foremost of the political institutions of that country.
>
> Alexis de Tocqueville, *Democracy in America* (1835)

"A new Adam in a new Eden"

In 1854, church historian Philip Schaff wrote that the United States offered "a motley sampler of all church history." [1] His analysis of religion in America was right on target, for no other nation on earth has had such a vital interactive relationship with more diverse religious beliefs and passions than this country. Although with Christopher Columbus' 1492 "discovery," America became the Great Frontier for the imperial designs of European Christendom, our religious roots truly begin in "mother England." The religious turmoil of England specifically (and Europe generally) was the major factor behind the "establishment" of America both religiously and colonially. [2] In no country was the travail of the Reformation more tumultuous than England, with Reformed and Puritan theology from their eighteenth century Evangelical Revival becoming the major catalyst behind the formation of America's religious heritage. [3]

It was the mustard seed of Puritanism which grew to be the fruitful tree of American religion and society. Sidney Ahlstrom writes that "the American colonies [became] the most thoroughly Protestant, Reformed and Puritan commonwealths in the world. Indeed, Puritanism provided the moral and religious background of fully 75% of the people who declared their independence in 1776 . . . If one were to compute such a percentage on the basis on all who bore the 'stamp of Geneva' in some sense, 85 or 90% would not be an extravagant estimate." [4] While the scattered colonial commonwealths (New England, Rhode Island, southern and middle colonies) chose to institutionalize it differently, all were marked by a similar Reformed and Puritan ethos. So, by the early eighteenth century, as evangelical historian Mark Noll says, "the dominant Christian theologies in America were quite similar to dominant theologies prevailing in Scotland, Northern Ireland, the Netherlands, and Switzerland. Theology was primarily Calvinistic or Reformed, and at least overwhelmingly theistic." [5]

31

"Puritanism for Dummies"
A widely ramified late sixteenth-century movement of religious reform in the Church of England among an increasingly literate population

Foundational beliefs
- Scripture as both practical and theoretical source of guidance
- Faith and conversion to Jesus Christ is experiential and personal
- Emphasis on Law and discipline in personal and public realms
- Purging of all "popish" remnants from Anglican tradition
- Establishing apostolic principles of worship and church order
- Implementation of Reformed doctrine

But by the early nineteenth century, America's religious situation had changed markedly from its Protestant European forebears. Revivalism had come upon the American scene again—the Second Great Awakening began in the 1790s in scattered New England towns, then spread to truly "cataclysmic" outbreaks around the country such as the Cane Ridge, Kentucky camp meetings of 1800–1801. As Mark Noll notes, this Revival brought "evolutionary changes" in Christian doctrine as well as a shift in America towards a Protestant evangelical theology shaped and molded by America's unique history.

Three "churches of the people" made this revivalism serve a communal purpose, as they gathered converts into churches, and spread their organizational networks around the country. Baptists, Methodists and Presbyterians now became the largest and most influential American denominations—replacing the Congregationalists and Episcopalians, who had been the largest churches in the 1790s. These three bodies enrolled millions who knew no other club or company, and no other organizations were in closer direct contact with more people. "With their simplified doctrines, folksy preaching, emphasis on immediate experience, efficient organization, energetic promotion of revivals, and rapport with the common people, they had immense appeal to multitudes of Americans." [6]

But quietly in the background of American society, other modes of religious experience and theology were slowly emerging to contrast these dominant Calvinist-based modalities. Roman Catholics, Lutherans, Jewish, African-Americans, and numerous uniquely American sects[7] all brought different mentalities, theologies and worship styles to the melting pot that was becoming American religious life. For example, the huge Irish migrations of the eighteenth and nineteenth centuries represented a slow yet powerful transforming movement that would ultimately change America's face. Thus by the time of the war, thanks to the enormous influx of Irish immigrants and a rising tide of Catholic periodicals, a distinct Roman Catholic religious presence was being felt on a national scene that had hitherto been almost exclusively Protestant. However, (as would be the case until well into the twentieth century) Catholics had little influence politically or socially except in heavily-populated Catholic areas.[8] It would unfortunately take a bloody civil war to reveal the painful truth that no one religious culture or experience could stand for all who called themselves Americans.

By 1850, Baptists and Methodists accounted for 90% of all churches in Georgia, and 80% in other leading slaveholding states (Virginia, South Carolina, Mississippi, Alabama). In the eleven seceding states of 1860–1861, Methodists claimed 45% of total number of churches, Baptists 37% and the Presbyterians 12%—which is a stunning 94% of all the churches in the heavily churched Confederacy!

Edwin Gaustad, *Historical Atlas of Religious America*, (1962)

The antebellum religious environment

As the Civil War era dawned, the most widely recognized American religious voices were Protestant, and the most prominent Protestant voices were self-consciously evangelical. Mark Noll speaks of the unique intellectual synthesis that had come about in antebellum America between religion, politics and culture. The key elements of this synthesis were visible in the strong links between religion and public life—*Protestant evangelical religious principles*, a *republican concept of politics* (where *"political power could be sanctified by the virtue of people and magistrates"*), and *"commonsense moral principles"* (such as a "mistrust of intellectual authorities," a "belief that true knowledge arose from the use of one's own senses").[9] This synthesis produced a society which stumbled into the Civil War rampant with religious beliefs and attitudes. Antebellum America had truly blended religion and culture in ways that might surprise our twenty-first century "political correctness" sensibilities.

As one writer remarks, "it was generally conceded that the great influences of life were religious. The primary purpose of existence for most people was eternal salvation. Therefore, it was deemed essential that the individual should conduct his everyday affairs in harmony with the wishes of a just and stern God."[10] In the mid-nineteenth century, the evidence for intellectual assent to the notion of a Divine being by most antebellum Americans was overwhelming. Simply put, nearly everyone believed in God and accepted the Presence of the Divine as one of Life's givens. One writer, James Turner, has done a fascinating study of how the notion of unbelief (i.e., the idea that there is no Deity, or that this Deity is unknowable) only slowly gained ground in America in the late nineteenth century. In Turner's words, unbelief "was a bizarre aberration," hardly part of any mainstream notions about the known universe of the time. Even by 1880, when *"unbelief had assumed its present status as a fully available option in American culture,"* Turner writes that agnostics by no means lurked under every blackberry bush, and only in the imaginations of overwrought bishops was there "a flood of infidelity sweeping over our land."[11]

Because antebellum Americans believed in God, and assumed the existence of a Divine Being, they engaged in various formal or informal "religious" rituals and patterns. There were the daily rituals of *organized religion*. The Second Great Awakening had left in its wake thousands of new evangelicals, and left a revived interest in all things religious. So, regular worship and Bible studies flourished, especially during the waves of religious enthusiasm of the early nineteenth century and the War years. Church attendance had risen—in 1800, only about 10% of the South's white population belonged to an organized church, but by 1860, 40% of the Southern white population did.

There were other religious rituals connected to *special life-events*—baptisms, marriages, deaths. Since it was assumed that Life came from God, it was presumed that one would celebrate those "cosmic moments" with religious ceremonies. "These observances, as much as formal worship, constituted the key rituals to that throng of antebellum Americans, both the formally and the informally religious, who shaped the major events of their day."[12] Simply put, there was no other cultural or voluntary organization that regularly brought together more people did than America's religious institutions.

Even America's *"public" rituals* were infused with religious connections. Religious instruction, or Bible study, was held in nearly every school in both North and the South—with America's public schools using the standard King James Version.[13] America's dominant Protestant majority had an enormous social influence upon the direction and content of education in antebellum America—with the creation of Horace Mann's public school system and William McGuffey's *Eclectic Readers* both reflecting historic Protestant values. In the North mainly, the "collective conscience of evangelical America" became the foundation of "social Gospel" humanitarian reform campaigns not only in education, but also in women's rights, prisons, hospitals, and even a "Peace Crusade."[14] Unfortunately, as we shall see, America faced one issue that all humanitarian efforts, vest-pocket utopias and shared belief in God could not solve. The greatest crusade of all would sunder the country, killing 620,000 Americans.

In summary, the simple fact was that no other antebellum group had as much power to influence the greatest numbers of citizens on a regular basis as did America's clerical religious leaders. Generally better educated than many of their members, clergy were highly influential community leaders, being (in Ahlstrom's words) "the official custodians of the popular conscience." As rhetoric in a very religious America heated up around the inflammatory slavery issue, clergy would lead the way in violence of statements and ultimacy of appeal, their pulpits "resounding with a vehemence and absence of restraint never equaled in American history."[15]

Thus the antebellum stage had been set for God to "go to war" in America. Both sides believed in God and prayed the Bible. Both Union and Confederacy expected Divine Blessing upon cause, country and comrades. Both Northern and Southern religious leaders preached, promoted and propagandized. Two examples from among many are illustrative. One of the powerful Southern religious and secessionist voices was *Rev. Benjamin Morgan Palmer* (First Presbyterian Church, New Orleans). In a dramatic sermon later published at the request of the New Orleans Confederate Guards, Palmer declared "Eleven tribes sought to go forth in peace from the house of political bondage, but the heart of our modern Pharaoh is hardened, and he will not let Israel go!" Because it was founded on "the immutable laws of God," the Confederacy was pre-eminently "the cause of God himself."[16] Influential Northern Methodist *Rev. Granville Moody* would certainly not have agreed, but was unapologetic for the clergy's role in helping instigate the conflict. "We are charged with having brought about the present contest. I believe it is true that we did bring it about, and I glory in it, for it is a wreath of glory around our brow."[17]

> In what would become a frequent linking of wartime fervor and religious convictions, when a South Carolina state convention met on Dec. 20, 1860 to formally dissolve their union with the United States, they met in a church to do so! It was a religious meeting place, the First Baptist Church of Columbia, South Carolina, that had the honor of hosting the group that blazed the trail out of union with the Federal government!

A shadow upon the land

Antebellum America may have been one of the world's most populous and powerful Christian nations, but it was also perhaps one of the most biased and prejudiced. Sidney Ahlstrom remarks simply that "The first half of the nineteenth century was the most violent period of religious discord in American history."[18] Few white Americans at the time thought it necessary to question their underlying presumptions and suspicions about the subhuman-ness of Blacks, or the national loyalties of Catholics, or the scorn they held towards Irish immigrants or freemasons or Mormons.

It was an era of nativism, of groups like the "Know-Nothing" party—an 1849 secret society born out of fear of the drastically rising emigration numbers of foreigners and Catholics. (The name came from the characteristic response members made when asked about their group—"I know nothing."[19]) In July 1863, mobs of New Yorkers (many of them Irish fueled by wartime losses, poor living conditions, job competition and a new conscription law) would spent four days in rioting, burning, and violence—newspapers and businesses being early targets, but unfortunate blacks receiving the full fury—before several regiments of Gettysburg veterans arrived to put it down with cannon and gunfire. After the Civil War, an anti-black and anti-Reconstruction group known as the Ku Klux Klan would begin to leave its ugly mark on American history.

In many ways, however, the nineteenth century was really just a logical step further down the historical chain from a spirit of prejudice latent in America both politically and religiously from its earliest days. Nathan Huggins remarks that America's founding document, the Constitution, itself speaks of "an unnamed category of humanity—not free, not bound for a term of service, not untaxed Indians [which] should count as three-fifths of a person for purposes of enumeration."[20] While this Constitution, with its famed Bill of Rights, became the model for the documents of many states, its guaranteed rights did not apply to slaves and, for the most part, did not apply to free blacks either.

Religiously, the framework underlying antebellum America continued to be Calvinistic and "Reformed"—and in John Calvin's severe discipline, anyone who could not fit into "sola fide" theology was considered condemned to hell, an "outsider" to Truth and eternal life. "There was a strong anti-Roman Catholicism animus to [the clergy's] pleading, as well as a fervent hope that 'errors of Popery' would not be sown in areas as yet unclaimed. In fact, a fierce tradition of anti-Catholicism, both visceral and dogmatic, is one of Puritanism's most active legacies to Anglo-American civilization."[21]

Thus, from the very beginning of the United States, early settlers who were Catholic or Jewish, blacks brought here freely or unwillingly through the "middle passage," even native Indians slowly pushed off ancestral lands, would all find and experience themselves as strangers in a strange land. America's dissenting Protestant colonists were indeed interested in religious freedom—but primarily for themselves. After having founded American communities where their own religious heritage and authority was firmly established, they were capable of vicious persecution towards any who might disagree with them. Thus, a spirit of religious intolerance, bigotry and at times blatant prejudice existed towards many foreigners, groups and religions in parts of antebellum America, and these attitudes were tacitly accepted and carried into the War by many soldiers and civilians on both sides.

James I. Robertson writes how the typical Northern troops simply reflected the national sentiments of the time. With one in four Union soldiers being either a first or second generation immigrant (the majority being either 200,000 Germans or 150,000 Irish), and foreigners being targets of blame for unwelcome changes in many time-honored traditions and customs, it is no surprise that prejudices ran strong with native-born Yankee and Rebel troops.

Although the foreign-born troops behaved no better or no worse than their American compatriots, they labored under an automatically bad reputation. In the summer of 1864, one of General Meade's staff officers sneered: "by the Lord! I wish these gentlemen who overwhelm us with Germans, negroes and the offscouring of the great cities, could only see—only see—a Rebel regiment in all their rags and squalor. If they had eyes they would know that these men are wolf-hounds, and not to be beaten by turnspits."

Ultimately, it would be only the bravery and courage of these "offscouring" and "turnspits" in the carnage of the battlefield that would bring them grudging acceptance as true American soldiers.[22]

Perhaps only the utterly candid, simple and blunt prayer of one North Carolina Confederate soldier captures that strange synthesis of Divine trust and regional sectionalism that marked the Civil War era. "Lord, we have a mighty big fight down here . . . and we hope, Lord, that you will take the proper view of the matter, and give us the victory."

As cited in Reid Mitchell, *Civil War Soldiers* (1988)

Further reading recommendations

Sidney Ahlstrom. *A Religious History of the American People*. New Haven, CT: Yale University Press, 1972.

C.C. Goen. "Chapter Two—Churches of the People." Pp. 43–63 in *Broken Churches, Broken Nation*. Macon, GA: Mercer University Press, 1985.

Eugene Genovese. "Religion in the Collapse of the American Union." Pp. 74–88 in *Religion and the American Civil War,* edited by Randall M. Miller, Harry S. Stout, and Charles R. Wilson. New York: Oxford University Press, 1998.

Mark A. Noll. *America's God—From Jonathan Edwards to Abraham Lincoln*. New York: Oxford University Press, 2002.

Phillip S. Paludan. Pp. 339–374 of *The People's Contest—The Union and the Civil War, 1861–65*. New York: Harper and Row, 1988.

Notes

1. As cited in Sidney Ahlstrom, *Religious History of the American People* (New Haven, CT: Yale University Press, 1972), 4.

2. Ahlstrom, *op. cit.*, 113. For analysis in this section, I am indebted to Sidney Ahlstrom's 1972 award-winning book, *The Religious History of the American People*, as well as to Mark Noll's more recent classic, *America's God* (New York: Oxford University Press, 2002).

3. Ahlstrom calls the time between about 1560–1685 in England the *"Puritan century"* because of the group's sudden rise to prominence. Prior to the English Civil War (1642–1649), the Anglican Church was unable to accommodate the increasingly strident concerns of this growing Puritan minority within their midst. The Church of England was seen as too hierarchical, ritualistic and "Armenian", and Puritan reformers demanded far-reaching changes in church government (e.g., removing bishops, a "purified" worship) which were ultimately unacceptable to the English Anglican Church. It was this intra-church conflict which helped give rise to the post-English Civil War influx of Puritans to the United States. Cf. Ahlstrom, *op. cit.*, 90–98 here.

4. Ahlstrom, *op. cit.*, 124. He is speaking here of the Reformed tradition among the German, Swiss, French, Dutch and Scottish people as well.

5. Noll, *op. cit.*, 7.

6. Cf. C.C. Goen, *Broken Churches, Broken Nation* (Macon, GA: Mercer University Press, 1985), 50. Goen's second chapter ("Churches of the People") is marvelous on this topic. *Presbyterianism* (whose stronghold had been the middle American colonies) actually were the third largest religious group in 1790, and were in Goen's words "poised to develop into a nationwide popular denomination." In an interesting modern interpretation of the Second Great Awakening, Mark Noll remarks that "I've come to believe there really was no such event. What did exist was a broad, intense and long-lasting turn to religion in a revivalistic Protestant form, but more led by the ongoing week-in, week-out activities of the Methodists than by any set revival events." (From a private conversation with the author).

7. Ahlstrom notes three notable American contributions to world religion that had American origins—"Christian restorationism led by Alexander Campbell, Seventh-Day Adventism and Mormonism." Cf. Ahlstrom, 387.

8. There were 1.75 million American Catholics in 1850, a number which doubled a decade later. By 1860, Catholics had expanded from 30,000 (in 1790) to 3.5 million (in 1860). However in 1860, statistics *also* show that there were only about 2500 Catholic churches compared to 20,000 Methodist churches—which leads Mark Noll to conclude that "while there may have been more baptized Catholic than full Methodist members, in terms of active adherents, there were still probably more Methodists than Catholics. [Certainly] the landscape was marked out as evangelical Protestant terrain, whatever may have been the actual count on the church rolls." (From Mark Noll's private notes). By 1866, Catholics made up 13% of America's population—though most were poor, and certainly considered near or at the bottom of the social ladder. Cf. *Eerdman's Handbook of Christianity in America*, (Grand Rapids, MI: Eerdmans Press, 1983), 235; also Ahlstrom, *op. cit.*, 8, 527, 542.

9. Noll's synthesis is much more polyvalent and nuanced than expressed here, and bears reading on its own. Cf. Noll, *op. cit.*, 5, 9 and 11. I particularly found insightful his reflections on "common sense" principles most engaging, for it seems to capture that

uniquely American spirit of independence both religiously and politically. As he says on page 11, Americans were united in the "conviction that people had to think for themselves in order to know science, morality, economics, politics, and especially theology."

10. James Silver, *Confederate Morale and Church Propaganda* (Tuscaloosa, AL: The Confederate Publishing Company, 1957), 25.

11. Turner's work is cited in Edward Crowther, *Southern Evangelicals and the Coming of the Civil War*, (Lewiston, NY: Edward Mellen Press, 2000), 2–3.

12. The church attendance statistic is from *Library of Congress Civil War Desk Reference*, ed. Mary Wagner, Gary Gallagher, Paul Finkelman (New York: Simon and Schuster, 2002), 85. Though this statistic may seem small, it should be remembered that many antebellum people especially in the South did not formally join a church for a variety of personal reasons—unwillingness to commit themselves to a particular theology, a deep sense of unworthiness in their Christian professions, an inability to submit fully to the stern demands of church attendance, lack of a preferred denominational church in their vicinity, etc. Nonetheless, these people went to preaching on Sunday and often during the week, sometimes attending two or three services daily. (Cf. Eugene Genovese, "Religion in the Collapse of the American Union," in *Religion and the American Civil War*, eds. Randall M. Miller, Harry S. Stout, and Charles R. Wilson (New York: Oxford University Press, 1998), 75–76. C.C. Goen also mentions that "nearly every [Southern] minister preached regularly to congregations three or four times the size of the church membership." In 1860, the census showed that America had one church for every 580 people, and had the facilities for seating three-fifths of the population at one time. (Goen, *op. cit.*, 55) For other references in this paragraph, cf. Edward Crowther, *op. cit.*, 2–3.

13. *Library of Congress Civil War Desk Reference*, ed. Mary Wagner, Gary Gallagher, Paul Finkelman, (New York: Simon and Schuster, 2002).

14. These Northern Reform campaigns grew from and were linked to church leaders and dedicated laymen. In *education*, perhaps the most far-reaching campaign, there was the liberal Unitarian Horace Mann (1796–1859) who created a public school system, and William McGuffey's (1800–1873) legendary *"Eclectic Readers"*. In *women's rights*, a movement which encountered resistance from traditional Protestant churches, there were Mary Lyon (1797–1849, founder of Mount Holyoke College) and Emma Willard (1787–1870, founder of a famous "Female Seminary" in Troy, NY). Women's roles in the temperance movement and anti-slavery crusade were very significant. Regarding *prisons and hospitals*, it was the Rev. Louis Dwight who led a prison reform movement in the 1820–1830s, the spinster schoolmistress Dorothea Dix (1802–1887) who was behind proper hospitalization and care for mentally ill, and Dr. Samuel Woodward (1787–1850) who worked for humane treatment and more successful cures for the Worcester, Massachusetts hospital. Lastly, *the Peace Crusade* was an idealistic campaign rooted in the Quakers (Society of Friends). Rev. William Channing organized the *Massachusetts Peace Society* in 1815, but his most pugnaciously pacifist disciple was William Lloyd Garrison (1805–1879), a disciple of radical non-resistance, pacifism and even anarchism. The *New England Nonresistance Society* was formed in 1838; and still other groups were formed. Cf. Sidney Ahlstrom for more details, *op. cit.*, 640–47.

15. Ahlstrom, *op. cit.*, 672.

16. "Sermons of Bishop Pierce and Rev. B.M. Palmer . . . Before the General Assembly" (Milledgeville, 1863), as cited in Silver, *op. cit.*, 27. Many of Palmer's powerful oratorical address were frequently reproduced, and circulated in thousands of. Some were said to have done more for the Confederate cause than an entire regiment of soldiers. Palmer would later bless the troops and flag of the New Orleans Washington Artillery from the steps of his cathedral, telling them that the war they went to fight was perhaps the most holy in all of human history, "a war of civilization against a ruthless barbarianism . . . ."

17. Moody's quote, as well as a summary explanation of the church's role in the war is cited in Ahlstrom, *op. cit.*, chapter 41 ("The Churches amid Civil War and Reconstruction"), 670–697.

18. Cf. Phillip S. Paludan, *The People's Contest—The Union and the Civil War, 1861–65* (New York: Harper and Row, 1988), 339–374; and Ahlstrom, *op. cit.*, 555.

19. The "Know-Nothing" platform of beliefs included opposing citizenship for any immigrant until after twenty-one years of living in America, and the banning of foreign-born citizens from holding political office in the United States. The group was strong in New York for a time, becoming in 1854 the "American" political party, taking control of the Massachusetts legislature and electing several members of Congress. However, their numbers splintered over disagreements over slavery, and was already fading in strength by the 1856 elections, when—although gaining over 20% of the vote in that election—it lost many of its adherents to the newly formed Republican party.

20. Nathan Irvin Huggins, *Black Odyssey—The African-American Ordeal in Slavery* (New York: Vintage Books, 1990), 93.

21. Ahlstrom, *op. cit.*, 114.

22. James I. Robertson, *Soldiers Blue and Gray* (Columbia, SC: University of South Carolina Press, 1988), 27–35.

Chapter Five

CATALYST FOR CONFLICT . . .
COMFORT IN WAR

> During the generation that culminated in the Civil War, no society on earth was as preoccupied with Scripture as the United States. And no comparable era in the history of Christianity ever witnessed so vigorous a defense of the simplicity of Biblical interpretation.
>
> Mark A. Noll, *America's God* (2002)

The Bible in antebellum America

Many veterans of Robert E. Lee's Army of Northern Virginia never forgot seeing one particular dead Confederate soldier on a Richmond battlefield. His hand was upon a Bible opened to the 23d Psalm, and resting on the words "Thy rod and staff they comfort me."[1] In the mid-nineteenth century, it would have likely been the King James Version that unfortunate soldier carried, and it would have been carried into battle by an overwhelming number of both Northern and Southern soldiers.[2] In fact, the one item that seemed to most survive deceased Civil War soldiers were Bibles. For many of these 620,000 deceased, the Bible would have been their spiritual bridge between the temporal and eternal, between this world and the next, between death and Life.

As the Civil War broke out, the Bible occupied an absolutely central place in American culture. In the early years of the country, Scripture had become the national book *par excellence*, and broad familiarity with its contents characterized both ordinary people and elites. "The overwhelming public attitude towards the Bible—even by those who in private never read it or heeded it, was one of reverential, implicit deference."[3] Antebellum Americans were products of the Second Great Awakening (a nationwide Protestant movement bringing revival to nearly every American church). An unadorned faith in Jesus Christ and the Word of God were at its core. Publications of the Bible dwarfed any other book of that time. Ordinary Americans read it frequently, accepted it as the Word of God, and saw it as an enormous personal resource in both life and death. Decades away yet were the twentieth century arguments and disagreements that would arise about Biblical authority, literalness, and interpretation.

For Civil War soldiers and armies as well, the Bible was indeed a precious cargo, with copies being produced almost as quickly as bullets during the war. The *American Bible Society* made the decision early on to supply Bibles to all soldiers. Sixteen presses in New York City worked for this purpose, and in the first year of the war alone 370,000 more Bibles were printed than the year before. Looking back in 1866, the ABS revealed that it had published 5,297,832 Bibles in different formats, with the 1862-formed United States Christian Commission becoming the main wartime distributor of these ABS Bibles.

It became clear early in the conflict that soldiers did not want to carry the heavier entire Bible, so "pocket Bibles"[4] quickly became available for soldiers desiring a "lighter load." Pastor Moses Hoge of Richmond became legendary for his "Bible-smuggling" exploits—running the Union blockade to smuggle 10,000 Bibles, 50,000 New Testaments, and 250,000 portions of the Psalms and Gospels from England back to the South.[5]

The common appeal of the Scriptures even led to strange displays of truce at times between the warring forces. In early 1862, a shipment of Bibles intended for Leonidas Polk's army in Kentucky was stopped as contraband by Union forces at Cairo, Illinois. But Polk and Ulysses Grant (the Federal commander) worked out a flag of truce so that the Bibles could be delivered unharmed to the Confederate forces. Shipments of Bibles under such flags of truce were sent regularly south from New York (because few if any Bible publishers existed in the wartime South) through Fort Monroe and City Point, under the approval of Secretary of War Edwin Stanton. As historian Ronald White phrases it well, such agreements could only have been worked out in a culture where indeed "both used the same Bible, and both prayed to the same God."[6]

But, contained within this enormous national respect and appreciation for the Word of God also lay disturbing seeds of dissension and disagreement. Just as with the differing divisive perspectives on slavery and secession, and the tensions underlying the predominant Calvinist tone of the country, in the same way a critical crisis was looming about how to read, interpret and apply these beloved words of Scripture. Indeed it can be said that, despite Scripture's heavenly promises of salvation and peace, in many ways it was the Bible itself which helped bring about the horrors of America's Civil War.

Comments about reading Scripture appear constantly in soldiers' diaries: "I have read five chapters in the testament today," "I must now read some in the Testament," "My Testament is my only companion," "I have finished reading the book of John." Many times, local citizens provided New Testaments for soldiers as they marched off to war.

Steven Woodworth, *While God is Marching On* (2001)

An "American way" of interpreting Scripture

Not only did most Americans read the Bible, it is highly significant that they read it *in the same way*. Through the 150 years of the "American experience," there had gradually emerged a uniquely American way of interpreting the Scriptures. The churches of America's predominant Reformed tradition (Baptists, Methodists, Presbyterians and Congregationalists) had encouraged a tradition of confidence in both reading and interpreting the Holy Bible. Thus, the vast majority of America's Protestant believers had grown up with two core foundational understandings of the Word—*first,* the traditional Reformed belief in "*sola scriptura*" (the Bible being the authority above all, a blueprint for how Christians should live their entire lives on earth); but *secondly,* a uniquely American "commonsense" democratic reading of Scripture (emphasizing that the ordinary believer could read and understand Scripture themselves, and did not have to rely on the words of kings, priests or church authorities).

As mentioned earlier, these broad "commonsense moral principles" had become part of an antebellum synthesis of religion, politics, and culture in America. By the time the Civil War rolled around, most Americans

> shared a mistrust of intellectual authorities inherited from previous generations and a belief that true knowledge arose from the use of one's own senses— whether external senses for information about nature and society, or the moral sense for ethical and aesthetic judgments. Most Americans were thus united in the conviction that people had to think for themselves in order to know science, morality, economics, politics, and especially theology. [7]

Evangelical historian Mark Noll mentions that "there was less theological borrowing from Britain and the continent in the period between the Revolutionary and Civil War than at any time before or since." Thus, in theology and hermeneutics[8], as in so many other areas of life, Americans had "done it their own way"—reading the Bible fervently, relying upon its Wisdom, becoming confident in their own ability to understand it, using it to shape their spiritual and ecclesiastical structures, and even define the nation itself.

But as the nineteenth century dawned, foundational flaws in this American hermeneutic began to appear. They were set in motion by our greatest unresolved national issue, the Jeffersonian "wolf being held by its ears" which had never gone away—race and slavery. What would happen if Americans disagreed on applying Scriptural words such as those relating to slavery? What would happen when people read the same Scripture yet concluded very different things? Again, Mark Noll best captures the gist of the issue. "The obvious crisis that bore directly on the nation was that 'simple' reading of the Bible yielded violently incommensurate understandings of Scripture with no means, short of warfare, to adjudicate the differences."[9] Simply put, by the 1840s, American churches, religious scholars, and preachers were at each others throats over Biblical teachings on slavery.

The common hermeneutic that had united America's Protestant majority now mired them in heated controversy and violent disagreement. The same Bible that had been the churches' foundation, offering people simple, democratic, "commonsense" interpretations, now became the catalyst for dividing America's churches long before it divided the country. Confidence over ordinary American people's ability to interpret the Bible correctly if only left to themselves proved to be misplaced. Division over the meaning and interpretation of the Bible became a major theological crisis, contributed immensely to the growing national crisis, and without a doubt helped start the Civil War.

This approach to Scripture dared common people to open the Bible and think for themselves. It even challenged them to limit religious discussion to the language of the Bible. Finally, this approach freed people from staid ecclesiastical traditions, thus befuddling the respectable clergy.

Nathan O. Hatch, *The Democratization of American Christianity* (1989)

The Bible and Slavery

The issue of the Bible and slavery was never a simple question. It involved a tangle of Reformed principles of Scriptural interpretation and passionate beliefs about the ultimate authority of Scripture and entrenched racism. The two cultures of North and South, so different socially, economically and religiously, both interpreted Scriptures "by canons deeply imbedded in American experience" and yet religious chaos was the result.[10] The following were the Scripture references (King James Version, of course!) used most often by proslavery preachers like Virginia Baptist Thornton Stringfellow (1788–1869):[11]

Genesis 9:18–27 [the "curse of Ham"] "a servant of servants shall he be unto his brothers; blessed be the Lord God of Shem, Canaan shall be his servant . . ."
Exodus 21:2–6 [Various laws about Hebrew servants, marriage, and children]
Exodus 20–21 "If he continue a day or two [smiting his servant], he shall not be punished, for he is his money"
Leviticus 25:44–46 "Both thy bondsmen, and thy bondsmaids . . . shall be of the heathen that are around you"
Colossians 3:22 "Servants, obey in all things your masters"
Colossians 4:1 "Masters, give unto your servants that which is just and equal"
Ephesians 6:5 "Servants be obedient to them that are your masters . . . with fear and trembling"

1st Peter 2:18–21 "Servants be subject to your masters with all fear . . . for this is thankworthy"

The Scriptural words on slavery are clear and obvious, but immensely difficult questions arise when *interpreting* these verses in antebellum Reformed fashion. Do believers therefore have to accept the legitimacy of slavery? If the Bible indeed sanctions slavery, does the Bible then have to be abandoned? Is the presence of slavery in the Bible necessarily a justification for the unique American form of slavery? Should believers distinguish here between the letter and the spirit of the Bible? Using the Bible to argue against slavery proved to be an extremely difficult theological task, for the proslavery argument was formidable.

Not only did one have to show that these "proslavery conclusions did not adequately exegete the biblical texts", but also one had to prove why "arguments against slavery should not be regarded as infidel attacks on the authority of the Bible itself." Noll concludes that, theologically speaking, "what was in fact a wide-ranging debate looked like it could be reduced to a forced dichotomy—either orthodoxy and slavery, or heresy and antislavery."[12] Nothing less than ultimate infallible authority of the Bible for all of life (at least as that authority had been formulated by Protestants since the Reformation) was at stake—thus intense emotion and deeply held dogmas dominated the slavery debate.

All of this should not lead to the impression that alternative interpretations of Scripture did not exist in America. They did—but unfortunately due to the marginal influence of the groups formulating them, they could not affect the growing theological and national crisis in a major way. *African-Americans* certainly loved the Scriptures, used them and believed in them as strongly as did white believers, but their unique approach of integrating Scripture into their lives,[13] and their socially marginalized position in society, kept their use of Scripture well outside the mainstream. *Roman Catholicism* had historically said[14] that to give the Bible to everyone was to take it away from everyone, but their appeal to a unified authority figure (the Pope and Church teaching) as a force above the American tumult was always offensive to the nation's Protestant majority. Other Protestant groups like *Lutherans* and *Old School Presbyterians* (from border and northern states) offered interesting alternative stances towards Scriptural interpretation as well, but couldn't influence theological reasoning during the War era.[15]

Meanwhile, the simple southern public (most who owned no slaves but had evangelistic backgrounds) continued to read their Bibles and listen to increasingly strident southern preachers. It was in the 1830s that a strong and uniquely Southern identity began to crystalize, and in this era of growing Southern nationalism, Southern proslavery advocates took up their fierce battle with Northern abolitionists.[16] In 1841, the above-mentioned Thornton Stringfellow wrote the bestselling proslavery tract of the time, giving therein the "authoritative" list of proslavery Scriptures—and the newly burgeoning religious presses spread the

45

proslavery "gospel." Southern ministers had by then developed an established place within the slaveholding elite, and their views on Scripture, slavery and the South resounded from both pulpit and press. In isolated rural areas, these itinerant preachers were often the only source of information about the outside world, and "the Bible was the only source of abstract ideas that many people in these areas encountered."[17]

The crisis over the Bible and slavery is summed up aptly by Noll when he says: "The North lost the exegetical war. The South certainly lost the shooting war. But constructive Christian theology was the major loser when Americans allowed bullets instead of hermeneutical self-consciousness to determine what the Bible taught about race and slavery."[18] Although the Bible was at the center of our religious imagination, Americans never found agreement about its application or interpretation to our aptly named "peculiar institution." Thus, the great American "debate" over the Bible and slavery was as much a battle over *how* to interpret the Bible as it was about *what* the Bible said. In the end, nearly every slavery argument came to naught, because the real issue blinding all parties involved (North and South) was not the authority or inerrancy of the Bible—but race and the Bible.

> Nobody at the North, we think, would defend Slavery, even from the Bible, but for this color distinction . . . Color makes all the difference in the application of our American Christianity . . . the same Book which is full of the Gospel of Liberty to one race, is crowded with arguments in justification of the slavery of another.
>
> Frederick Douglass, March 1861 speech

Race and slavery

In what is surely one of the great ironies of the time, it was only African-Americans who realized the essential flaw in all the antebellum slavery arguments. Only they clearly perceived that the Bible speaking about *race* was not the same issue as the Bible speaking about *slavery*. The great majority of white Americans were historically and psychologically incapable of recognizing that their intuitive racial assumptions (i.e., that blacks were inferior), and what the Bible said about slavery, were two distinct issues. The words that David B. Davis wrote about America's economic situation were just as true for its theological situation. "In the United States ... the problem of slavery ... had become fatally intertwined with the problem of race. Race had become the favored idiom for interpreting the social effects of enslavement and emancipation, and for concealing the economy's parasitic dependence on an immensely profitable labor system."[19]

The truth was that ingrained "common sense" racial assumptions and the culture's "intuitive racism" had clouded the pulpits and religious press of the time, crowding out conclusions of Biblical exegesis. The great Reformed scholars of the time had all fallen into the trap, leading "astray" the thousands whom they influenced. Charles Hodge (Princeton's renowned Presbyterian professor), James H. Thornwell (the South's most respected theologian), Robert L. Dabney (respected theologian but post-war "bitter Jeremiah") and others blithely brought racial assumptions into their work, or liberally cited non-Bible-based sources—as if these carried the same weight as their fine-tuned Scriptural conclusions and sources. All were rigorous in logic and analysis in purely Scriptural study—but became illogical, shallow and superficial in their beliefs about race. The certainty in their minds of black racial inferiority was the blind spot in all their biblical testimony.

Underneath all their proslavery theology lay one basic "common sense" presumption. "If the Bible were to justify the racial slavery that existed in the United States—and if faith in Bible-only literalism was to be preserved," then that one presumption would have to be true—the "deeply ingrained conviction that among the peoples of the earth only Africans were uniquely set apart for chattel bondage."[20]

Thus in the end, the drama of the highly popular Bible in antebellum America concluded as a complex and confusing tragedy with a horribly sad ending. The same force which "enabled evangelicals to contribute so much to constructing the national culture prevented [them] from offering a scriptural Word from God to address the crisis that ripped apart the country that they, as much as any other group, had created."[21] In a manner that the Deity surely did not appreciate, this tragedy was only resolved by "the most persuasive theologians" of the day—the Rev. Drs. William Tecumseh Sherman and Ulysses S. Grant.

Congregationalist pastor Henry Ward Beecher became an unwittingly symbol of how mid-nineteenth century Americans fell into using militaristic ends to solve religious issues. In 1854, his activist Plymouth Church in Brooklyn, New York sent boxes of Sharp's rifles to new settlers in Kansas to help them resist proslavery radicals. These guns became known as "Beecher's Bibles."

Further reading recommendations

John Patrick Daly. "Holy War—Southern Religion and the Road to War and Defeat, 1831–1865." Pp. 34–35 in *North and South* 6, no. 6 (Sept. 2003).

John Patrick Daly. *When Slavery Was Called Freedom—Evangelicalism, Proslavery, and the Causes of the Civil War, 1830–1865*. Lexington, KY: University of Kentucky Press, 2002.

Stephen Haynes. *Noah's Curse—The Biblical Justification of Slavery*. New York: Oxford University Press, 2002.

Mark A. Noll. "The Bible and Slavery." Pp. 43–73 in *Religion and the American Civil War*, edited by Randall M. Miller, Harry S. Stout, and Charles R. Wilson, New York: Oxford University Press, 1998.

Mark A. Noll. *America's God*. New York: Oxford University Press, 2002.

Mark A. Noll. *The Civil War as a Theological Crisis*. Chapel Hill, NC: University of North Carolina Press, 2006.

Ronald White Jr. Pp. 102–106 in *Lincoln's Greatest Speech—The Second Inaugural*. New York: Simon and Schuster, 2002.

Notes

1. James I. Robertson, *Soldiers Blue and Gray* (Columbia, SC: University of South Carolina Press, 1988), 189.

2. Though the King James Version (literally, the 1767 revision of the old 1611 "Authorized" or "King James" translation) was the standard Protestant version, Catholics used the Douay Version, a vernacular translation of the official Latin version (Jerome's Vulgate) authorized by the Catholic Church. In an interesting gesture of wartime ecumenism, one Union Protestant chaplain, Rev. Fredric Denison, once returned from his leave with 300 Douay Testaments for the Catholic men of his regiment!

3. Mark A. Noll, "The Bible and Slavery," in *Religion and the American Civil War*, edited by Randall M. Miller, Harry S. Stout, and Charles Reagan Wilson (New York: Oxford University Press, 1998), 44. I am indebted to Mark Noll for his crisp and precise terminology, as well as his exegetical and hermeneutical insights throughout this section. His above-mentioned article, as well as his 2002 award-winning book *America's God* (New York: Oxford University Press, 2002) are marvelous resources for the entire area of Scripture and the Civil War.

4. Printed versions of smaller portions of the Bible, usually Psalms and Proverbs from the Old Testament, and several New Testament books, such as Luke, John, Romans, 1st and 2nd Corinthians, etc, Cf. Ronald White Jr., *Lincoln's Greatest Speech—The Sec-*

ond Inaugural (New York: Simon and Schuster, 2002), 102–106. This section is an excellent short summary of the powerful role that the Scriptures played for soldiers in the Civil War era.

5. Noll, "The Bible and Slavery," *op. cit.*, 48.

6. White, *op. cit.*, 107.

7. Noll, *America's God, op. cit.*, 11.

8. The professional study of the principles and practice of Scriptural exegesis and interpretation.

9. An insightful statement by Mark Noll helps further clarify this issue: "It was not merely the Bible but a particular way of reading the Bible that provided the rationale for the institution [of slavery]." Noll, "The Bible and Slavery," *op. cit.*, 46, 49.

10. Noll, *America's God, op. cit.*, 396.

11. John Patrick Daly, "Holy War—Southern Religion and the Road to War and Defeat, 1831–1865," in *North and South*, vol. 6, no. 6 (Sept. 2003), 34–45. Daly's fine article and his book, *When Slavery Was Called Freedom—Evangelicalism, Proslavery, and the Causes of the Civil War, 1830–1865*; (Lexington: University of Kentucky Press, 2002) are excellent and detailed studies of this issue.

12. Noll, *America's God, op. cit.*, 392–395.

13. This is described by Noll as "dramatic narrative . . . prophetic . . . adapted to African traditions" in his description of the African-American alternative hermeneutic in *America's God, op. cit.*, 404–06.

14. This was through people like the sainted sixteenth century theologian Robert Bellarmine.

15. Again, Mark Noll's development of these two failed alternatives are well worth studying. Cf. Noll, "The Bible and Slavery," *op. cit.*, 53–61, and the fuller development outlined in *America's God, op. cit.*, 402–417.

16. Cf. Daly, *op. cit.*, 36. Cf. also on this point Samuel S. Hill, Jr., *The South and North in American Religion* (Athens, GA: University of Georgia Press, 1980). The next chapter will develop this separate Southern identity both religiously and politically.

17. Daly, *ibid.*

18. Noll, *America's God, op. cit.*, 421.

19. David Brion Davis, "Reconsidering the Colonization Movement, Leonard Bacon and the Problem of Evil," in *Intellectual History Newsletter* 14 (1992), 4.

20. I have drastically simplified Mark Noll's arguments on the how America's "common sense" consensus on race was the main reason why both the Reformed and alternative hermeneutics failed. His fuller presentation can be found in *America's God, op. cit.*, 417–421.

21. Noll, *America's God, op. cit.*, 17.

Chapter Six

THIRD COUSINS ALIENATED

Many Northern evangelicals viewed the South as a region of barbarity and irreverence, blighted by the odium of slavery, where true religion could never be practiced. Southern Christians replied with a critique of the deplorable religious state of the North . . . [claiming they] harbored a dangerous religious heterodoxy that sought its basis not in the Bible, but in shameful and irresponsible movements for social reform. Christians of both sections denounced the churches of the other region as being riddled with corruption, and praised [themselves] for maintaining the essence of the gospel.

Gardiner Shattuck, *A Shield and a Hiding Place* (1987)

From cousins to strangers

In January 1861, Georgia's Charles C. Jones was worried. The wealthy state of South Carolina had already seceded from the Union; and was soon followed by the further January secessions of Alabama, Mississippi, Louisiana and his own state, Georgia. Noting the increasing separation between North and South, Jones feared that there was now actually two races in America, "which, although claiming a common parentage, have been so separated by climate, by morals, by religion . . . that they cannot longer exist under the same government." [1] His words were prophetic and his worries justified—for within months, America's always serious sectarian divisions would finally become deadly serious. Brother would face brother in vicious battle, and Bible-believing Northerners would be killing Bible-believing Southerners.

What could have led to victorious, fully independent America of 1783 becoming within one lifetime so divided and hopelessly split between North and South? Certainly there were many factors—slavery being the most obvious, but crucial factors such as economics, culture and politics must be accounted for as well. But once again, in many written accounts of the reasons behind the sectarian divisiveness that led to Civil War, the role of religion is often ignored as a motivating factor. But when examining the facts, it is hard to ignore the fact that religious and theological differences between North and South were a crucial backdrop and hauntingly prophetic prelude to the later political division of America. The unique variations in religion (theological and denominational, as well as social and experiential) that grew up between the two halves of post-Revolutionary America truly helped set the stage for the inevitable military conflict that would soon rip the country asunder.

We have already seen that the individual states which became "united" began under the auspices of a Protestant Christianity that was predominantly Calvinist and Reformed. The North and South were simply two different regions of the one and same nation, with the same basic society, culture and religious underpinnings. Thus, "in their disparate ways . . . [both] North and South began with basically Christian visions for society—for moral society as well as for moral individuals."[2]

But as the nineteenth century began, a growing sectional distinctiveness began to creep into these two geographic halves of the whole country. The fine scholar of comparative religious history, Samuel S. Hill, insightfully delineates the process by which this occurred, discerning three epochs in the religious history of America's two geographic sections. While the second epoch is our concern (unfortunately he ignores the War years), I share his outline here for the purpose of a larger perspective:

1795–1810 *("First cousins separated")* One federal union with common traditions, but two regional cultures with little interaction. Religion slowly becomes a powerful force, though in different ways for each section.

1835–1850 *("Third cousins alienated")* Still close in many ways, North and South begin to diverge due to differing views on slavery, religion, society and more. Religious homogeneity in the South's unique culture holds it together.

1885–1900 *("Strangers in the same household")* Religion in the North trends towards church unity, liberal theology, and the "social Gospel." The religion of a nationalistic South becomes insular, antagonistic, and conservative.[3]

Using Hill's paradigm, in the first decades of the Republic, "neither enmity nor alienation, not even aloofness, accompanied apartness and separation at this early stage." The notion that America as a whole was God's chosen country, a "New Israel" and a "city upon a hill," helped nurture national unity despite the pervasive localism that existed. But in the second epoch, a distinctively Southern ethos and self-consciousness began to emerge, with a slowly increasing antagonism and enmity towards a North that was increasingly perceived to be different in many ways, including religion. Due to unique regional influences, the diverging development of organized religion in America's two halves helped reinforce a growing divisiveness—in this case a *spiritual* divisiveness that would all to soon provide volatile fuel for the heated theological and Scriptural debates over slavery.

> Visitors to America noticed the growing sectarian differences. "In 1831–
> 1832 de Tocqueville had found little differences between North and the
> South in respect to tolerance . . . [but] By the 1850s the northern states
> seem to attained a freer intellectual climate with regard to religion and
> social reforms; the South, in the meanwhile, had regressed in the matter
> of intellectual freedom."
>
> Clement Eaton, *The Leaven of Democracy* (1963)

Religion in the North

The colonizing Puritans who left England arrived with a vision of a "Place where
the Lord will create a new Heaven and a new earth . . . new Churches and a new
Commonwealth." They saw themselves as a covenanted people with a providential
mission to create a new community affecting the entire social and spiritual order.
Hence, New England villages became tightly-knit and well-ordered societies, with
the church holding a position central to the community in everyday life. There was
a strong emphasis on personal moral standards, as well as on civic responsibilities
to larger society. But as Samuel Hill notes, "the New England religious situation
was constantly changing," and as the country expanded these prosperous tight-knit
communities were stretched and challenged by new Enlightenment theories about
human rights and government.

A massive influx of "dissidents" (German Lutherans, Irish Catholics, Quakers,
Jews, Dutch Reformed, Anabaptists of different sorts) altered the Northern environment, giving a broader and more diverse flavor to religion. Secular forces began
to emerge which radically transformed the North—industrialization, immigration,
and westward migration to the "frontier." Then, early nineteenth century revivalism
shook up the "traditional" Northern churches (Congregationalists, Presbyterians),
giving fuel to the sudden rise of "popular churches" (Baptists, Methodists), and
making most Northern Protestants (Anglicans and Lutherans excepted) heavily
evangelical. Still, overall, the North remained strong in their theological traditions,
pious lifestyles, and socially oriented tone to church life.[4]

By the nineteenth century, Northern theological thought had also begun to develop down slightly different paths than their Southern cousins. Church historian
James Moorhead speaks of the "*post-millennialism*" that came to dominate in the
four major Northern Protestant denominations [5]—namely, the belief that the Second
Coming of Jesus would occur *after* the millennium foretold in Revelations 20. Thus,
while the immediate coming of the Master was not expected, people could by their
deeds and actions fulfill the necessary conditions for that Second Coming, thus has-
tening the date. It is not hard to see how this line of religious thinking could feed
into the concept that the Civil War *was* that long-awaited Armageddon. Thus, one

frequent wartime preaching theme was reminding people that by pushing on to Northern victory, righteous Christians might indeed hasten the coming of the Lord's Kingdom.[6]

> One with God is always a majority.
>
> Wendell Phillips, abolitionist

The evangelical North's concern for the larger social injustices of society continued to grow. Among other Northern religious social concerns (e.g., education, voting/women's rights, reforms in prisons and hospitals) it was inevitable that sooner or later slavery would surface. It was in the 1830s that abolitionism rose to national attention, posing a serious challenge for clergy and church leaders.[7] Many religious denominations (most mainstream Protestants) recognized that slavery was an evil in itself, but found other reasons to tolerate or justify its existence. Some saw it "as an institution woven into the fabric of the nation, and not easily rooted out by moral suasion or constitutional actions." [8] Doubts existed as to whether slaves were ready to be free, with some ministers questioning whether blacks "had the same God-given capacity as whites to perform the duties of democratic citizenship."

Thus, before the war, Northern churches and preachers were far from unanimous in their attitude towards slavery; and generally speaking, in the 1830–1840s they rejected abolitionist demands for immediate emancipation. However, by the 1850–1860's this had changed—many northern clergymen had slowly become far more militant about anti-slavery causes, and increasingly strident political and sectionalist preaching began to become the norm. After the outbreak of war, Northern churches did generally become strongly unified in their support for the Union and its causes. James Moorhead says that subsequently "the churches contributed to the radicalizing of the Northern war efforts . . . churches made what had started as a war for the preservation of the Union into a war of liberation [from slavery]."

As the three leading Protestant churches divided and war drums beat, both North and South turned on each other religiously with the same zeal usually reserved for "popery" and heresy. Northern preachers became patriotically passionate about the rightness and ultimate vindication of their cause, emphasizing that the Union had to be preserved because of the special place America occupied in world history. "With its republican institutions, democratic ideals and Christian values, the United States stood in the vanguard of civilization's forward progress. The success of the Confederate rebellion would imperil that progress."[9] Theirs was a battle of right against wrong (the eternal battle prophesied in Revelation 16:16), with the 1860–1861 secession of all Southern states only confirming beliefs in the ultimate moral rightness of their cause. Northern churchmen thus became crucial propagandists as the Civil War broke out, focusing on loyalty, patriotism and the cause of Union. "Ministers succeeded in giving the war a religious sanction . . . It seems likely, in fact, that the Protestant pulpit was the single most important source of northern patriotic exhortation."[10]

> God is calling to the nations! The despotic thrones are growing weary! It is an age of liberty! God is mustering the great army of liberty under his banners! In this day, shall America be found laggard?
>
> Henry Ward Beecher, *Patriotic Addresses* (1887)

Religion in the South

South of the Mason-Dixon line, as with many other things, religion looked and felt a little different, for (as Samuel Hill points out) what was originally a *region* was gradually becoming a *culture*. The colonial South, while being birthed in the same idea of providential mission, was affected by different social factors and a strong agricultural tradition. Large towns were virtually non-existent, and the population highly scattered around the countryside. There was a much stronger sense of independence and individualism in the generally isolated, rural and agricultural South. The forces of institutional Puritanism which shaped New England were never really felt in Virginia and the Carolinas.

The rise of the Virginia tobacco culture with its concomitant dependence upon slavery, unique topography and culture, helped give early pre-eminence to a southern Church of England that was inescapably associated with social privilege but had little popular influence.[11] But it was the immense and intense Cane Ridge, Kentucky revivals of 1801 which changed the face of Southern religion forever, affecting as they did mostly the *"common folk"*—the poor, those of lower social standing, normally cut off both politically and economically. It was the less structured and more evangelical Methodists and Baptists who reaped the results, growing rapidly in the two "Great Awakenings" of America's early history.

By 1860, in the eleven seceding Southern states, Methodists could claim 45% of all churches and Baptists 37%, with both groups drawing heavily from the common people of the country and small towns. *Baptists* proliferated in the South because of their spiritual vitality, individualistic emphasis on conversion and "fluid" evangelistic structure. It could be said that the Baptists "pioneered" America's revivalistic tradition, with preaching that was strictly Reformed in spirit and Calvinistic in theology. *Methodism* spread because of an amazingly well-organized system of circuit preaching stations and camp meetings, and their simple preaching of the

Wesleyan message of God's sovereignty, man's depravity, and the route to salvation being opening of one's heart to God's love. Methodists especially (but Baptists as well) were successful because they did not wait for the masses of people to come to church, but rather took the faith to wherever they might be. This technique had great results, tapping into a spiritual hunger perhaps ignored by the religious establishment. Thousands of people flocked to hear Wesley and others, "some gaping, some laughing and some weeping" according to one witness.[12]

A Confederate soldier wrote his wife in early 1862, "when we lay all upon this altar of our country, the God of Nations will give us a permanent happy existence. How near akin is patriotism to religion!"

Hattaway and Hunter, "The War Inside the Church" (1988)

Because of the evangelical roots of Baptists and Methodists, and the slave-based economy underlying their society, Southern theology developed differently from Northern. Well-educated ministers helped create a Scripturally-based moral consensus accepting and even sanctifying slavery, using it as an ethic to guide the conduct of Christian masters and a challenge to convert slaves. James I. Robertson notes that "religion in the South was more conservative and orthodox than anywhere else in the nation. The Bible was the authoritative Word of God, and that was all there was to it. New denominations spawned by the Enlightenment—Unitarians, Congregationalists and Universalists, for example—never took root below the Potomac River." [13]

Southern spirituality was seen as essentially private and personal (after all, salvation is an *individual* choice), not having the component of *social* Christianity which was emerging in the North. Sin was defined more personally (Sabbath-breaking, intemperance, gambling, political corruption, dueling), and not socially (slavery, inequities of women's and voting rights). In fact, as the war neared, Southern churches became outspoken in chastising their Northern cousins for straying from their spiritual roots with liberal theological trends such as the Enlightenment "evils" of rationalism, deism, and infidelity.

Though the relationship between Southern religion and Southern politics is complex and symbiotic, without a doubt religion had an enormous social impact on the Southern populace as the shells fell on Fort Sumter in April 1861. Donald Matthews remarks that "Religion became identified with an essential public reaffirmation of social solidarity. Going to church became not merely a religious act, but a civic responsibility." [14] Therefore, as war-fever descended upon the South, congregations and pastors were not about to take a back seat to the rhetoric of their Northern relatives. While Southern pulpits rang out with charges of "tyranny against the

North," they would also "preach political liberty for the South with a ferocity—and frequency—unmatched in the North."[15] James Silver writes that

> the church in the south constituted the major resource of the Confederacy in the building and maintenance of civilian morale. As no other group, Southern clergymen were responsible for a state of mind which *made* secession possible, and as no other group they *sustained* the people in their long, costly and futile War for Southern Independence. [16]

By 1861 the depth of alienation between northern and southern churches suggests that the two halves of the Union no longer shared the same religion, or at least that evangelicals in the two sections offered two very different solutions to the question of how to be part of the world.

Richard Carwardine, *Evangelicals and Politics* (1993)

The foundation is cracked

By 1861, a "Gospel of disunion" had divided North and South, creating fundamental (and literal) religious divisions which stimulated and fueled the already superheated controversy over race-based slavery. Whereas public and private religion should be a factor unifying people in prayer and petition, in pre-War America it had become a deep source of deep divisiveness. If America's *churches* could not even agree on the divisive issues, could there be any hope at all for the country's politicians and secular institutions? America's religious foundation had cracked, and for at least two reasons was irretrievably beyond mending.[17]

First, there was fundamental divergence on the *Church's proper responsibility to the larger society.* In the North, a vision of God's Truth developed which for many people necessarily began to *include* social and public responsibility for the transformation and morality of the larger society. Bringing God's sovereignty to bear on the public order was as much a suitable religious response as yielding one's heart to grace and redemption.[18] However, the South's evangelical vision was the opposite—seeing individual spirituality and morality as the primary task of Faith, not the responsibility for changing the larger society. That was God's proper domain and a matter of divine sovereignty.

This attitude came to be known as the doctrine of the *"spiritual church,"* and was often used to defend against Northern condemnations of slavery. Developed by James Henley Thornwell (a Presbyterian minister and the south's greatest theologian), the church was defined as a "spiritual body whose purposes are only the dispensation of eternal salvation, not the creation of morality, decency and good order, which may . . . be secured without faith in the Redeemer."[19] Thus, the church

57

really had nothing to say to the larger human society (certainly not to the issues of slavery or abolition), and should be blissfully unconcerned about what happened there.[20]

Second, two unique Southern factors made sectarian religious divisiveness and the War that followed nearly inevitable—the *presence of Negroes* (with their special fixed roles in society), and a *rural lifestyle based upon the slave-holding economy.*[21] Issues of blacks and their "peculiar institution," unresolved since the Constitution, forced the breach between America's churches—which in turn would force a horrific and deadly breach in national unity. The presence in America of that one unresolved faith issue, and the economy that became based upon it, was in the end too great a force for even our most sacred institutions to avoid.

With America's religious foundation cracked, and its churches in disagreement, what occurred next was probably inevitable—the largest and most influential American denominations split in two. That is the subject of our next chapter, but before delving into those divisions, one final quote captures the significance of this moment in time:

> If there was one condition *sine qua non* leading to the final disruption, according to many, many commentators, it was the severing of ecclesiastical ties. As the Civil War began, a Southern Presbyterian editor surveyed the event with grim satisfaction: "this present revolution," he declared, is nothing less than an "uprising" of Southern Christians. "Much as is due to many of our sagacious and gifted politicians, they could effect nothing until the religious union of the North and South was dissolved." [22]

If religious people who valued forgiveness, reconciliation and love could not resolve their differences, what hope for compromise was there for politicians—most of whom were lawyers—whose philosophy of social action was based on an adversary view of issues?

Donald Matthews, *Slavery & Methodism* (1965)

Further reading recommendations

Sidney Ahlstrom. Pp. 429–454 in *A Religious History of the American People.* New Haven, CT.: Yale University Press, 1972.

Richard Carwardine. *Evangelicals and Politics in Antebellum America.* New Haven, CT.: Yale University Press, 1993.

George Frederickson. "The Coming of the Lord: The Northern Protestant Clergy and the Civil War Crisis." Pp. 110–130 in *Religion and the American Civil War*, edited by Randall M. Miller, Harry S. Stout, and Charles R. Wilson. New York: Oxford University Press, 1998.

C.C. Goen. Pp. 1–42 in *Broken Churches, Broken Nation—Denominational Schisms and the Coming of the Civil War.* Macon, GA: Mercer University Press, 1985.

Samuel S. Hill. "Religion and the Results of the Civil War." Pp. 360–381 in *Religion and the American Civil War*, edited by Randall M. Miller, Harry S. Stout, and Charles R. Wilson. New York: Oxford University Press, 1998.

Samuel S. Hill Jr. *The South and the North in American Religion.* Athens, GA: University of Georgia, 1980.

Donald G. Matthews. *Religion in the Old South.* Chicago: University of Chicago Press, 1977.

James H. Moorhead. *American Apocalypse—Yankee Protestants and the Civil War, 1860–1869.* New Haven, CT: Yale University Press, 1978.

Notes

1. Gardiner Shattuck, *A Shield and a Hiding Place—The Religious Life of the Civil War Armies* (Macon, GA: Mercer University Press, 1987), 1.
2. Samuel S. Hill, *The South and North in American Religion* (Athens, GA: University of Georgia, 1980), 5.
3. *Ibid.*, cf. especially his Introduction on pp. 1–12.
4. I am greatly abbreviating Samuel Hill's thesis here, expounded in *The South and the North in American Religion.* Cf. pages 10–11 for his summary of this major theme of his fine book. Cf. also James Moorhead, *American Apocalypse—Yankee Protestants and the Civil War, 1860–69* (New Haven, CT: Yale University Press, 1976), 2–4.
5. The Congregationalists, the Presbyterians (both Old and New School), the northern Baptists (later renamed American Baptists) and the Methodist-Episcopal Church (North). Cf. Herman Hattaway and Lloyd A. Hunter, "The War Inside the Church," in *Civil War Times Illustrated* 26 (January 1988).

6. Moorhead's book *American Apocalypse* is foundational on this topic. Cf. James Moorhead, *op. cit.,* 1–22.

7. America's Quaker community was heavily involved in abolitionism, and were "lonely voices in the desert" crying out against it even as far back as pre-Revolutionary War times. Cf. James Moorhead, *op. cit.,* 85. Also cf. Samuel S. Hill, "Religion and the Results of the Civil War," in *Religion and the American Civil War,* edited by Randall M. Miller, Harry S. Stout, and Charles R. Wilson (New York: Oxford University Press, 1998), 378–80.

8. George Frederickson, "The Coming of the Lord," in *Religion and the Civil War, op. cit.,* 114.

9. James Moorhead, "Religion in the Civil War: The Northern Side," http://nhc.rtp.nc.us:8080/tserve/nineteen/nkeyinfo/cwnorth.htm (2001).

10. Frederickson, *op. cit.,* 118.

11. Cf. Samuel. Hill, "Religion and the Results of the Civil War," *op. cit.,* 374; also cf. Sidney Ahlstrom, *Religious History of the American People* (New York: Oxford University Press, 1972), 191–92.

12. Ahlstrom, *op. cit.,* 435–445.

13. James I. Robertson, *Soldiers Blue and Gray* (Columbia: University of South Carolina Press, 1988), 171.

14. Donald G. Matthews, *Religion in the Old South,* (Chicago: University of Chicago Press, 1977), 249.

15. Harry Stout, *Upon the Altar of the Nation—A Moral History of the Civil War* (New York: Viking/Penguin, 2006), 49.

16. James W. Silver, *Confederate Morale and Church Propaganda* (Tuscaloosa, AL: Confederate Publishing Company, 1957), 101.

17. I am thankful to Mitchell Snay's insights here, as expressed more fully in his *Gospel of Disunion—Religion and Separatism in the Antebellum South* (New York: Cambridge University, 1993). Cf. also Richard Carwardine, *Evangelicals and Politics in Antebellum America* (New Haven, CT: Yale University Press, 1993).

18. Hill, *op. cit.,* 35.

19. *Library of Congress Civil War Desk Reference,* edited by Mary Wagner, Gary Gallagher, and Paul Finkelman (New York: Simon and Schuster, 2002), 685.

20. This "spiritual church" argument was a two-edged sword—if Christians took no interest in *defending* slavery/abolition, then neither should they take any interest in *supporting* or encouraging it! Many Southern ministers betrayed their logic here by their enthusiastic support of both slavery and the Confederacy. The 1862 Georgia Methodists are an example, declaring that "The Church has a right to be heard in all legislative questions, to have a voice in all the deliberations of cabinets and councils." I am grateful to Steven Woodworth for his insight on this point. Cf. Woodworth, *While God is Marching On—The Religious Life of Civil War Soldiers* (Lawrence: University Press of Kansas, 2001), 119 and 125.

21. Hill, *op. cit.,* 16.

22. C.C. Goen, *Broken Churches, Broken Nation—Denominational Schisms and the Coming of the Civil War* (Macon, GA: Mercer University Press, 1985), 107.

Chapter Seven

PAVING THE WAY FOR SECESSION

> There are good arguments to support the claim that the split in the churches was not only the first break between the sections, but the chief cause of the final break.
>
> William Sweet, *Story of Religion in America* (1950)

Setting the scene

In 1852, a member of America's pre-eminent religious family (the Beechers[1]), published a book which none less than Abraham Lincoln called "the book that began this great war." Harriet Beecher Stowe, an able lay theologian herself, confronted a religiously divided county with *Uncle Tom's Cabin*, remarking that it was God who wrote the book. If indeed it was the Almighty who "wrote" that influential novel, it makes one wonder what the Almighty was telling his churches and clergy at the same time—for although they sang from the same hymnbook, they certainly were not singing the same hymn.

The years 1837–1860 were crucial years in American history, with momentous events occurring in religious and moral spheres that sent the runaway sled of American slavery crashing into a ghastly Civil War. *First*, never before or after was organized religion more active politically than in those twenty years before the Civil War. Religious rhetoric around slavery and abolition became self-righteous, vehement and almost without restraint. If, as Sidney Ahlstrom posits, the clergy were "official custodians of the American conscience," then their volatile pre-War writing and preaching indicated that America's conscience was in deep trouble.[2]

Second, a slow ripping of the seamless garment of American national and religious unity had begun—and God's "official" representatives were doing the ripping. As many religious historians recognize, it was America's churches and clergy who helped bring about the final break between North and South. In the *North*, the anti-slavery movement became a juggernaut driven and inspired by religious fervor. In the *South*, churchmen were the group most responsible for preserving a Biblically supported social order with slavery at the core. This would lead to denominational and national chasms that would not be resolved without the archetypal salvation of a horrendous "baptism of blood."[3]

Third, the immensely influential churches and clergy of antebellum America fumbled away a unique opportunity to resolve a national crisis. Because lawyers

61

and politicians had been unable to resolve the slavery controversy, America's clergy had a historic opportunity to step into the breach. Their social and political leadership had the potential of making a critical difference in avoiding what lay ahead. When public questions like those of slavery became defined as *moral* issues (rather than matters of legality or practicality) then the authority of ministers was enhanced—because they were recognized as having special competence on such ethical questions. But with America watching, listening, and searching for a way out of a national quagmire many were even unaware of, America's churches failed—morally, theologically, and Scripturally. Not only were they unable to help the nation, they were even unable to help themselves. Thus, some twenty-five years before South states would secede, America's churches "seceded" from each other.[4]

A British visitor to antebellum America observed that of American churches, Methodists and Baptists were the most numerous, "Episcopalians the most fashionable; and the Preeminence of wealth and intelligence was thought to lay with the Presbyterians."

Max Berger, *The British Traveller in America, 1836–1860* (1943)

The "elite" Presbyterians lead the way

In the 1830s, despite only being America's third largest denomination, Presbyterians dominated the intellectual and theological scene from their pulpits and presses. More than any other denomination, their communications network was nation-wide (particularly with their religious newspapers) and their educational influence dominant in both North and South (with educational centers in Columbia, Richmond, Princeton, Cincinnati, Chicago, and New York). Considered somewhat of an elite church among evangelicals because of their affluence and highly educated clergy, they had great leadership influence, and exercised it through a smoothly functioning organization (with structured presbyteries, synods, and assemblies).[5]

But at the 1837 General Assembly, seemingly innocuous issues of doctrine and missionary methods raised by a "New School" of thinkers had aroused great resistance in an "Old School" coalition of traditionalists and moderates. The insurgent New Schoolers were promoting more liberal measures for revivalism and interdenominational cooperation, seeking to move away from traditional interpretations of their old Calvinist roots.[6] But coincidentally, they also happened to represent most of the Presbyterian abolitionists, and were interested in speaking more to the antislavery feelings of their flocks. But in 1837, the Old School had carefully planned their move, and with little remorse they voted to remove the four "offending" synods—thus ridding themselves of so-called "heresy" and abolitionists in one fell swoop. The New School organized their own General Assembly a year later, but further divisions would unfortunately follow—an 1857 departure of 15,000 Southern New School members again, over increasing antislavery views (they ultimately joined the Old School, South); and an 1861 Old School split along northern and southern lines.[7]

While the New School had heeded the increasing volume of anti-slavery voices, the Old School could rejoice in a welcome victory over abolitionism. But despite the doctrinal and "heretical" overtones, no one was fooled about what lay at the bottom of the 1837 division. New School scholar Lyman Beecher (himself earlier acquitted in a heresy trial) wrote that "John Calhoun was at the bottom of it. I know of his doing things . . . It was a cruel thing—it was an accursed thing, and 'twas slavery that did it." The Cincinnati Journal and Luminary also knew what the issue was. "The real question is not between the new and old school—it is not in relation to doctrinal errors; but it is slavery and anti-slavery. It is not the [doctrinal] standards which were to be protected, but the system of slavery."[8]

Presbyterians on both sides clearly recognized where all this led. William Plummer warned in an August 1837 religious paper that "the Potomac will be dyed with blood" over the issue of slavery. James Henley Thornwell (staunch Old School defender) wondered aloud "Are our country, our Bible, our interests on earth and our hopes for heaven to be sacrificed on the altars of a fierce fanaticism? Slavery is implicated in every fibre of Southern society; it is with us a vital question . . . We would save the country if we could."[9]

But a desire to "save the country if we could" is different than *taking action* to actually do the saving. While New School Presbyterians attempted vainly to maintain peace among themselves, their 1857 split of twenty-one Southern and border presbyteries fully completed the split of America's most influential evangelical group. The southern-dominated Old School had long since retreated into self-righteous false peace, remarking in 1845 that she could not possibly "legislate where Christ has not legislated, nor make terms of membership which He has not made . . . the proper thing for the church to do is remain silent on the subject." By 1845, the silence and disunity of the Presbyterian "older brothers" had opened the door for trouble in the homes of their evangelical cousins.[10]

My religious belief teaches me to feel as safe in battle as in bed. God has fixed the time for my death. I do not concern myself about that, but to always be ready, no matter when it may overtake me.

Thomas J. "Stonewall" Jackson,
Presbyterian deacon

Chapter Seven

Methodists, Baptists, and slave-owning bishops

The largest pre-war Christian denomination was the Methodist Episcopal Church, followed closely by the Baptists. In 1850, in twenty-three of the thirty-two states in the Union, *Methodists* had more churches than any other denomination, with Baptists leading in eight others (Catholics led in newly admitted California). Because of the Methodist's highly successful and well-defined structure of conferences, traveling preachers, and societies, they were literally the most extensive national institution in antebellum America other than the federal government. Their national network of itinerant preachers and conferences brought Methodists unity, prosperity and a powerful influence in the country. The comment of an 1836 Oberlin divinity student is revealing about the great influence that Methodism could have. "Citizens mostly turned out to hear. They were not willing to form a society [to oppose slavery] immediately. The reason was they were chiefly Methodists, and were afraid to move until their minister should say—*move.*"[11]

Baptists in America grew from less than 900 churches in 1790 to more than 12,000 in 1860. In the years following the Civil War, they became the largest denomination in the south (Southern Baptists remain today America's largest Protestant denomination). While Baptists were close behind Methodists in pre-war membership numbers, their greater "congregationalist" tendencies (mistrust of authority, passion for individual freedom, belief in the autonomy of the local church) minimized a deeper bonding within their churches and a broader national influence.

Still, the majority of Baptists did band together in regional associations for fellowship, information sharing and mutual counsel, and these groups had a respected moral authority. Baptist periodicals and tracts circulated widely across the country, keeping church members well-informed of broader national and denominational events. Thus, although less "formally connected" than the Methodists, the Baptists had a strong national network of denominational relationships—and their societies covered a wide constituency of committed evangelical believers.[12]

Curiously, it was the same issue acted out in similar scenarios which led to the division of both evangelical groups. Abolitionism began to rise as a major issue in the 1830s in both denominations, as primarily northern ministers grew more and more outspoken in their condemnations of slavery. In April 1840, Northern Baptist abolitionists issued *An Address to Southern Baptists* denying the standard biblical justifications for slavery, urging Southerners to "confess their sinfulness" and to immediately begin action for legal emancipation. Stung by the attack, Baptists in the South warned that "unless aspersions upon their character ceased they would cut off their benevolent funds to the general Baptist agencies and, if necessary, even separate from them altogether."

The 1836 Methodist Conference was forced to address the growing slavery controversy (they acknowledged its evil but declined to legislate), but as hostilities over the issue continued to crystallize, twenty-two abolitionist ministers (and 6,000

64

members) left in 1843 and formed a new denomination—the Wesleyan Methodist Church. Finally, in 1844–1845, following years of intra-denominational debate, heated letters and publications, position papers and dire warnings, the intense ecclesiastical war over slavery (mixed now with church authority questions) brought the crisis to its boiling point.

> As its greatest social institution, the church in the South constituted the major resource of the Confederacy in the building and maintenance of civilian morale. As no other group, Southern clergymen were responsible for a state of mind which made secession possible . . .
>
> James Silver, *Confederate Morale and Church Propaganda* (1957)

Methodists: It was debate over the qualifications of potential denominational leaders that was the catalyst for division in both denominations. The new Methodist bishop of Georgia, James O. Andrew, owned slaves as a result of both an inheritance and his second marriage to a slave-owning woman. A group of delegates at the 1844 Methodist Conference instructed him to desist from exercising his office while this "impediment" remained—bringing a howl of protest from Andrews (who argued that Georgia law forbad masters to free slaves), all the Southern delegates and a few Northern as well. Following a lengthy and heated series of debates, the Conference ended in a strange blend of peace and drama—with a formal motion (approved by delegates from both sections) to separate the church into two parts.

Thus, in May 1845, the *Methodist Episcopal Church, South* was formally born—soon including several highly acclaimed universities and colleges, as well as a religious influence second only to the Southern Baptist Convention. Three years later, however, angry Northern Methodists condemned the Southern delegates' actions, declaring them "null and void," and beginning what historian Sydney Ahlstrom called the "gory and ghastly Methodist border warfare."[13]

The division in the Methodists was not without irony. The founder of Methodism, John Wesley, had in 1785 denounced slavery as "that execrable sum of all villainies," describing American slavery as "the vilest that ever saw the sun." Reflecting the split personality of the southern white mind, Methodists also had the best-known and organized outreach for bringing slaves to Jesus, beginning in the 1830s and continuing right up to the division. But despite seventy years of post-war meetings about their differences, Methodists would continue to live with appendage "comma South" until 1939 when the two groups finally united to form *The Methodist Church*. However in the bloody Civil War to come, until America's central unresolved moral issue was resolved by the "theologians" Sherman and Grant, each Methodist branch would be an unwavering cheerleader for their respective sides.[14]

Baptists: The 1845 Baptist separation had been brewing for years because of the abolitionism of Northern members. In November 1844, Alabama Baptists demanded that the Baptist General Convention declare that slaveholders were as eligible to become missionaries as non-slaveholders. The Acting Board (a small group located in Boston) demurred at this "hypothetical question" but maintained its right to judge the competency or fitness of any applicant, and then opined that they could "never be party to any arrangement that which would certainly imply approbation of slavery." Southerners then declared that the Board had overstepped its authority, and when proslavery advocates assembled in Augusta, Georgia on May 8, 1845, the *Southern Baptist Convention* was born. Included in the 293 delegates from eight states (and the District of Columbia) were governors, judges, congressmen and other high functionaries—all defending slaveholding as Biblically sanctioned, even as they expressed "profound responsibility" for the "integrity of the nation, the institutions of truth, and the sacred enterprise of converting the heathen."[15]

The northern Baptists convention would refashion itself in a more congregationalist way, calling itself the "American Baptist Missionary Union." After the war, although every other denomination would eventually re-unite, Baptists would prove the exception—the Southern Baptists remained staunchly independent. In fact, post-war Southern Baptists became a culture and a way of life—their message included social conservatism, white supremacy and preservation of a strict racial hierarchy. In conclusion, John Patrick Daly remarks about Baptists that "the birth of the Southern Baptist Convention and the birth of the Confederacy were closely linked; southern ministers who built the antebellum southern churches were also instrumental in building the Confederacy . . . Southern religion thus became the ideological foundation both of secession and of the war effort."[16]

> Much as is due to many of our sagacious and gifted politicians, they could effect nothing until the religious union of the North and South was dissolved, nor until they received the moral support and co-operation of Southern Christianity.
>
> A.A. Porter, 20 April 1861 editorial in *Southern Presbyterian*

America reacts to the evangelical "civil war" [17]

Three evangelical "popular churches" dominated in the mid-nineteenth-century, and were America's most formidable subculture. What Presbyterians, Baptists and Methodists wrote, taught, preached and believed had enormous influence upon every aspect of American religious, social and political life. When these denominations divided, ecclesiastical shock waves rolled over the country. Reacting to the divisions, political leaders of all persuasions wondered aloud about the country's future, asking how long north and south could share the same political union if they no longer even worshiped in the same Christian churches.[18]

Senator *Henry Clay* of Kentucky was not a practicing Christian most of his life, but joined the Episcopal Church in 1847. The final years of his life were devoted to efforts of pacification and compromise, and he seems to have brooded frequently over the political consequences of the church schisms. In April 1845, he warned Southern Methodists who were planning their separation: "I will not say that such a separation would necessarily produce a dissolution of the political union of these States; but the example would be fraught with imminent danger." After both Methodists and Baptists had separated, and shortly before his 1852 death, Clay said in an interview: "I tell you, this sundering of the religious ties which have hitherto bound our people together, I consider the greatest source of danger to our country. If our religious men cannot live together in peace, what can be expected of us politicians, very few of whom profess to be governed by the great principles of love?"[19]

Perhaps the most famous yet ironic warning came from *John C. Calhoun*—a man whose rhetoric helped bring the churches and country to the boiling point in the first place. On 4 March 1850, his eloquent message was read in the United States Senate (he was too feeble to deliver it himself), and centered on how the cords that bound the States together were now snapping.

> Some cords are spiritual or ecclesiastical; some political; others social . . . The strongest of those of a spiritual and ecclesiastical nature, consisted in the unity of the great religious denominations, all of whom originally embraced the whole Union. All these denominations . . . were organized very much upon the principle of our political institutions.

Calhoun then carefully reviewed the snapped cords—the first had been the Methodist Episcopal Church, the second Baptists, the third Presbyterians ("not entirely snapped, but some of its strands have given away"). The Episcopalians were the only major Protestant denomination "who remain unbroken and entire . . . ." Calhoun was clearly worried about this, as he concluded "If the agitation goes on, the same force, acting with increased intensity . . . will finally snap every cord, when nothing will be left to hold the States together except force."[20]

But the damage had been done. With the religious cords gone, the political cords, when they broke, snapped quickly and in rapid succession. In November 1860 Abraham Lincoln was elected President. On December 20, 1860, South Carolina delegates voted unanimously to secede from the Union. By February 1, 1861 six other Southern states had left. On April 12th, Confederate Captain George James ordered his batteries to open fire on Ft. Sumter. On April 14th, the first two soldiers died of some 620,000 that would follow—killed accidentally in an ammunition explosion. Political secession had followed religious secession—and the churches of God had paved the way.

Chapter Seven

Further reading recommendations

Richard Carwardine. *Evangelicals and Politics in Antebellum America.* New Haven, CT: Yale University Press, 1993.

John P. Daly. *When Slavery Was Called Freedom: Evangelicalism, Proslavery, and the Causes of the Civil War.* Lexington: University Press of Kentucky, 2003.

George Frederickson. "The Coming of the Lord." Pp. 110–130 in *Religion and the American Civil War*, edited by Randall M. Miller, Harry S. Stout, and Charles R. Wilson, New York: Oxford University Press, 1998.

Eugene Genovese. "Religion in the Collapse of the American Union." Pp. 74–88 in *Religion and the American Civil War*, edited by Randall M. Miller, Harry S. Stout, and Charles R. Wilson, New York: Oxford University Press, 1998.

C.C. Goen. Pp. 65–107 of *Broken Churches, Broken Nation.* Macon, GA: Mercer University Press, 1985.

Mark A. Noll. Pp. 1–29 of *The Civil War as a Theological Crisis.* Chapel Hill: University of North Carolina Press, 2006.

Notes

1. At the time of the War, no American religious family was as prominent as the Lyman Beecher family. *Lyman Beecher (1775–1863)* himself was an ordained Presbyterian minister, a Yale graduate, a stern Calvinist moral author and reformer and a well-known revivalist preacher. He married three times (Roxanna Foote in 1799, Harriet Porter in 1817, Lydia Beals in 1835), and had 13 children between them. After pastoring briefly in a Congregationalist Church, he returned to his Presbyterian roots and in 1832 became president of Cincinnati's Lane Theological Seminary. Son *Edward Beecher (1803–1895)* was a college president, and pastor of churches in Boston, Galesburg and Brooklyn. *Catharine Esther Beecher (1800–1878)*, a teacher and popular writer, was physically frail but indefatigable in her fight for women's issues. At odds with her father's stern Calvinistic beliefs, she transferred her membership from the Congregationalist to Episcopal Church. *Thomas Beecher (1824–1900)* was chaplain of the 141st NY Vols., defended slavery, and opposed temperance and women's rights movements. *Henry Ward Beecher (1813–1887)* was a prominent New York Congregationalist pastor, becoming one of America's most renowned preachers. In 1854, his Plymouth Church in Brooklyn sent boxes of Sharp's rifles to new settlers in Kansas to help them resist proslavery radicals. They became known as "Beecher's Bibles." *James Chaplin Beecher (1828–1886)* became the Civil War colonel of a black volunteer regiment, committing suicide in 1886. *Harriet Beecher Stowe (1811–1898)* married a Congregational professor of the Old Testament, wrote the classic *Uncle Tom's Cabin* and nu-

merous other works (averaging one a year until her death). *Uncle Tom's Cabin* was described by one critic as "a verbal earthquake, an ink-and-paper tidal wave." Cf. Sidney Ahlstrom, *A Religious History of the American People* (New Haven, CT: Yale University Press, 1972), 657; Chris Armstrong, *Christian History and Biography*, "People Worth Knowing," 43–45; John W. Brinsfield, William C. Davis, Benedict Maryniak, and James I. Robertson Jr. *Faith in the Fight—Civil War Chaplains* (Mechanicsburg, PA: Stackpole Books, 2003), 7–8; and Mark Galli, "Firebrands and Visionaries," in *Christian History* 11, no. 1 (1992).

2. For more details on the topic of the inflammatory pre-War preaching and writing of America's clergy, see George Frederickson, "The Coming of the Lord—The Northern Protestant Clergy and the Civil War Crisis," in *Religion and the American Civil War*, edited by Randall M. Miller, Harry S. Stout, and Charles R. Wilson (New York: Oxford University Press, 1998), 110–113; James Moorhead, *American Apocalypse—Yankee Protestants and the Civil War, 1860–1869* (New Haven, CT: Yale University Press, 1978).

3. Harry Stout speaks at length of the post-War significance of this "baptism in blood" for both North and South. He refers to the great Civil War effusion of blood being the core "sacrifice" that brought about a new and unifying post-war civil religion centered around the "sacred" cause of patriotism and Union. Cf. Harry S. Stout, *Upon the Altar of a Nation* (New York: Viking/Penguin, 2006).

4. I am grateful to George Frederickson for his insights in this section. (Cf. George Frederickson, "The Coming of the Lord—The Northern Protestant Clergy and the Civil War Crisis," in *Religion and the American Civil War, op. cit.*, 112.) As mentioned earlier, not only did antebellum Americans attend church, but they sought divine approbation for their social and political views. Eugene Genovese speaks of this in his essay "Religion in the Collapse of the American Union," when he says "the country's most socially and politically influential leaders were either committed Christians themselves, or demonstrated that they knew their politically decisive constituents to be so. Both abolitionists and slaveholders appealed to Scripture." (Eugene Genovese, "Religion in the Collapse of the American Union," in *Religion and the American Civil War, op. cit.*, 75.) Cf. Mark Noll's book *The Civil War as a Theological Crisis* (Chapel Hill: University of North Carolina Press, 2006) for a marvelous description of the intense Scriptural and theological problems posed by the American Civil War. In this book, Noll outlines how mid-nineteenth century religious divisiveness not only paralyzed the dominant Protestant Reformed theology of the time, but also crippled its development well after the war.

5. Presbyterian theological seminaries were Richmond Theological (Virginia), Princeton (New Jersey), Lane Theological (Cincinnati), McCormick Theological (Chicago, known pre-war as the "Presbyterian Theological Seminary of the North West") and Union Theological (New York). After the war, although they declined in denominational numbers, Presbyterians continued their strong national influence. They were almost over-represented in the ranks of the architects of the Lost Cause. James Henley Thornwell, Benjamin Morgan Palmer, Robert L. Dabney (who unabashedly promoted the "sanctity" of his deceased Presbyterian commander "Stonewall" Jackson) and others were all forces to be reckoned with. For more details here, see Samuel S. Hill, "Religion and the Results of the Civil War," in *Religion and the American Civil War, op. cit.*, 375; and Harry Stout and Christopher Grasso, "Civil War, Religion and Communications—The Story of Richmond," *ibid.*, 317; C.C. Goen, *Broken Churches, Broken Nation—Denominational Schisms and the Coming of the Civil War* (Macon, Ga.: Mercer University Press, 1985), 61–61 and 68–78.

6. Eugene Genovese remarks that New Schoolers had "retreated from Calvinistic orthodoxy, and tolerated abandonment of longstanding commitment to doctrines of predestination, original sin, human depravity and much else" (Cf. Genovese, "Religion in the Collapse of the American Union," in *Religion and the American Civil War, op. cit.*, 78.)

7. For more details, see George Marsden, *The Evangelical Mind and the New School Presbyterian Experience: A Case Study of Thought and Theology in 19th Century America* (New Haven, CT: Yale University Press, 1970), 65–66. C.C. Goen, *op. cit.*, 68–78 was foundational for me in laying out these scenarios.

8. Lyman Beecher, vol. 2 of *The Autobiography of Lyman Beecher,* ed. Barbara Cross, 2 vols.; (Cambridge, Mass.: Harvard University Press, 1961), 323. Also *Journal and Luminary* (Cincinnati), 15 January 1837; *Biblical Repository and Princeton Review* 9 (1837), 479.

9. Cf. the 1851 article by James Henley Thornwell, "Relation of Church to Slavery," in *The Collected Writings of James Henley Thornwell,* edited by John B. Adger and John L. Girardeau, 4 vols. (Richmond, VA: Robert Carter and Bros., 1871–1873); vol. 4, 394–96.

10. By 1870, Old and New School divisions had healed, but the deep geographical divide lasted years longer. In 1983, Louisville Presbyterian Theological Seminary played a key role in helping re-unite the branches, after decades of pushing in that direction. Prominent war-time Presbyterians included *Charles Hodge* (Princeton's Old School seminary); *Moses Drury Hoge* (prominent Richmond pastor); *Thomas Smyth* (Presbyterian *"divine"* from South Carolina); *James Henley Thornwell* (the "Calhoun of the southern church"); *Thomas Cobb* (Georgia politician, fiery secession advocate); *Robert Lewis Dabney* (future Confederate staff officer, ordained minister, later unreconstructed theology professor at Union Seminary in Virginia); *Benjamin Morgan Palmer* (renowned Louisiana preacher); *Lyman Beecher* (moral reformer, president of Lane Theological); and *George H. Stuart* (Philadelphia layman/merchant who was the first President of the Christian Commission).

11. The quote is from Gilbert Barnes and Dwight Dumond, eds., *Letters to Theodore Dwight Weld, Angelina Grimke-Weld and Sarah Grimke,* 2 vols., Gloucester, MA, 1965, as cited in Goen, *op. cit.*, 58. As mentioned in a previous chapter, by the time of secession Methodists had 45% of the total number of churches in seceding states and Baptists 37%. Cf. C.C. Goen, *op. cit.*, 54–59; also Mark Noll, *op. cit.*, 26–27 for his insightful summary of the influential role that Methodists and evangelicals played prior to the war.

12. Cf. C.C. Goen, *op. cit.*, 59–61. Though Baptists had no central governing authority or any supreme judicatory, they did have several "extra-church" organizations which, although having narrowly-defined purposes, had great national influence and financial support from individual contributors. The unity of these national groups, however, was disrupted first by a feeling that home-missions agencies within the body had failed to evangelize Southern territory, and then later by the slavery arguments. Examples of such Baptist societies were two large national missionary groups, a tract society (later known as the American Baptist Publication Society), an education society and the Baptist Young People's Union. In fact, probably the single most popular piece of religious literature in the war (*A Mother's Parting Words to her Soldier Boy)* was written by a Virginia Baptist minister, Jeremiah Bell Jeter—over 250,000 copies were eventually distributed. (Cf. Paul Harvey, "Yankee Faith" and Southern Redemption," in *Religion and the American Civil War, op. cit.,*171.) Cf. also Frank S. Mead and Samuel S. Hill, *Handbook of Denominations in the United States* (11th edition) (Nashville, TN: Abingdon Press, 2001).

13. Sidney Ahlstrom, *Religious History of the American People* (New Haven, CT: Yale University Press, 1972), 660. Cf. also Samuel S. Hill, *The South and North in American Religion* (Athens: University of Georgia Press, 1980), 62; Steven Woodworth, *While God Is Marching On—The Religious Life of Civil War Soldiers* (Lawrence: University Press of Kansas, 2001), 20; and C.C. Goen, *op. cit.*, 90–98.

14. 500 of the Union's 2000 chaplains were Methodist. In the South, so many Methodist ministers enlisted that by spring 1862, Methodist Bishop Anderson and other prominent clerics were greatly concerned, worrying that too many pulpits were empty! Southern Methodists suffered greatly from wartime privations, while their Northern namesakes prospered in membership and wealth. Methodist denominational strength declined in the second half of the nineteenth century, slipping to second behind the Baptists—but they remained a power because of their sheer numbers. (There were one and a half million members by 1906 in the main Methodist Episcopal South branch alone.) Some prominent wartime Methodists were: *Jesse T. Peck* (minister and quasi-official historian of antebellum evangelical Christianity); *Matthew Simpson* (bishop known as the "evangelist of patriotism" for his itinerant Northern revivals); *William G. Brownlow* (circuit rider for ten years, editor of the Knoxville *Whig*, fiery pro-Union orator, post-war Tennessee Governor and Senator—all the while insisting slavery was the right and natural condition of persons of color!); *John Cowper Granberry* (well-known CSA chaplain) and *Oliver O. Howard* (Union General, active layman, leader of the Freedman's Bureau; Howard University was named after him.) Cf. George Frederickson, "The Coming of the Lord," in *Religion and the American Civil War, op. cit.*, 115; Webb Garrison, *Civil War Curiosities—Strange Stories, Oddities, Events and Coincidences* (Nashville, TN: Rutledge Hill Press, 1994), 50; and Ahlstrom, *op. cit.*, 677, footnote #16.

15. Of the 293 delegates at the May 1845 meeting, 139 were from Georgia and 102 from South Carolina. John Patrick Daly speaks of how the birth of the Southern Baptist Convention and the birth of the Confederacy were closely linked—for the same ministers who broke away to form the Baptist Convention were instrumental in building and supporting the Confederacy. Daly goes on to remark that "in 1995 the largest Protestant denomination in the United States, the Southern Baptist Convention, apologized for their church having promoted slavery and segregation. Even more remarkably, the Convention finally acknowledged the obvious: that it had been founded in 1845 in order to defend slaveholding as biblically sanctioned." John Patrick Daly, *When Slavery Was Called Freedom: Evangelicalism, Proslavery, and the Causes of the Civil War* (Lexington: University Press of Kentucky, 2003), 34. Cf. also Samuel Hill, *op. cit.*, 64–65; and C.C. Goen, *op. cit.*, 90–98.

16. John Patrick Daly, *op. cit.*, 34. Cf. also Paul Harvey, "Yankee Faith" and Southern Redemption," in *Religion and the American Civil War, op. cit.*, pp. 180–181; and Sidney Ahlstrom, *op. cit.*, 664–665. Some prominent war-time Baptists were *Basil Manly Sr. and Jr.* (prominent Alabama planters and ministers, Manly Sr. was also a college President and strong secessionist); *Richard Fuller* (prominent South Carolina leader); *John Broadus* (late nineteenth century southern educator, renowned Confederate preacher); *W. F. Broadus* (renowned Confederate preacher); *John William Jones* (author of *Christ in Camp*, chaplain of Army of Northern, Virginia, postwar "Lost Cause" apologist); *Jeremiah Bell Jeter* (Richmond, Virginia pastor, teacher, co-founder of Southern Baptist Conference, "*reluctant slave owner*"); *James B. Gambrell* (President of Southern Baptist Conference); *Barnas Sears* (minister and president of Brown University). Cf. *Religion and the American Civil War, op. cit.*, 93, 122, 176; 327, 348.

17. Aside from Baptists, Methodists and Presbyterians, several other churches did divide over Civil War issues. The *Episcopalians* split for the duration of the war (forming the Protestant Episcopal Church in the Confederate States, and using a Southern-oriented version of the *Book of Common Prayer*), but quickly reunited at war's end. The *Lutherans* saw several serious breaks around the war years, but only one was directly connected to the War - the 1863 formation of the United Synod of the South. In 1918, they merged with the Lutheran General Synod and the General Council to form the United Lutheran Church. *Roman Catholics* and *Jews* (due to their unique church polities) did not formally split, rather individual churches, temples, priests and rabbis generally lined up with the section of the country they were in. *Congregationalists* did not split, nor did the strongly Northern and liberal *Unitarians* and *Universalists*—in fact these two would themselves merge in 1961 to form the Unitarian Universalist Association. Cf. Frank S. Mead and Samuel S. Hill, *Handbook of Denominations, op. cit.*

18. Richard J. Carwardine, *Evangelicals and Politics in Antebellum America* (New Haven, CT: Yale University Press, 1993), 44. Eugene Genovese, "Religion in the Collapse of the American Union," *op. cit.*, 78–79. Cf. also C.C. Goen, *op. cit.*, 98–107.

19. Henry Clay letter to William A. Booth, 7 April 1845, in *The Works of Henry* Clay, ed. Calvin Colvin, 6 vols., (New York, 1857); and Chester F. Dunham, *The Attitude of Northern Clergy Towards the South, 1860–1865* (Toledo, OH: Gray Company, 1942). Both works are cited in C.C. Goen, *op. cit.*, 101 and 105–106.

20. Richard K. Cralle, ed., *Speeches of John C. Calhoun* (New York, 1968); as cited in C.C. Goen, *ibid.*

Chapter Eight

THE INVISIBLE INSTITUTION

> Missus, don't cry; it vex the Lord. I had t'irteen children, and
> I ain't got one left to even put a coal in my pipe, and if I did not
> trust de Lord Jesus what would become of me?
>
> Old Georgia ex-slave to her master

Out of the motherland

The Africans who were to become Americans came from a vast region of Western Africa stretching inland for two to three hundred miles. They came from villages where agriculture, farming and nature were at the center of life, where spirits dwelt in each thing around them, and where isolation was unthinkable since the self was always in relationship to others. Thus, the ordeal of being captured by another tribe, sold to European merchants, transported through a horrendous "middle passage" and ultimately enslaved as a marketable object in the New World—these were events that were a radical rupture of one's entire spirit, soul and universe.[1] As the transplanted Africans struggled to comprehend the evil that had befallen them, their intrinsic spiritual natures discovered something unique in America they had not seen before—a "fully articulated ritual relationship with the Supreme Being, who was pictured in the book Christians called the Bible not just as Creator and Ruler, but also as the God of History, a God who lifted up and cast down nations and peoples." They discovered a God, a gentle Savior, and a theology of history, that could help make sense of their enslavement.[2]

Early colonial planters had scant interest in converting their slaves, because it was generally believed that Christianity spoiled slaves, making them impudent and rebellious. But in 1701 (136 years after Spanish black Catholic slaves landed in St. Augustine, 82 years after African slaves arrived at Jamestown), the Anglican Church set up a society to support missionary work among slaves in the colonies. They accomplished this only after convincing masters of their duty to catechize slaves, and by reinforcing the fact (later a colonial law) that baptism would not imply emancipation. Master need not fear changes in their systems—on the contrary, Christianity actually made *better* slaves by convincing them to obey their masters out of moral duty, and not just fear. As one historian summed it up, "These clergymen had been forced by the circumstance of racial slavery in America into propagating the Gospel by presenting it as an attractive device for slave control." Thus from America's earliest roots, a central symbiotic connection was created between Scripture, slavery and the South. It would remain our heritage for over 200 years.[3]

Anglican missionaries had only mixed success with slave conversions for the first 120 years of black slavery in British North America. While a few successful missions were established, many could report only vague intentions instead of concrete accomplishments. It was the 1740's First Great Awakening sweeping through the colonies which saw the first large numbers of slave conversions. In contrast to the slow Anglican process of indoctrination, evangelicals like Edwards, Whitefield and Tennent preached the immediate experience of conversion as the primary requirement for baptism, thus making Christianity more quickly accessible. The evangelical's downplaying of instruction and learning as pre-requisites for the Christian life encouraged the poor, illiterate and even the enslaved to participate in the highly charged prayer meetings and revival services.

From 1790–1815,[4] an increasing number of slaves converted to Christianity, influenced by the powerful revival preaching of both Baptists and Methodists. In the emotional and sometimes ecstatic expressions of Faith found there, slaves found a form of worship that touched their roots. The native spirit of the motherland found a connection with the Holy Spirit of American evangelical worship, and thus, in both Civil War America and today, these two denominations continue to predominate in African-American communities.

> The white people retired, and the meeting was continued by the black people. Friday was the greatest day of all. We had a Lord's Supper at night . . . three of the preachers fell helpless within the altar, and one lay a considerable time before he came to himself. From that, the work of convictions and conversions spread, and there was no intermission until the break of day. . . .
>
> 1807 Georgia revival preacher

"Come ye out from among them" [5]

As Andrew Billingsley points out, from the beginning, black Americans were involuntary adherents to a "host society" in which their own creative participation was severely limited by law, tradition and even religion. So, it was only natural that relatively early on black Christians became cramped by white church styles, stifled by requirements of racial conformity found even there, and that they heeded the Scriptural call to "come ye out from among them." In the post-Revolutionary spirit of religious independence, it had become possible to organize all-black churches. Under the auspices of the Great Awakening evangelists, a considerable number of black preachers had been ordained, licensed and begun to pastor their own flocks.

Thus several "African" churches (as they were then called) grew up even before 1800—with the Baptists of Silver Bluff, South Carolina being credited as the first black American church (founded 1773–1775). Evidence indicates that at least a dozen others had been formed by 1800, many in the South and mostly Baptist, but some Methodist and Presbyterian as well.

The free black communities of the North (specifically African Methodists in conflict with white elders) gave birth to a new independent black denomination, the *African Methodist Episcopal Church* in Philadelphia in 1816 (led by former slave and Bishop Richard Allen). Another African Methodist denomination was also organized in 1821 in New York. In the decades ahead, freedman from these groups would be some of the most articulate and sophisticated spokesmen for black freedom in America. In Southern slave states, because of restrictive laws, the usual Methodist practice was to compose local churches of both black and white members, with special seating allotted to blacks (who actually often outnumbered the whites). In 1790, the Methodist church reported 11,862 "colored" members (almost a fifth of the church's total), with Baptists believed to have converted many more.

> We had prayer meetings on the plantation once or twice a week. We went to the white folks church on Sunday. We went to both Methodist and Presbyterian. The preacher told us to obey our marsters.
>
> Henry James Trentham,
> former North Carolina slave

However, after 1830, events changed the religious mood in the South. The vocal anti-slavery movement had grown far more intense, and along with insurrections like those of Denmark Vesey (1822) and minister Nat Turner (1831), the Southern planters became far more defensive and reactionary. Ironically, this led to a burst of enthusiasm for promoting religion among slaves, for whereas planters had previously been fearful of slaves *with* religion, now they feared slaves *without* it! While resisting black literacy and independent religious worship (and enforcing that with laws), they now encouraged black church activity—with white ministers or under white supervision, of course—as a means of social control. As Eugene Genovese phrases it, they "had the good sense to know that if the slaves were listening to a reliable white preacher, they could not—at that moment, at least—be off in the woods listening to some suspect black exhorter." By the 1850s, Christianity had spread rapidly throughout the slave quarters, although most slaves never held formal membership in regular churches.[6]

In this situation, as Sydney Ahlstrom points out, clearly "only the most incomplete kind of Christianization could be carried out. One ex-slave described the situation when he said that 'the colored folks had their own code of religion, not nearly so complicated as the white man's.'"[7] What that ex-slave meant was quite simple—resisting attempts at social control, effectively shut out of church in all but formal ways, southern blacks went ahead and held their own religious gatherings anyway. Meeting in secret, outside of white control, risking punishment if caught, black believers held their own unique worship—in slave quarters, brush arbors, wherever they could get away.

At these meetings, the slaves expressed their own interpretations of Christianity, connected it with folk beliefs from African culture, and empowered it by their unique tragedies, yearnings and hopes. Their spiritual songs were songs of faith and hope, invested with intense meaning. Their Christian worship necessarily contradicted that of their masters—for no matter how religious they might be, the faith of their masters was compatible with slavery, while that of the slaves was not. In a great irony, the very same Biblical stories of Exodus that inspired the Puritan leader John Winthrop and his 1640 colonial American flock, now gave hope, conviction and perseverance to 1850 black Southern Americans on the eve of war. The image-laden prayer uttered by a female house slave whose daughter had just been brutally whipped was typical. "Thar's a day comin'! I hear the rumblin' ob de chariots! I see de flashin' ob de guns! . . . Oh, Lor'! Roll on de chariots, an' gib de black people rest an' peace."[8]

> The black church has always been considered the most formidable bastion of black solidarity . . . It remains so today: The black church is the uncontested mother of black culture.
>
> Andrew Billingsley, *Mighty Like a River* (1999)

The "invisible institution" of slave religion

With the institutions of the country against them and the institution of slavery oppressing them, black slaves needed something to anchor them, to encourage them to "keep on keepin' on" and to wait for the "Jubilee day" ahead. Religion became that *invisible institution,* albeit a highly unique one, giving them "the one thing they had to have if they were to resist being transformed into the Sambos they had been programmed to become. It fired them with a sense of their own worth before God and man." Religion protected slaves against a destructive self-hatred by emphasizing their sense of Divine worth. Religion gave a perspective with which to look upon themselves and white men—one that taught them they were in God's hands despite their fears, and there was a truth and standard for all humanity. Religion taught Christian slaves standards of dignity and integrity which obliged them to be honest, and which, in confronting their Christian masters, provided them with techniques that could undermine the master's power over them.[9]

The slave religion which was their solace and strength was truly unique. Combining evangelistic Christianity with African elements, a distinctive black American religion started to come together—one that was the chief means by which these former Africans, bereft of native culture, language and religion, could define their personal and social existence in America. W.E.B. Du Bois' classic research explains the three elements which characterized "the religion of the slave"—preacher, music and frenzy. The *preacher* "is the most unique personality developed by the Negro on American soil. A leader, a politician, an orator, a 'boss,' an intriguer, an idealist." Then, of *music* he wrote "the music of Negro religion is that plaintive rhythmic melody with its minor cadences which, despite caricature and defilement, still remains the most original and beautiful expression of human life and longing yet born on American soil." Lastly, the third characteristic: "Finally, the *Frenzy* or "Shouting', when the Spirit of the Lord passed by, and seizing the devotee, made him mad with supernatural joy . . . [it is] the one more devoutly believed in than all the rest." Thus, the slaves did not simply become Christians, they fashioned Christianity into a unique institution which fit their own distinctive experiences of enslavement in America.[10]

> Oh, Jesus tell you once before,
>   Babylon's fallin' to rise no more;
>   To go in peace an' sin no more;'
>   Babylon's fallin' to rise no more.
>
>   Sung at fall of Richmond

The outbreak of the Civil War disrupted the normal religious work carried out by churches, especially in the South, where 14% of eligible clergy became chaplains. Despite difficulties, estimates show that between an eighth and a sixth of the South's slave population of four million may have been affiliated with some church in at least a vague way. Slaves in the war-time south became increasingly aware of the issues at stake, and despite the problems this entailed, a certain jubilant hopefulness could be heard in their songs. Booker T. Washington remembered those days vividly. "As the great day drew nearer, there was more singing in the slave quarters than usual. It was bolder, had more ring, and lasted well into the night."

Northern black churches became major proponents of the anti-slavery cause, with many pastors and parishioners getting heavily involved with the Underground Railroad. Sojourner Truth, Harriet Tubman and Frederick Douglass were all members of the A.M.E. Zion Church who guided runaway slaves to freedom in Canada (often using church buildings as safe houses along the way).[11]

Finally in 1863, as momentum in the North grew politically, a dream was fulfilled for the many black churchmen and community leaders like Frederick Douglass who had been its promoters—the first black Union troops were recruited and saw action. They went on to play a crucial role in the Civil War both symbolically and actually, with approximately 200,000 blacks fighting in the Union Army and Navy. James McPherson writes that "without their help, the North could not have won the war as soon as it did, and perhaps it could not have won at all. The Negro was crucial to the whole Union war effort."[12] As they fought, they brought pride to their race, and carried their religion with them. Many used spare time learning to read and write, with the Bible being first on their list of books.

Thomas Wentworth Higginson's masterpiece, *Army Life in a Black Regiment*, captures the power that this "invisible institution" had on soldiers he came to love:

> Never, since Cromwell's time, had there been soldiers in whom the religious element held such a place. "A religious army," "a gospel army," were their frequent phrases. A few men . . . belonged to the ancient order of hypocrites, but not many. The most reckless and daring fellows in the regiment were perfect fatalists in their confidence that God would watch over them, and that if they died, it would be because their time had come. This almost excessive faith, and the love of freedom and of their families, all co-operated with their pride as soldiers to make them do their duty . . . It was their demeanor under arms that shamed the nation into recognizing them as men.[13]

In their unique black religion, with its praise meetings, ecstatic worship and transcendent spirituals, black Americans had found a way to survive. In doing so, they discovered a source of strength and endurance that would enable them to triumph not just the slavery of the past, but the Jim Crow prejudice yet to come.

Sunday was a great day around the plantation. The fields was forgotten, the light chores was hurried through, and everybody got ready for the church meeting. It was out of doors, in the yard fronting the big lot ... Master John's wife would start the meeting with a prayer and then would come the singing—the old timey songs. But white folks on the next plantation would lick their slaves for trying to do like we did. No praying there, and no singing.

As cited in Eugene Genovese, *Roll, Jordan, Roll* (1976)

Further reading recommendations

Paul Finkelman, editor in chief. Volume 3 (*Religion*) of *Encyclopedia of African-American History 1619–1895*. New York: Oxford University Press, 2006.

Eugene Genovese. *Roll, Jordan, Roll—The World the Slaves Made*. New York: Vintage Books, 1976.

Thomas Wentworth Higginson. *Army Life in a Black Regiment and Other Writings*. New York: Penguin Books, 1977.

Nathan Irvin Huggins. *Black Odyssey—The African-American Ordeal in Slavery*. New York: Vintage Books, 1990.

Belinda Humence, editor. *My Folks Don't Want Me to Talk About Slavery*. Winston-Salem, NC: John H. Blair Publisher, 1984.

Paul Johnson, editor. *African-American Christianity—Essays in History*. Berkeley: University of California Press, 1994.

James M. McPherson. *The Negro's Civil War*. New York: Ballantine Books, 1991.

Hugh Thomas. *The Slave Trade: The Story of the Atlantic Slave Trade, 1440–1870*. New York: Simon and Schuster, 1997.

Notes

1. At the height of the slave trade, healthy young African men could be bought for as low as $10 in Africa, and sold for as much as $600 in America. Thus, there was enormous profit to be made for transporting a human cargo of some two or three hundred slaves. The numbers of Africans actually exported to the Americas is a highly discussed subject. Based on figures in the excellent and thorough 2006 *Encyclopedia of African-American History*, specialists agree that between 125,000—340,350 were brought to the Americas in the sixteenth century, and about 1.5 million in the seventh century. The difference between slaves in the United States and those in the Caribbean and Brazil is insightful. In those latter areas, slaves had an extremely high mortality rate because of the labor-intensive work of primarily sugar plantations and mining. The average slave's life-span there was only ten years, and thus the slave population could not replenish itself. In America, by contrast, slaves had relatively less labor-intensive work, worked less, largely in food-crop plantations, and were fed better than their counterparts. In the eighteenth century, about 400,000 slaves were brought to the United States, but by 1770 there were two and a half million working slaves, and by the Civil War, four million. Cf. Paul Finkelman (editor in chief), *Encyclopedia of African-American History 1619–1895* (3 vol.) (New York: Oxford University Press, 2006), 118. See

also Nathan Irvin Huggins, *Black Odyssey—The African-American Ordeal in Slavery* (New York: Vintage Books, 1990), 38. The first three chapters of Huggins' book has an excellent and moving description of the African native world, the process of being captured, sold, transported and "adapted" to American slave conditions.

2. Cf. Albert Raboteau, "African-Americans, Exodus, and the American Israel," *African-American Christianity—Essays in History*, edited by Paul Johnson, (Berkeley: University of California Press, 1994), 1–9. The 1701 Anglican missionary outreach was entitled the *Society for the Propagation of the Gospel in Foreign Parts*, and it centered on the plantations in the South.

3. Winthrop D. Jordan, *White over Black: American Attitudes toward the Negro, 1550–1812* (Baltimore: Penguin Books, 1969), 191.

4. Pioneering black historian Carter Woodson calls this era "the Dawn of the New Day" in the Christian history of black Americans, a period in which the Revolutionary War had lifted most hindrances to freedom of religion. It is highly ironic, however, that in this very period he describes came the invention of the cotton gin, new breeds of cotton and westward expansion—all of which breathed new life into a declining slave system, re-making it into the political, economic and moral juggernaut that it became by the mid-nineteenth century Civil War. Cf. Carter Woodson, *History of the Negro Church*, as cited in Sydney Ahlstrom, *Religious History of the American People* (New Haven, CT: Yale University Press, 1972), 701.

5. I am indebted for my insights in this section from the following works: Albert Raboteau, "African-Americans, Exodus, and the American Israel," *op. cit.*; Andrew Billingsley, *Mighty Like a River—The Black Church and Social Reform* (New York: Oxford University Press, 1999), xiv–9; Eugene D. Genovese, *Roll, Jordan, Roll—The World the Slaves Made* (New York: Vintage Books, 1976); and Sydney Ahlstrom, *op. cit.*, 698–714.

6. Genovese, *op. cit.*, 189. Genovese has excellent insights on this topic in *Roll, Jordan, Roll*, *op. cit.*, 183–193. W.E.B. Du Bois and other scholars estimated that only about one out of every six adult slaves considered himself attached to a Christian sect. But as blacks did not hold formal church membership, neither did southern whites—who often did not attend services regularly either. More often than not, many supposedly staunch Christians only joined a church late in life. "In the rural, quasi-frontier slave states good Christians went to the services that were available and had little opportunity to join the churches that most suited their theological preference." Cf. Eugene D. Genovese, *op. cit.*, 184.

7. Ahlstrom, *op. cit.*, 703.

8. Raboteau, *op. cit.*, 8. Thomas Higginson's war-time memoirs *Army Life in a Black Regiment* contains an excellent chapter entirely devoted to the words and spirituals that his soldiers sang during the Civil War. Cf. Thomas Wentworth Higginson, *Army Life in a Black Regiment and Other Writings* (New York: Penguin Books, 1977), 149–173.

9. Eugene Genovese, *op. cit.*, 283. Genovese's reflections on the religious foundations of the black nation on pp. 280–284 of *Roll, Jordan, Roll* are excellent, but the entire Book Two ("The Rock and the Church") is foundational for its deep research and insights on this entire area. Cf. also Nathan Irvin Huggins, *op. cit.*, 180–182 for what religion taught and did for the attitudes and images of slaves.

10. Cited in Andrew Billingsley, *op. cit.*, 7. Cf. also Albert Raboteau, *op. cit.*, 8–9.

11. Ahlstrom, *op. cit.*, 706–07, and Paul Finkelman (editor in chief), *Encyclopedia of African-American History 1619–1895*, Volume Three, *op. cit.*, 24–25. James McPherson estimates that approximately 500,000 slaves came within Union lines during the war, most of whom went to work as laborers or soldiers for the North. Cf. also Monroe Fordham, *Major Themes in Northern Black Religious Thought, 1800–1860* (Hicksville, N.Y.: Exposition Press, 1975) who captures the strong social Gospel themes of African-American religion in the North before the war.

12. In *January 1863*, the Governor of Massachusetts was authorized to raise a regiment of black soldiers, resulting in the formation of the famed 54th MA, followed soon after by the 55th. The *spring of 1863* saw Gen. Nathaniel Banks recruiting a "Corps d' Afrique" from the black population of Louisiana, and drawing in by the end of August some 15,000 soldiers. In *March 1863*, Adj. Gen. Lorenzo Thomas was sent to the lower Mississippi valley to organize as many black regiments as possible from around the area's freedmen—resulting in the First TN Infantry (African descent) being formed around Memphis (renamed the 59th USCT in March 1864). In *May 1863*, the War Department gave official sanction to a new Bureau of Colored Troops. The *summer of 1863* brought a hard-earned respect for these often-reviled black troops, as two regiments of New Orleans free blacks and Louisiana ex-slaves showed a desperate courage at the failed assault on Port Hudson on May 27th. The charge of the 54th MA made famous in the movie *Glory* took place at Fort Wagner near Charleston Harbor in July 18, 1863. By *October 20, 1864*, there were 140 black regiments in the Federal service, with a total strength of 101,950 men. Black troops participated in every major Union Campaign in 1864–1865 except Sherman's invasion of Georgia. Ironically, Charleston, South Carolina fell at the hands of the black troops Sherman would not have accepted in his army. Cf. James M. McPherson, *The Negro's Civil War* (New York: Ballantine Books, 1991), 175–196, 227. The cited quote is found on page xvii.

13. Thomas Wentworth Higginson, *op. cit.*, 197–98, 206.

Section Three

RELIGION DURING THE CIVIL WAR

A fervently pious nation was at war, and amidst the carnage and slaughter, amidst the heroism and weariness, men on both sides hungered for inspiration and peace with God. Dedicated men and women on both sides responded to their hunger with wide-ranging ministries. On both sides, the soldier's sense of duty was deepened, his morale improved, his loyalty intensified. More cynical commanders and more despairing men might have been less sure that the Almighty was with them and that victory must come. They might have felt as strong desire to compromise. Perhaps piety lengthened the war. Certainly it deepened the tragedy and made the entire experience a more enduring scar on the national memory.

Sidney Ahlstrom, *Religious History of the American People* (1972)

Chapter Nine

RELIGIOUS SUPPORT SYSTEMS

William McCarter of the 116th PA lay wounded and cold [and] was startled to see a man enter the tent carrying a generous supply of hot biscuits and a 'tin bucket full of strong, hot coffee.' Inquiring where these 'God-sent luxuries' had come from, he learned that the source was the U.S. Christian Commission. It was the first he had heard of the organization, and he was deeply impressed.

Stephen Woodworth, *While God is Marching On* (2001)

"There's a good deal of religion in a warm shirt . . ."

From Fort Sumter in 1861 through the last engagement at Palmito Ranch, Texas in 1865, approximately three million men (and a clandestine 400-600 women) served in Civil War armies. Some 620,000 died in the conflict (diseases killing twice as many as battle), considerably more were rendered unfit due to illness, and nearly all experienced the loneliness, suffering and deprivations of four long years of difficult and unfamiliar military life. The personal needs and demands of these millions were great, and the task of caring for them far too immense for the governments alone, and thus before long an army of civilians grew up to address the needs the military was unable or unwilling to. Aside from the requisite hospitals[1] and related medical staffs, there were sutlers, photographers, newspapermen, morticians, actors/actresses, laundresses, bakers, barbers and more. But right alongside this group was a veritable "religious army"—a multi-denominational mix of concerned individuals and charitable organizations who volunteered in vast numbers to meet both the spiritual, medical and physical needs of soldiers.

Whatever else the Civil War did, it brought about a literal mountain of charitable religious support for soldiers, and saw an astounding increase in fund-raising at all levels of American society. The War led to nothing less than a philanthropic revolution—with every town and church involved, innumerable societies being formed, and countless churchmen involved as never before in both public and secular undertakings. In his 1864 book *The Philanthropic Results of the War in America*, Linus P. Brockett presents statistics showing that an incredible $212 million was raised in the North alone—and that by only 1864! He maintains that "neither in ancient or modern times, has there been so vast an outpouring of a nation's wealth for the care, the comfort, and the physical and mental welfare of those who have fought the nation's battles or been the sufferers from its condition of war."[2]

One wartime writer saw all this charitable giving as a "new Chapter in Church History," with another describing it as "sort of a pentecostal gathering wherein [all denominations] forgot all their differences, and poured into one common reservoir their thank offerings."[3] The patterns of charity developed in the Civil War formed the foundation for the widespread claims that a moral awakening was happening within America, and also helped give impetus to the "social Gospel" message that would later radiate through the North. Although the patterns and structures of aid would vary between North and South, still it can be said that rarely has American religious charity been so great. Perhaps George Stuart, founder of the Christian Commission, summed up wartime religious charity best: "there is a great deal of religion in a warm shirt and a good beefsteak."

> Crackers and oats are more necessary to my army than any moral or religious authority.
>
> William T. Sherman, in 1864,
> denying ministers passes to ride the railroad

Northern aid efforts

The philanthropic spirit was strong in the North from the very beginning of the war. There were few towns or villages which did not have a Soldier's Aid Society, usually staffed by women volunteers who sewed garments, collected packages, and ran fairs to obtain money for the work among the troops. Every major town also had its freedmen's relief association who supplied material, schools and teachers for impoverished ex-slaves, as well as maintaining an especially crucial relationship with the federal government's slowly evolving policy towards blacks.[4] But probably the most enduring and visible contribution of Northern churches to the Union war effort was the creation of two powerful organizations that channeled the benevolence of individual churches and members.

One was the *United States Christian Commission*, founded by Protestant evangelicals to provide religious ministry to soldiers. After the discouraging battle of Bull Run, a special meeting was called by the YMCA to organize local charity efforts. George H. Stuart (a deeply religious Presbyterian Philadelphia banker) became the permanent chairman of this new philanthropic group, which by war's end had virtually absorbed the YMCA into itself.

The nearly 5,000 unpaid delegates sent to the army spent their time visiting sick and wounded, presiding at revival meetings, sponsoring chaplain meetings, operating lending libraries, providing religious materials, running soup kitchens, supporting chaplains and surgeons, and offering a broad range of assistance wherever needed. In conjunction with women's auxiliaries, the Commission received and distributed over $6 million in cash, goods and services; and passed out about one and a half million Bibles, a million hymnals and 39 million tracts. By 1865 they had become a vast interdenominational fellowship including in its ranks the representatives of all major denominations.[5]

Although the main focus of the Commission had been to bring the Gospel to the soldiers, they were flexible and wise enough to eventually minister to all the soldiers' physical needs. Despite early unenthusiastic support from army officers, the Commission's strong attempts at seeking approval from men like Lincoln and Stanton resulted in their faring better in the government's eyes than their "cousins" in the Sanitary Commission. Though anecdotes abound of the good done by the Christian Commission, one story will have to suffice for our purposes. Daniel Crotty, a desperately ill soldier from the 3d MI, was away from his regiment, and did not have the strength to get back.

> Staggering along, he saw "some tents pitched in front of a house." Making his way to the gate, he finally passed out. When he came to, he found "some kind nurses bending over me, and looking anxiously for my recovery." These turned out to be "the ladies of the Christian Commission, who had left home and all its luxuries to administer to the poor soldier in the field. God bless all those devoted women," Crotty wrote, "and if they do not receive their reward on earth may they receive it in heaven."[6]

Dorothea Lynde Dix (1802–1887)
Though not a nurse, this stern and often difficult Unitarian became Superintendent of Women Nurses. She ruled on the acceptability of all nursing applicants, always fighting to retain independent control over the women nurses. Among those who ran across her prejudices were Catholic nuns, for in Dix's eyes, only Protestants were acceptable nurses. After the war, she continued her crusade to provide more human treatment for institutionalized people.

The *United States Sanitary Commission* was, in the words of one historian, "the largest, strongest, and most tightly organized philanthropic body that America had ever seen." This commission was also religious at its base (liberal Protestantism), but had the more focused initial concern of assisting the work of the army's Medical Bureau. The Sanitary Commission employed salaried employees, used professional fund-raisers and disdained more sentimental notions of giving. Members said that it was more important to save lives and leave souls in God's hands. Begun in June 1861, largely through the energetic efforts of Unitarian minister Henry W. Bellows in New York City, the Sanitary Commission focused its attention on "systematic, scientific and impersonal charity." They dispatched medical inspectors to the front, who helped expose problems of sanitation, drainage, faulty diet, rest camp needs, hospital mismanagement, etc.—and offered preventive medicine. One historian described its work as "a vast composite Florence Nightingale, and an essential component of the war effort." [7]

Initially unwanted by the army, by 1865 the War Department had not only accepted the Sanitary Commission's position with the soldiers, but come to depend upon it to increase the army's supplies and improve the methods of the Medical Bureau. Commission workers gradually became involved in all aspects of practical aid to soldiers, as well as in public lobbying until they secured a much needed streamlining of sanitary practices in the armed forces. James Moorhead remarks that their "systematized benevolence may be justly cited as one of the progenitors of the American Red Cross." [8]

Thus, despite their different religious motivations and leadership styles, both Northern Commissions were highly successful at helping Union soldiers. Both groups raised about $6 million in funds, were well-organized and efficient, relied on prewar societies for local participation and leadership, kept very fine records of materials delivered and controlled their distribution effectively. In his wartime journal, Chaplain Louis Beaudry (5th NY Cavalry) frequently mentions his regular contacts with both the Christian Commission and the Sanitary Commission. Sharing a few sample excerpts from but one month (July 1864) will reveal the almost mundane regularity with which he grew to depend upon both groups. [9]

July 1–8, 1864 Traveled with 5th NY Cavalry on the Reams Station VA raid, then returned to camp.

July 10, 1864 "We then visited the Christian Commission where I met some of the agents with whom I am familiarly acquainted. I secured large stores; all I wanted or could carry . . . At the Sanitary Commission, I found an old schoolmate, Sydenan Keese, Chief Clerk in this department. We had a happy greeting. By him, I had free access to the stores."

July 13, 1864 "Dr. Armstrong and I started off in search of Sanitary Commission stuff for regiment . . . we secured several items of vegetables, viz, 1 bbl. Potatoes, 1 bbl. Beets and canned fruits."

July 20, 1864 "Stopped at the Christian Commission where we took dinner and got a few things"

July 23, 1864 "At City Point got reading matter from the Christian Commission, met there my old college friend George A. Hall, now agent of the Commission. Short, pleasant visit. Got some postage stamps."

July 27, 1864 "We visited our friends of the Christian Commission where we got some things, fed our horses and took dinner."

July 31, 1864 "Went to the Christian Commission. Got a few things."

Southern aid

The devastating effect of the Civil War impacted all Southern institutions, as well as the local populace and area economies. Southern churches in areas invaded by Union troops usually suffered horrible desecration and damage—with buildings, equipment, records and parsonages often attacked and destroyed to a degree "far exceeding military necessity," in the words of one writer. Thus, in contrast to the well-organized national relief agencies of the North, Southern relief efforts to soldiers were necessarily more limited and localized. A great many civilian aid societies did spring up to assist the Confederate war effort, but none had the overall impact or broad organization as the two Northern commissions. In 1861, Felicia Grundy Porter of Nashville formed the *Women's Relief Society* in Tennessee, which soon spread throughout the South. This society raised money through concerts and spent it largely on artificial limbs for amputees. In early 1862, the citizens of Richmond began the *Richmond Ambulance Committee*, and for the remainder of the war, its one hundred members organized the transportation of Confederate wounded from area battlefields to Richmond hospitals using thirty-nine ambulances.[10]

Almost every town had its *Ladies Aid Society* (also called *Soldier's Aid* societies) which coordinated efforts to help the troops of that town in the field. The societies made all sorts of clothing for the soldiers—underwear, shirts, uniforms, overcoats, scarfs, socks and blankets. Local tailors in some towns would often help the women—as did the tailors of Athens, Georgia, who cut the heavy cloth for the uniforms before the ladies sewed the garments. These societies were generally made up of middle and upper-class women, but poorer women also made clothing on an individual basis for their relatives and sent them food when they had it to spare. Aside from furnishing clothing for soldiers, the societies also at times helped provide food, medicines and hospital supplies. The efforts of these local groups could be quite impressive in size and quantity. On November 10, 1861, the *Dallas Herald* reported that the Lancaster Ladies Aid Society had sent $1,676.50 worth of coats jeans, flannel and linsey shirts, winter drawers, winter vests, boots, shoes, woolen mittens, blankets and 'bed comforters' to the men of the 6th TX Cavalry.[11]

Southern clergy were quick to blame extortioners, "men of greed who stirred up an egregious yearning of the bowels after filthy lucre." Before Christmas 1863, a "prayer of the Extortioner" was circulated in North Carolina: "Our father who art in heaven—I wonder what will be the price of wheat this summer. My crop is fine, very fine. I think I might get at least four dollars for it. I should like to get ten—Hallowed be thy name—If the season continues I shall make a tremendous crop of corn, and as my cribs are now sufficient to last me two years, it will be a clear profit."

James Silver, *Confederate Morale and Church Propaganda* (1957)

Southern churches were also active in aiding soldiers and caring for their dependents. Of course, many Southern churches become temporary hospitals, but the buildings of some colleges and seminaries were converted into more permanent hospitals for wounded of both armies. All Southern denominations organized committees or agencies to solicit funds and supplies for needy soldier families; and in hospital centers like Richmond, many church women served as nurses. Georgia Episcopal bishop Stephen Elliot mandated the formation of committees to prepare bandages, clothing, medicine and foodstuffs for use in military hospitals.

In 1864, Alabama Episcopalians began a program to establish orphanages for the children of deceased and disabled soldiers, and a new order of "Deaconnesses" was created to staff them and care for the children. That same year, Southern Methodists created a Soldier's Orphan Association, directing all presiding elders to gather the names of orphans and suggest places for their care. Baptists in Virginia and Georgia likewise had strong concerns for war orphans, and in 1865, the secretary of one Baptist committee could report that $200,000 had been raised, and between seven and eight hundred children had been assisted.[12]

The churches of the heavily evangelical South also worked hard to provide soldiers with "soul food." With soldiers becoming terribly bored and eager for reading of any kind, churches labored to get religious literature (especially "Testaments") into their hands. *Colporteurs* were missionaries whose chief job was to carry and distribute religious literature to soldiers; and tracts such as the famous *A Mother's Parting Words to Her Soldier Boy* were deeply uplifting to many Southern soldiers. Rev. B.B. Ross found hospital patients "greedy, yea ravenous, in their appetite for something to read . . . they take the tracts with delight." When their tracts stirred up the soldiers reading them, some colporteurs wound up being drawn into deeper ministry. "A notice of a few moments will give me a large congregation," wrote one colporteur, who reported handing out 41,000 pages of tracts and preaching nearly daily in one month of ministry alone. Numerous agencies were formed to meet these "spiritual nourishment" needs, with the *Evangelical Tract Society* of Petersburg, Virginia being the largest and most prolific. During the war, it issued more than one hundred different tracts with a total print run estimated at some fifty million copies![13]

Vicksburg civilians suffered greatly in the June 1863 battle there. During one bombardment, Margaret Lord (wife of Episcopal rector Rev. Dr. William Lord) tried to comfort her daughter as they crouched in the church basement. "Don't cry my darling" she soothed the girl, assuring her that "God will protect us." But the little girl could not be calmed, as she spoke in tears "But, momma, I's so 'fraid God's killed too!"

Terry Winschel, *Triumph and Defeat* (2004)

"Angels of Mercy"

In the entire history of the Civil War, perhaps only one group of religious people achieved such hard-earned, deeply appreciated respect from soldiers and officers of both sides as Roman Catholic nuns. The role of these Catholic women can be better appreciated by recalling that in 1861 there was no Red Cross, and that the first trained nurses in the United States graduated long after the war was over. "The country had only 600 trained nurses at the start of the Civil War. All were Catholic nuns. This is one of the best-kept secrets in our nation's history." [14] From the standpoint of charity alone, the nuns' work stands out more boldly when remembering that they served both Catholics and Protestants alike—despite the lurid calumnies about convents which were so popular before the war. While Catholic chaplains were only tolerably welcomed on the war scene, Catholic nuns who were nursing sisters were in actual demand.

The war had just begun when the *Sisters of Mercy* (New York) and the *Sisters of Charity* (New York) volunteered to send over a hundred sisters to the service of the country. At first, Archbishop John Hughes did not think much of the idea, but thankfully his viewpoint did not prevail. [15] These *Sisters of Mercy*, along with the *Daughters of Charity* (Emmitsburg, Maryland) and the *Sisters of the Holy Cross* (Notre Dame) all served in Northern camps and military hospitals throughout the country. There are records indicating that at least 232 nuns from the Daughters of Charity helped nursed troops during the war. It should also be noted that the navy's first hospital ship (*USS Red River*), deployed on the Mississippi River, had Catholic nuns serving as volunteer nurses. [16]

The Confederacy also realized the value of Catholic religious women, repeatedly asking the help of the *Sisters of Charity* (Charity Hospital in New Orleans). The order responded by sending several teams of nuns—one to Florida (later Corinth, Mississippi), and the other to Holly Springs. Likewise, six *Sisters of Mercy* had come from Baltimore to Vicksburg, MS, in 1859 as teachers, but when the battle began, their school quickly became a hospital for wounded and dying soldiers. There were also three sisters from the *Daughters of Charity* who ministered at Vicksburg (after having cared for wounded at Natchez in 1862), and numerous other *Sisters of Mercy* at several other Mississippi hospitals. By war's end, a very conservative estimate is that well over 600 sisters (mostly of foreign birth), from at least twelve different Catholic religious orders, had served the soldiers of both sides. [17]

It would take another book to relate all the stories of the tremendous impact these nuns had upon many soldiers—including formerly some staunch Southern Protestants—because of their expertise and dedication. One amusing yet poignant tale among the many found in journals and diaries will have to suffice for my purposes here, however. Confederate chaplain Fr. John Bannon (1st Missouri CSA) had been ministering in Vicksburg after the battle there, attempting to baptize a badly wounded Southern soldier. But this tough, battle-hardened Confederate veteran utterly refused to accept what Fr. Bannon was saying until the Catholic nun who had been gently taking care of him confirmed that the priest was correct! After speaking with his nun/nurse first, and determining that what the priest had said *was* accurate, the soldier then turned back to Bannon and said, "'Very well, all right. Go ahead, Mister, what's next.'" Fr. Bannon later added "In the end I baptized him, although it may be said that perhaps it was rather *in fidem Sodorum* [in the faith of the nuns] rather than *in fidem Ecclesia* [in the faith of the Church]."

The post-war description given of Sr. Anthony O'Connell (a Sister of Charity from Cincinnati) might well have been applied to many of these truly amazing women, called often "angels of mercy": "She was reverenced by Blue and Gray, Protestant and Catholic alike; and we conferred on her the title of the 'Florence Nightingale of America.' Her name was a household word in every section of the North and South." [18]

In 1862, when New York City officials turned over to the Federal government a large building in Central Park for a hospital, they requested this of Secretary of War Edwin Stanton: "We want the nurses of this hospital to be the Sisters of Charity, the most faithful nurses in the world."

R. J. Murphy, *The Catholic Church During the War* (1928)

Further reading recommendations

Benjamin Blied. Pp. 117–121 of *Catholics and the Civil War*. Milwaukee, WI: Bruce Publishing Company, 1945.

W. Harrison Daniel. "The Effects of the Civil War on Southern Protestantism." *Maryland Historical Magazine* 69, (1974): 44–63.

Michael F. Fitzpatrick. "The Mercy Brigade—Roman Catholic Nuns in the Civil War." *Civil War Times Illustrated* 36, no. 5, (October 1997): 35–40.

Joseph O. Henry. "The United States Christian Commission in the Civil War." *Civil War History* 6 (1960): 374–77.

Philip Katcher. *The Civil War Sourcebook*. New York: Facts on File Publishers, 1992.

Edward P. Smith. *Incidents of the U.S, Christian Commission*. RMJC Publications, Concord VA, 2003. [Reprint of the original 1869 version]

Margaret Wagner. Gary Gallagher and Paul Finkelman, editors. *Library of Congress Civil War Desk Reference*. New York: Simon and Schuster, 2002.

Steven E. Woodworth. "To Labor for the Souls of Their Fellow-Men." Pp. 160–174 in *God is Marching On—The Religious Life of Civil War Soldiers*. Lawrence: University Press of Kansas, 2001.

Notes

1. By 1865, there were 204 Federal general hospitals with 136,894 beds, treating more than 1 million soldiers in the course of the war. In the South, by 1865, 154 hospitals had been created, and in Virginia alone 293,165 soldiers were treated in general hospitals between September 1862 and December 1863. During the war, the United States Medical Department staff grew to include some 12,000 doctors of various kinds. The Confederate Medical Department was much smaller, with an estimated 3,200 surgeons and assistant surgeons (not counting contract physicians and navy doctors). Cf. *Civil War Desk Reference*, edited by Margaret E. Wagner, Gary W. Gallagher and Paul Finkelman (New York: Simon and Schuster, 2002), 627–638 and 652–654.

2. Brockett's quote is cited in James H. Moorhead, *American Apocalypse—Yankee Protestants and the Civil War, 1860-1869* (New Haven, CT: Yale University Press, 1978), 68.

3. *Ibid.*

4. When the Lincoln administration agreed to create a pilot project for the education of freed blacks on the Sea Islands off South Carolina, these private freedmen's groups provided the workers and paid their salaries. From Freedmen's Relief Societies came the stream of

requests that eventually led to the creation of the Freedmen's Bureau in March 1865 under the direction of Gen. Oliver O Howard.

5. Cf. *Civil War Desk Reference, op. cit.*, 686. Also see Gardiner H. Shattuck Jr., *A Shield and a Hiding Place—The Religious Life of Civil War Armies* (Macon, GA: Mercer University Press, 1987), 24–33; Phillip Shaw Paludan, *'A People's Contest'—The Union and the Civil War, 1861–1865* (New York: Harper and Row, 1988), 352–354; and Sidney Ahlstrom, *Religious History of the American People* (New Haven, CT: Yale University Press, 1972), 697ff. The Christian Commission also worked to promote religious revivals in the Army and sponsored regular chaplains meetings, some of which curiously reflected the same pettiness which always seems to exist between ministers and churches. Rev. Louis Beaudry comments about a particular 1863 meeting, saying "Chaplains are men of like passions with other men too much. A great portion of the time was taken up [at the Chaplains meeting] by useless controversies and general arguments, especially against the idea of a Chaplain having any military rank whatever. We adjourned at 4:00 PM to meet tomorrow at one again, without having accomplished anything." Cf. Louis N. Beaudry, *War Journal of Louis N., Beaudry, Fifth New York Cavalry*, edited by Richard E. Beaudry (Jefferson, NC: McFarland & Company Publishers, 1996), 92.

6. Steven Woodworth; *While God is Marching On* (Lawrence: University Press of Kansas, 2001), 171. Such well-known Civil War-era women as Dorothea Dix, Louisa May Alcott and Jane Swisshelm served as nurses under the auspices of the Christian Commission, as did thousands of other women.

7. Quotes here are cited in Shattuck, *op. cit.*, 29; and Sidney Ahlstrom, *op. cit.*, 680.

8. James Moorhead, *op. cit.*, 66.

9. Louis N. Beaudry; *op. cit.*, passim. I am grateful to Phillip Shaw Paludan for his concise summary of the consistencies between the two groups.

10. Philip Katcher, *The Civil War Sourcebook* (New York: Facts on File, 1992), 242.

11. *Ibid.* Cf. also *Encyclopedia of the Confederacy*, vol. 4; Richard N. Current (editor in chief) (New York: Simon and Schuster, 2003), 1501–02.

12. W. Harrison Daniel, "The Effects of the Civil War on Southern Protestantism," in *Maryland Historical Magazine* 69 (1974); 44–63.

13. Steven E. Woodworth, *op. cit.,* 163–167.

14. William Barnaby Faherty, *Exile from Erin* (St. Louis, MO: Missouri Historical Society, 2002), 77.

15. In a May 9, 1861 letter to Bishop Francis Kenrick (Baltimore), Archbishop John Hughes wrote this about the Sisters of Mercy's desire to serve: "I have signified to them, not harshly, that they had better mind their own affairs until their services are needed." Reflecting on overall American Catholic history, this would certainly not be the first nor last time that Catholic women religious would act in spite of their bishop's opinion!

16. Cf. Benjamin Blied, *Catholics and the Civil War* (Milwaukee, WI: Bruce Publishing, 1945), 117–121; and Ellen Ryan Jolly, *Nuns of the Battlefield* (Providence, RI: Providence Visitor Press, 1930); 4th edition. For an account of the Mercy Sisters in Vicksburg, cf. Sr. Ignatius Sumner, *Angels of Mercy—An Eyewitness Account of the Civil War and Yellow Fever* (Baltimore: Cathedral Foundation Press, 2000).

17. Faherty, *op. cit.*, 77–8, 111–12. Cf. also Benjamin Blied, *op. cit.*, 118.

18. The Fr. Bannon quote is from Faherty, *op. cit.*; 79–80; the quote about Sr. O'Connell is from Robert Joseph Murphy, "The Catholic Church in the United States during the Civil War Period," in *Records of the American Catholic Historical Society* 39, no. 4 (December 1928), 315.

Chapter Ten

SOLDIERS OF THE LORD— CIVIL WAR CHAPLAINS

> A tablet honoring Chap. Aaron H. Kerr (9th MN) erected in 1897 read "A faithful preacher of the Word of God; a sympathetic pastor, his ministry in peace and war a constant benison, his presence a benediction, his life an impressive sermon."
>
> Brinsfield, Jr., *et. al., Faith in the Fight* (2003)

"Holy Joes" on the battlefield

"A chaplain's work is enough to fill an angel's heart" wrote Chap. John Burgess (30th IA), but during the Civil War such angels were few and far between. Some who filled that role were called chaplain, preacher, Father, "Holy Joe" or "Holy John"—but by whatever name, Civil War chaplains came to play a crucial role in comforting and emotionally supporting many soldiers. They could have enormous impact (either for bad or good!) on the morale and spirit of the normal soldier. But their first Civil War battle was simply for recognition. Chaplains had served in the American army ever since the Revolutionary War—but it was the Civil War that provoked new debates about the unique role that the "church" side of the church-state equation should play in military matters.

An anti-clerical strain had long existed in American religion, with churchmen often seen as being petty and conniving. Chaplains did not enjoy universal good opinion in antebellum America, and many would have agreed with Ambrose Bierce's definition of a clergyman as "a man who undertakes the management of spiritual affairs as a method of bettering his temporal ones."[1] Some Civil War commanders openly opposed their presence among the troops.[2] A humorous story in Gen. Dan Sickles' Excelsior Brigade (composed of several regiments) about the 73d NY's vote for a chaplain captures the sentiment of many soldiers. The Jesuit Fr. Joseph B. O'Hagan (the eventual chaplain) described the results: "Over 400 voted for a Catholic priest, 154 for any kind of a Protestant minister; 11 for a Mormon; and 335 said they could find their way to hell without the assistance of clergy."[3]

Early in the war, there were some very poor chaplains, men who used position for personal gain. Some were too old or physically unfit, and some simply were neer-do-wells and misfits who had chosen the wrong profession. One Union officer summed up the challenge facing him and said "the chaplain's post was one of the easiest to fill, and one of the hardest to fill well."[4] Some early ministers simply had what could politely be called a lack of scruples—one minister entered a stud-poker game with the 2nd CT Heavy Artillery and cleaned out the entire company; another slept in a brothel while his regiment was in the field; and yet another deserted with $90 of regimental funds.[5] But after the first two years, most poor candidates were weeded out, so that by 1865, it generally could be said that "chaplains performed well in the war . . . and fared well in earning the respect of the soldiers."[6]

The one duty specified for *all* chaplains (formally in the North, but not in the South) was holding regular worship services—most often on Sunday afternoons to avoid conflict with drilling. At times this was hard to do (due to weather, drills, being on march, about to do battle), so chaplains had to have flexibility and adaptability. Many meetings were held spontaneously when troops were available. If no chapels were around (many were built by soldiers when they were encamped for a period of time), religious gatherings were held outdoors in front of a tent or in the woods, with the listeners sitting on logs or boxes, or standing in irregular fashion.

Chaplains played a wide variety of roles in both armies, and the best chaplains were those who became "jacks of all trades" for their men—comforting the homesick, counseling the sorrowful, teaching reading and writing, writing letters for hospitalized, maintaining libraries, becoming postmaster, carrying men and equipment on marches, foraging, digging wells and rifle pits and more.[7]

These were men like the Rev. Charles Quintard (1st TN CSA), who filled his canteen every morning with whiskey and, throughout the regiment's advance, dispensed drinks "to help the wearied and broken down to keep up in the march;"[8] or like the legendary Fr. Peter Cooney (35th IN) who regularly traveled taking thousands of dollars from soldiers to their families (including $24,000 on one occasion alone in November 1863!)[9]

Despite the intense support for the work of chaplains from some high places (like Abraham Lincoln), there was a shortage of chaplains in both armies throughout the war, with even Stonewall Jackson (a great proponent of chaplains) never having sufficient religious representatives. The Northern War Department announced in June 1862 that of 676 regiments in the field, only 395 had chaplains on official assignment. Of that number, twenty-nine were absent on detached service while another thirteen were absent without leave. A third of Union regiments had no chaplains.

In the Confederacy, each regiment was intended to have an active chaplain assigned to it, but in reality an 1863 CSA Chaplains Association report reveals that half of the Southern units were without a minister.[10] Perhaps Chaplain John S. Paris (54th NC) summed it up best in one letter home. "Can't you find a man who will volunteer as a chaplain? There are fifteen regiments from North Carolina without chaplains. I am the only one in the brigade. Such a life is rough."

Union chaplains

Very early on, Abraham Lincoln and the War Department recognized the value of religion and need for chaplains for Union troops. Beginning in 1861 (with Orders #15 and #16), a series of wartime regulations were passed which dealt with various aspects of chaplain life—from their commissioning and purpose, to details like pay, forage, clothing, professional standards, etc. Since the military chaplaincy had been small prior to 1861, many special issues had to be worked through gradually—such as pay scales, officer status, and non-Christian chaplains.

For the first year of the war, Jewish rabbis were ineligible for official chaplaincy, because of legislation defining chaplains as "regularly ordained ministers of a Christian denomination." After public agitation, and a personal interview between Rabbi Arnold Fischel and President Lincoln in December 1861, the words "*religious* denomination" were substituted for "*Christian* denomination," and the issue was resolved.[11]

There were three types of Union chaplains: *post* (connected to a specific military post or facility), *regimental* (one specific regiment), and *hospital* (one specific hospital).[12] Wherever they ministered, great flexibility was required, because chaplains were confronted with a wide variety of needs and duties. As Warren Armstrong remarks in his excellent book, "the duties of the chaplaincy demanded endless energy and unlimited patience, devotion to duty, and constancy of conviction," this "the man who could not bend to the extraordinary circumstances . . . could not gain the confidence of his men and ultimately found himself rejected by those whom he had hoped to serve."[13] Many Union chaplains did resign in disgust, disappointment or disillusionment, but "far greater was the number who remained to serve . . . and captured the affections and respect of their comrades."[14]

Thousands of chaplains enlisted when the war began, one per regiment, and headed south with their units. Given the antagonism of a few officers, the irreligion of others, and other early challenges in defining their duties, "they were hardly there for the pay [but] believed their service would be needed, and that religion was an imperative part of the soldiers life."[15] As the largest Northern religious denomination, Methodists had the largest contingent of chaplains (more than a third), but all major denominations were represented. Baptists were at least equal in membership to Methodists, but preferred to stay away from the church-state involvement that the chaplaincy represented, instead preferring to serve as "volunteer missionaries" for their denomination.[16]

By war's end, 2398 ministers, priests and rabbis had rendered service to the Union armies—including over seventy Catholics, seventeen blacks,[17] one Jewish chaplain and even a very controversial female chaplain! Here are a few vignettes of some of these more colorful and well-known Union chaplains:

James F. Jacquess (73d IL). Although formally not its chaplain, he organized this "Preacher's Regiment," because at least fifteen of the original officers were licensed Methodist ministers. Leaving Illinois as one of the largest regiments, they returned as one of the smallest. A soldier wrote later that "of course none in the Preacher Regiment played cards." [18]

Ellen (Gibson) Hobart. This outspoken freethinker, feminist trailblazer and spiritualist was the wife of 8th WI chaplain John Hobart. When turned down herself for a chaplain's commission by Secretary Seward, she went through Wisconsin governor James Lewis to become chaplain of the 1st WI Heavy Artillery, but was never allowed to formally muster in. [19]

Samuel Harrison (54th MA). This 6 foot, 5 inch black Congregational pastor served for seven and a half months, before being forced to resign because the paymaster general refused to pay him more than $10 a month. It took twenty months and the Attorney General's help before Harrison got his entire back pay. [20]

Thomas L. Ambrose (12th NH). A Church of Christ pastor, Ambrose stayed behind after Chancellorsville to help wounded Union soldiers who fell into Rebel hands. He worked around the clock, even going to Lee's headquarters to obtain the promise of a wagonload of cornmeal, and carried a 50-lb bag nearly two and a half miles back by himself. [21]

John Eaton Jr. (27th OH). While beginning as a chaplain, he was made a colonel in charge of black troops, later becoming brevet brigadier general. Grant appointed him to work with runaway slaves, and his great initiative provided a model for the later Freedman's Board (established Mar. 4, 1865). [22]

Charles C. McCabe (122nd OH). When this Methodist was confined in Libby Prison, he antagonized his captors but lifted the spirits of Union soldiers by singing the "Battle Hymn of the Republic" and inviting them to join him. [23]

Civil War "clergy-generals"

(CSA)	Ellison Capers	(postwar Episcopal bishop)
	Alexander T. Hawthorne	(postwar Baptist missionary)
	Mark Perrin Lowrey	(Baptist minister)
	William N. Pendleton	(Episcopal minister)
	Leonidas Polk	(Episcopal bishop of LA)
	Francis Shoup	(postwar Episcopal priest)
(USA)	John Eaton	(Congregational minister)
	Green Clay Smith	(postwar Baptist minister)
	William A. Pile	(Methodist minister)

Jon Wakelyn, *Biographical Dictionary of the Confederacy* and *The Civil War Book of Lists*

Union Chaplains—Facts and Statistics

Numbers[24]

2,398 chaplains (for 2.1 million Union troops)
Less than **600** chaplains were in service at any one time
2,154 were Regimental chaplains (with the remainder being Hospital & Navy)
73 died in non-combat deaths
    11 killed in action
    4 mortally wounded[25]
    4 awarded Medal of Honor[26]

Denominations

Methodist 38%
Presbyterian 17%
Baptist 12%
Episcopal 10%
Congregational 9%
Unitarian/Universalist 4%
Catholic 3%
Lutheran 2%
All others 1% or less

Support systems

After eighty-five years of merely having United States "customs" for military chaplains, in 1861 it was mandated that officers of Union regiments would first elect a regimental chaplain, who then would be formally appointed by the government. They were to "hold worship services whenever possible."

Salary—$145 monthly originally, but later cut to $100 monthly plus three daily rations and forage for one horse. They were not officially treated as officers until 1864, and then their rank was equated with captains.

Dress—stipulated in 1861 to be "plain black frock coat, with standing collar, one row of nine black buttons, black pantaloons, black felt hat or Army forage cap without ornament."[27] However, there were many wartime exceptions made to this "official" uniform.

Comments—U.S. regulations supported and came to govern many aspects of Union chaplain's roles. Some chaplains thought they were combatants and did fight, but in 1863 Congress officially declared chaplains non-combatants, announcing that the Union would not hold Confederate chaplains as prisoners of war.

Confederate chaplains

Unlike their Northern counterparts, providing for the spiritual support of *their* soldiers was not a high Confederate priority, and indeed the chaplaincy was excluded from initial Southern military structures. Legislation passed by the Confederate Congress in the spring of 1861 directed President Davis to assign as many chaplains as needed, but prescribed no duties and offered nothing for forage, horse, supplies, quarters or a uniform. The monthly $85 salary was cut to $50 within two weeks, with even that being too much for some legislators. There were several unique factors which accounted for this "less recognized" role of clergy in the South.

First, Southern leaders like Jefferson Davis and James Seddon (Secretary of War) had a low opinion of clergy, and saw fighting soldiers as being of a higher priority than praying chaplains. Davis particularly had not been impressed with the chaplains he had encountered at West Point—of the five who served in his years there, three resigned and two were discharged.[28]

Second, many Southerners were believers in the strict separation of church and state, believing that churches should support their ministers, not the government. In fact, throughout the war, southern Baptists consistently sought to pay their own chaplains rather than have the government do it.

Third, a foundational tenet of the Confederacy had been decentralized power— so as Gardiner Shattuck aptly states, "many aspects of the military and political life were either poorly organized or left intentionally to individual initiative." Thus the confusion surrounding chaplains fell very much into a larger confusion that plagued the entire Confederate bureaucracy.[29] Bertram Wyatt-Brown remarks that

> the Southern government did not take very seriously the need for clergymen on the battlefield. Davis thought paid chaplaincies a misallocation of scarce resources. Eventually the Confederate government grudgingly provided chaplains with a private's level of wages and rank. As a result, few clergymen took up the labor for long . . . Only fifty ministers served for the duration of the war.[30]

It is all of this that helps account for the fact that there was always a chronic shortage of Southern chaplains.[31] By March 1863, even the pious Presbyterian "Stonewall" Jackson himself had chaplains in only forty-four of his ninety-one regiments; with Episcopal Bishop Leonidas Polk in the West being even worse off, having only fifteen regiments of forty supplied with chaplains.

This Southern "confusion" about the role and duty of chaplains may perhaps lend some insight into why the South seemed to have more "fighting parsons" than the North. Wartime letters and diaries show a large number of those who were chaplains "did not hesitate to take up arms in the ranks or even to lead soldiers in assaults."[32] Some had first served as enlisted men and were accustomed to weapons, others perhaps wanted to show their dedication or patriotism, but certainly the bias towards fighting soldiers seemed to be more acceptable in the South. Again, let us share a few vignettes of some of the colorful wartime Confederate chaplains.

Isaac Taylor Tichenor (17th AL). A Baptist preacher, this post-war college president impressed his men by his sharpshooting at Shiloh—killing a colonel, a captain and four privates! It apparently didn't hurt his religious reputation, as he later became known as the "father of Southern Baptist Sunday School literature."[33]

Charles T. Quintard (1st TN). This Episcopal priest (and later bishop) was one of the most prominent Southern chaplains. A medical doctor who later studied theology, his biography reads like a "Who's Who" of the Confederacy, as he knew and associated with nearly all of the most well-known Confederate leaders.[34]

J. William Jones (13th VA). After serving as a wartime chaplain, the Baptist Jones became the "evangelist of the Lost Cause," editing fourteen volumes of the *Southern Historical Papers*, authoring influential post-war books (e.g. *Christ in Camp*) and was "one of the most popular Southerners in late nineteenth-century Dixie."[35]

Moses Drury Hoge (Camp Lee, VA). A prominent Presbyterian pastor in Richmond from 1845–1899, Hoge preached weekly to Confederate troops, ran the blockade to smuggle Bibles and religious materials from England into the South, and accompanied President Davis from Richmond before that city fell.[36]

Robert Lewis Dabney (18th VA and Jackson's Staff). His friendship with Jackson perhaps kept Dabney around longer than his military skills should have allowed. After the war, this Presbyterian intellectual became a Lost Cause and Jackson apologist, as well as a bitter advocate of the old Southern ways.[37]

William E Wiatt (26th VA). After resigning two pastorates, Wiatt became the only chaplain the 26th VA ever knew—one of few such situations in the war. This Baptist preacher joined as a private, and was appointed chaplain shortly after.[38]

"How Firm a Foundation" was a favorite wartime hymn. Published in London in 1787, it was sung in America to a traditional tune. It spoke of God's many precious promises, emphasizing that all were found in the Bible. There Christians had a "firm foundation" for the godly life they needed. "How firm a foundation, ye saints of the Lord / Is laid for your faith in His excellent word! / What more can he say than to you He hath said / To you who for refuge to Jesus have fled?"

Steven Woodworth, *While God is Marching On* (2001)

Confederate Chaplains—Facts and Statistics

Numbers[39]

938 chaplains of recognized denominations (**1308** served with commissions at some time during the War)

14% of all eligible Southern clergy became wartime chaplains.

41 are known to have died in the Civil War:

    32 died from exhaustion or disease
    17 were killed between 1861–1862 alone
    12 killed were Methodists[40]
    21 were wounded but survived

Denominations

Methodist 47%
Presbyterian 18%
Baptists 16%
Episcopalian 10%
Catholic 3%
Others 1% each (for 5 denominations)

Support systems

Initially there were no positions for military chaplains authorized by the Confederate government, but in May 1861 some "bare bones" legislation was passed authorizing chaplains to be commissioned. However, there were no formal duties defined for them, and they received no rations, supplies, forage,[41] quarters or horse.

Salary—$85 then $50 monthly (finally raised in 1862 to $80).[42] Chaplains had to provide their own transportation to camp and their own horse, but they could carry a gun if they wished. Eventually they were allowed to draw a private's rations.[43]

Dress—There were no regulations about rank, insignia, age, physical condition or uniform. Many dressed in a plain gray uniform coat with gray trousers, and such hats, belts, buckles and pouches as they could find. While some attempted a common uniform, generally Confederate chaplains "wore whatever they could buy, borrow or manufacture." [44]

Comments—There was no chief of chaplains or any overall supervisory body to coordinate chaplain's efforts.[45] Many ministers entered army as soldiers or officers not chaplains, thus there were more "fighting chaplains" in the South. Of one hundred clergy in the Army of Tennessee in 1863, only half held the chaplain's post.[46]

Lasting influences of Civil War chaplains

The long-term influence that war-time chaplains had on the men they served is difficult to estimate precisely. Certainly there were both good and bad chaplains, with some men gaining far more respect among soldiers than others because of their dedication, work, and war-time attitudes. Indeed as Warren Armstrong summarizes in his excellent book on Union chaplains, "in all probability, the degree of influence varied with the personality and character of the individual chaplain. It may be concluded quite reasonably, however, that in many cases, the influence was profound. The vast majority of chaplains served commendably." [47]

Certainly as the war drew to a close, the chaplains who were then in place—the men who had borne the rigors of the field with their weary troops—seemed to stand higher in the regard of the troops than did the average chaplains present at the war's beginning. For some soldiers, perhaps more than can ever be known, a chaplain's impact could be truly profound.

Methodist chaplain *John Brouse* (100th IN), by his bravery at the battle of Missionary Ridge, becomes a paradigm for the great good that truly spiritual and dedicated men could do amidst the horrors of war. "Without a thought of his personal safety, he was up on the firing line assisting the wounded, praying with the dying, doing all that his great loving heart led him to do." It is no surprise that a Union soldier who was there with him later wrote "no wonder our boys love our gallant chaplain."[48]

One Confederate chaplain tried to improve his condition by commandeering a horse from a Virginia farmer. He rejoined his regimental commander, who asked him where he got the horse. "Down the road there," the chaplain replied. Angrily, the colonel told the chaplain to return it. The chaplain protested, saying in response "Why Jesus Christ, when he was on earth, took an ass to ride to Jerusalem." The colonel snapped back "You are not Jesus Christ; that is not an ass; you are not on your way to Jerusalem; and the sooner you return that horse to its owner, the better it will be for you."

James I. Robertson, *Soldiers Blue and Gray* (1988)

Further reading recommendations

Warren Armstrong. *For Courageous Fighting and Confident Dying—Union Chaplains in the Civil War*. Lawrence: University Press of Kansas, 1998.

John Wesley Brinsfield, Jr. *The Spirit Divided—Memoirs of Civil War Chaplains, The Confederacy*. Macon, GA: Mercer University Press, 2006.

John W. Brinsfield, Jr., William C. Davis, Benedict Maryniak, and James I. Robertson, Jr. *Faith in the Fight—Civil War Chaplains*. Mechanicsburg, PA: Stackpole Books, 2003.

Kent T. Dollar. *Soldiers of the Cross—Confederate Soldier-Christians and the Impact of War on Their Faith*. Macon, GA: Mercer University Press, 2005.

Charles F. Pitts. *Chaplains in Gray—The Confederate Chaplains Story*. Concord, VA: R.M.J.C. Publications, 2003.

Gardiner Shattuck, Jr. "Holy Joes: The Experience of Clergy in the Armies." Pp. 51–72 in *A Shield and a Hiding Place: The Religious Life of the Civil War Armies*. Macon, GA: Mercer University Press, 1987.

There are also many chaplain diaries and letters published, as well as a number of chaplain biographies. Cf. the bibliography of this book for specific titles here.

Notes

1. John Brinsfield, Jr., William C. Davis, Benedict Maryniak, and James I. Robertson; *Faith in the Fight* (Mechanicsburg, PA: Stackpole Books, 2003); 28.
2. James I. Robertson, *Soldiers Blue and Gray* (Columbia: University of South Carolina Press, 1988), 175. Some officers felt that the presence of chaplains made men more fearful of death; others worried about their preaching against sin and vice, as well as the potential challenge to blind discipline that they represented.
3. Brinsfield, Jr., *et al.*, *Faith in the Fight*, *op. cit.*, 14.
4. *Religion in the American Civil War*, edited by Randall M. Miller, Harry S. Stout, and Charles R. Wilson (New York: Oxford University Press, 1998), 149.
5. Robertson, *Soldiers Blue and Gray*, *op. cit.*, 177–78.
6. Steven Woodworth; *While God is Marching On* (Lawrence: University Press of Kansas, 2001), 159.
7. Cf. chapter two in Warren Armstrong; *For Courageous Fighting and Confident Dying* (Lawrence: University Press of Kansas, 1998), 16–42.
8. Robertson, *op. cit.*, 179.
9. From *The War Letters of Father Peter Paul Cooney*, the unpublished 1930 dissertation paper of Rev. Thomas McAvoy, at Notre Dame University Library, 61.

10. Robertson, *op. cit.,* 179 and Shattuck, *Shield and a Hiding Place*, 47.

11. Cf. Brinsfield, Jr., et al., *op. cit.*, 31—35 for the full story of how Lincoln's July 1862 legislative change was reached. Only one rabbi is known to have served as a regimental chaplain during the War—Ferdinand Sarner (54th NY). Cf. also Shattuck, *op. cit..*, 54; and Bertram Korn's fine book *American Jewry and the Civil War*, (Philadelphia, PA: Jewish Publication Society of America, 1951).

12. Warren Armstrong; *op. cit.,* 18–41.

13. *Ibid.*, 41–42.

14. *Ibid.*

15. Philip S. Paludan, *A People's Contest—The Union and the Civil War* (New York: Harper and Row, 1988), 349.

16. Shattuck, *op. cit.*, 63.

17. I am following Brinsfield's numbers in *Faith in the Fight, op. cit.*, 37.

18. Elizabeth Rissler, "The Preachers Regiment," *Illinois Civil War Sketches*, June 1963. Also Woodworth, *op. cit.*, 94, 122.

19. Brinsfield, Jr., et al., *op. cit.*, 39–43. Mrs. Hobart finally received $1200 for back pay in 1876, but was never approved for disability benefits. She died in 1901, effectively written out of history, likely because she was somewhat eccentric despite her remarkable energies and talents.

20. Armstrong, *op. cit.*, 11; and Brinsfield, Jr., et al., *op. cit.*, 37.

21. Rice Bull, *Soldiering: the Civil War Diary of Rice Bull, 123d New York Volunteers*, edited by K. Jack Bauer (San Rafael, CA: Presidio Press, 1977), 70–81.

22. Garrison, *op. cit.*, 51, and Armstrong, *op. cit.*, 85–86.

23. Armstrong, *op. cit.*, 64. I am grateful to Bruce Allardice of the Chicago Civil War Round Table (*More Civil War Generals in Grey*, Baton Rouge: Louisiana State University Press, 1985) for additional names on the following "Civil War "clergy-generals" insert.

24. Shattuck, *op. cit.,* 50–56, 62; and Brinsfield et al. *op. cit.*, 43–47.

25. John L. Lenhart (Methodist Navy chaplain); Bovell McCall (13th TN Cavalry); Ozem B. Gardner (13th KS) and John R. Eddy (72nd IN).

26. Two Medals of Honor were given for helping wounded under fire (Francis B. Hall, 16th NY, and John M. Whitehead, 15th IN), and one Medal was given to Milton L. Haney (55th IL) more for his military actions than his spiritual. When a hole suddenly appeared in Union lines at the Battle of Atlanta, Haney temporarily took command of fifty soldiers to halt a Rebel counter-attack, and then resumed his normal chaplain's duties. Cf. also Shattuck, *op. cit.*, 51; Honeywell, Col. Roy J.; "Men of God in Uniform," in *Civil War Times Illustrated* 6, (Aug. 1967); 31–36.

27. Shattuck, *op. cit.*, 55.

28. Brinsfield, Jr., et al., *op. cit.*, 55.

29. Shattuck, *op. cit.*, 63-64.

30. Bertram Wyatt-Brown, "Church, Honor and Secession," in *Religion and the American Civil War, op. cit.*; 104.

31. Chaplains had to be recruited because officially appointed pastors were exempt from the 1862 Conscription Act, and (after 1863) those who had enlisted as soldiers were not allowed to transfer to a vacant chaplain's position (fighting soldiers were more important than praying chaplains).

32. Brinsfield, Jr., et al., *op. cit.*, 83.

33. Brinsfield, Jr., et al., *ibid.*; and Pitts, *op. cit.*, 132–33.

34. It was Charles Quintard who was responsible for the conversion of Braxton Bragg, baptized Ben Cheatham and buried Pat Cleburne after the battle of Franklin. Brinsfield et al., *op. cit.*, 63 and 73. Cf. also Roy Honeywell, *op. cit.*, 31–36.

35. Charles Reagan Wilson, *Baptized in Blood—The Religion of the Lost Cause* (Athens, GA: University of Georgia Press, 1980), 119–138.

36. Pitts, *op. cit.*, 125.

37. Wilson, *op. cit.*, 85–86; and Wallace Hettle, "The Minister, the Martyr and the Maxim – Robert Lewis Dabney and Stonewall Jackson," in *Civil War History*. 49, no. 4 (December 2003), 353–369.

38. William Wiatt, *Confederate Chaplain William Edward Wiatt—An Annotated Diary* (Lynchburg, VA: The Virginia Civil War Battles & Leaders Series, 1994).

39. Brinsfield, Jr., John W., "Chaplains of the Confederacy," in *Faith in the Fight, op. cit.*, 85. Cf. also John W. Brinsfield, Jr., *The Spirit Divided—Memoirs of Civil War Chaplains* (Macon, GA: Mercer University Press, 2005), 10–11.

40. "The majority of Methodist clergy in 1861 in the South seemed to prefer fighting to preaching." Cf. Brinsfield, Jr., "Chaplains of the Confederacy," *op. cit.*, 62.

41. In 1864 they were allowed to draw forage "if they had a horse" and a stationery allowance for letter-writing. Charles Pitts, *Chaplains in Gray* (Concord, VA: R.M.J.C. Publications, 2003), 41. Also Brinsfield, Jr., "Chaplains of the Confederacy," *op. cit.*, 58.

42. Brinsfield, Jr., "Chaplains of the Confederacy," *op. cit.*, 58.

43. This was considered to be an insult and slur by chaplains. "The sad manner in which the Confederacy supported its clergy insured that there simply would not be a large enough supply in the army." (Shattuck, *op. cit.*, 65).

44. Brinsfield, Jr., "Chaplains of the Confederacy," *op. cit.*, 73–74; Brinsfield, Jr., *The Spirit Divided, op. cit.*; and Pitts, *op. cit.*, 44–45.

45. William Faherty, *Exile in Erin* (St. Louis: Missouri Historical Press, 2002), 47.

46. Robertson, *op. cit.*, 175.

47. Armstrong, *op. cit.*, 114.

48. Woodworth, *op. cit.*, 157. A good rebuttal to a study done on chaplains' "limited" effectiveness during the war is found in Warren Armstrong's *For Courageous Fighting and Confident Dying, op. cit.*, 55.

Chapter Eleven

SOLDIERS OF THE CROSS—
CATHOLIC CHAPLAINS

> This was one of my most laborious days: it being spent from morning till late at night hearing confessions, administering Extreme Unction, baptizing, and in washing and dressing wounds. Late this night we received orders to prepare to march in the morning. I threw myself down for a few hours in the open air but slept little.
>
> Fr. James Sheeran (14th LA), May 7, 1864 after Battle of Wilderness

Challenges to the Catholic Chaplaincy

While all Civil War chaplains faced troubles early in the war regarding issues of pay, status, and roles, Roman Catholics experienced special challenges in providing religious care, as well as having priests appointed as official chaplains. Being a religious minority within the predominantly Protestant armies of both sides, the larger Catholic struggle for recognition and acceptance had a significant impact here as well. As previously mentioned, Civil War armies were perhaps the most religious armies of all American history—but the strong evangelistic attitudes of many Protestant churchmen posed a challenge for Catholic leaders. James Moorhead has written how many Protestant organizations saw the wartime army as a fertile ground to "win souls" for Jesus, thus leading to a flood of Christian literature, Bibles, and religious-based relief efforts (U.S. Sanitary Commission and the Christian Commission). Already well aware of Protestant efforts at "sheep-stealing," the Catholic hierarchy (especially in the north) realized that it had to act quickly to supply chaplains for their Catholics soldiers.[1]

An immediate and ongoing concern was the adverse attitude of Protestants in the army. Some Protestant officers simply refused to accept Catholic priests as chaplains for their Catholic men. In the spring of 1862, only twenty-two priests served among the 472 Union chaplains then on duty, when the ratio of Catholic to Protestant soldiers was actually about one to nine. Thus Catholic chaplains were chosen only for regiments that were nearly exclusively Catholic (e.g., the 69th NY, heart of the Union "Irish Brigade," and the 10th TN CSA). It was a rare situation indeed when a Catholic would chaplain a predominantly Protestant regiment.[2] Chaplains like future bishop John Ireland (5th MN) and James Gombettelli (13th PA Cav) both served only very short chaplain stints because of the predominantly Protestant nature of their regiments. Protestant "sheep-stealing" efforts always remained a problem. As Randall Miller says, "Catholics chafed at the Protestant prodding of such men as 'the one-wing devil' General O.O. Howard, who wanted to convert their armies into Protestant crusaders."[3]

The responsibility for selecting Catholic chaplains generally lay with Church leaders. Requests went out from both Union and Confederate governments to bishops and religious superiors, and Catholic leaders responded. Archbishop John Hughes received an appeal from the Governor of New York, as did Bishop James Wood from the Pennsylvania Governor. Religious orders such as the Jesuits, Redemptorists and Holy Cross (CSC) requested volunteers from their members to serve as chaplains—and all received positive responses. Many Catholic priests volunteered on their own without being asked to serve as chaplains.

In the end, over seventy "official" Catholic chaplains served in both armies (fifteen serving more or less "full-time" throughout the entire war), with many other Catholic clergy playing part-time "unofficial" roles to assist soldiers in the practice of their faith.[4] "Maryland Province Jesuits from the French missions of New York and the South, Holy Cross priests from Notre Dame, Redemptorists from New Orleans, and secular priests from a score of dioceses" were among those who served.[5] Still, the Catholic response was not without its difficulties.

The mid-nineteenth century was a time of booming immigration, particularly of the Irish, the great majority of whom were Catholic. Understaffed even in peacetime, already stressed with divergent ethnic needs, it was often difficult for the American Catholic Church to spare priests for chaplaincy purposes. Thus, despite being allowed to chaplain, some priests were later recalled to their dioceses or congregations after serving for a while (e.g., John Ireland, Joseph O'Hagan SJ, Joseph Prachensky SJ).[6] Many priest/chaplains served for only a short time.

Some priests, like the St. Louis priest Fr. John Bannon (1st MO CSA Infantry), never even sought formal permission from their bishop to become a chaplain, knowing that they would not receive it (although Bannon did leave a farewell letter with Bishop Peter Kenrick, which he never opened). Other priests attempted to balance both parish responsibilities with "informal" chaplain duties—Oscar Sears (CSA) in Lynchburg, Virginia, and Innocent Bergrath (CSA) in Eastern Tennessee are examples here, although many more served in this capacity than can likely be known without great research.

It is estimated that some 200,000 Catholics served in Civil War armies (145,000 of whom were Irish).[7] But because of inequities and shortages, many in non-Catholic regiments went without the services of a priest for long periods of time. The Cincinnati-based German Catholic paper *Der Wahrheitsfreund* complained in 1862 that "There are regiments where one-third are Catholic, and yet there is no Catholic chaplain in the brigade, or in the whole division. There are only a few regiments in which there are no Catholic soldiers, and we do not believe that the tenth part of these Catholics can receive the sacraments when they have most need to them."[8] The few but excellent war-time journals of Catholic priests are full of stories of their meeting Catholics (soldiers both Confederate and Union) who had not had the services of a Catholic priest for long periods of time. Fortunately, occasional long encampments allowed a few priests to circulate more among the different regiments, and thus offered opportunities for sacraments to be received and ministry to be engaged in for those who chose.

I suppose you expected me home before now. When I left I did not think that I would be so long in the army. I could not think of leaving my brave fellows in the face of the enemy without a priest—not knowing what day a battle would be fought . . . I came very near being killed four or five times during those battles. Nothing but the protecting hand of God could have saved me for which I can never be sufficiently thankful.

December 1864 letter from Fr. P.P. Cooney CSC to his brother
[after the battles of Franklin and Nashville]

Daily Catholic chaplain life

Catholic chaplains slept on the same hard ground, wrestled with the same life and death issues, and performed many of the same ministries as did their Protestant counterparts. They visited hospitals, followed soldiers into battle, provided comfort to the sick and dying, helped instruct people on various religious points, offered counsel to the condemned and dying, and became "jacks of all trades" to help the soldiers they worked for. But Catholic priests had the further important and unique ministry of Sacramental administration for their soldiers. They heard soldiers' confessions (at times for hours on end throughout the night), and sometimes in dangerous situations offered a mass "general absolution" to the gathered troops. (Despite Fr. William Corby becoming legendary for this on the second day of Gettysburg, he did this on at least one *other* occasion, as did other Catholic priests from time to time.)

Arranging for the regular celebration of Mass for the troops was a chief responsibility for priest/chaplains—despite the uncertainty of drill and camp life, exhaustion, fatigue and "worldly distractions," priests learned to adapt and celebrate Mass "on the fly," as well as at makeshift altars in open-air settings. When celebrating Mass for his troops, Fr. Corby was fond of mentioning in his *Memoirs* that "thus we sanctified another spot in Virginia on our march, as we had done a hundred times before and which we continued to do until we reached the *end* on the banks of the Appomattox."[9]

> As fast as our men dropped, they were seen first by the priest, at the request of the sufferer, and if his wound was fatal, the priest heard his confession on the spot, and then he was conveyed to a place called a hospital. All know that Catholics, when about to die especially, desire to become reconciled to God, not merely by contrition for sins, but also by the use of the Sacrament of Penance . . . .
>
> Fr. William Corby, *Memoirs of Chaplain Life*

Other issues unique to Catholic theology and heritage also followed them around. With the stress of army life leading to over-indulgence in "John Barleycorn," Catholic priests frequently found themselves administering the traditional "pledge" to those soldiers (many of them Irish) who had indulged too freely for too long. Priests on both sides also constantly struggled to find the necessary resources to celebrate Mass—namely an altar, vestments, chalice, hosts, wine, etc. When (for whatever reason) a priest would lose his Mass kit, it almost always occasioned a short leave to pick up new supplies for this key sacramental work.

An early and cumbersome burden for Catholic chaplains was the standard requirement to obtain "faculties" to minister from bishops of areas in which they traveled, and of communicating their whereabouts to their superiors. This was ultimately resolved by a February 1862 prescription from Rome allowing priests to perform their ministry wherever they traveled, but to attempt to present themselves to the local Ordinary within two months if possible.[10]

A final unique opportunity that Catholic chaplains (and religious sisters as well) had was to help break down the anti-Catholic bias so prevalent in America, and to perhaps help begin a deeper understanding and acceptance of Catholics. Deep anti-Catholic bias would certainly continue on for decades after the Civil War, but without a doubt many inroads were made with countless individuals by the wartime ministry of Catholic chaplains. A fine example of this is seen in Congregationalist chaplain William Eastman, who in the post-war years wrote eloquently of the impact that priests like John Ireland (5th MN), Joseph O'Hagan (73d NY) and William Corby (88th NY) had upon himself and others:

There were chaplains of all denominations, and the spirit of oneness among them would have seemed rather remarkable at home. We who were Protestants, used to think that the Roman Catholic chaplains had some advantage in the firm grip they had upon their men. One can hardly fail to hear in the memory of such times the echo of that fine classic:

By communion of the banner
Battle scarred but victor banner
By the baptism of the banner
Brothers of one church are we.[11]

Catholic clergy as war-time emissaries

By its nature, the Catholic Church is an international institution, with ecclesial connections throughout the world. This fact was not lost on both Northern and Southern governments during America's Civil War, as both attempted to use Catholic bishops as emissaries to build alliances overseas. Rome was the place both the Union and Confederacy looked towards for support, but (like other European capitals of that time), "it was a hotbed of intrigue,"[12] and in the end the final results were uncertain, with success difficult to evaluate with any precision. Still, it is worth noting the respect that both governments had for the efforts and potential effect these bishops could have for their government's causes.

For the Union, it was prominent New York *Archbishop John Hughes* who was summoned to Washington in October 1861, and asked to sponsor the Union cause abroad. While refusing any official position, Hughes consented to serve in a private capacity, and so sailed for France on November 6, 1861, having conversations with French royalty (Napoleon III and Empress Eugenie) as well as other ambassadors and officials. He later wrote that he was uncertain if his efforts had served to prevent either England or France from entering the American conflict, emphasizing there was no love for the United States beyond the Atlantic. However President Lincoln was pleased with Hughes' efforts, saying that he turned sympathy our way in Europe more than any one else could have done.[13] In Rome, the United States requested through Hughes that the Vatican follow a policy of non-intervention in the conflict, an approach which offered no difficulties for Rome.[14]

> On Oct 18, 1862, Pius IX wrote a letter to Archbishops Hughes and Odin (New Orleans) asking both to labor strenuously for peace. "Neglect nothing as long as it is compatible with your office . . . We hope that our paternal exhortation will be the more graciously accepted . . . because we are moved, not by any political motives nor by any earthly considerations, but solely by fatherly love."

In response to this, Jefferson Davis sent his own letter to the Pope on Sept 23, 1863, obtaining a Papal response phrased in general terms of charity, but using the title "Your Excellency." Despite later discussion over the deeper ramifications of this, it is best seen as sheer formality, with no deeper political meaning. In 1864, Davis himself commissioned *Bishop Michael Lynch* of Charleston to do what Hughes had attempted to do several years before. He visited Ireland first, then London, Paris and Rome—meeting Catholic hierarchs along the way, as well as Napoleon III (who was friendly but said nothing of real substance). By 1864 attitudes of people overseas had hardened regarding the situation, and Lynch (though always greeted favorably) did not receive much active support for his cause.[15]

Other Catholic clergy were sent overseas in various emissarial capacities as well. In 1863, *Fr. John Bannon* (Confederate chaplain and former St. Louis MO pastor) went to his native Ireland to explain the causes of the Confederacy, and help prevent more Irishmen from migrating to the U.S. to fight for the Union. By the spring of 1864 he had finished his work, and temporarily joined Bishop Lynch in his emissarial role; but after the war, radical Republican lawmakers had not forgotten Bannon's wartime efforts, and blocked his return to America.[16] Other efforts at influencing European nations were carried out by *Bishop Michael Domenec* (Pittsburgh), a Spaniard by birth who played a minor role in attempting to influence Spain against the Confederacy[17]; Benedictine *Abbot Bonifaz Wimmer* (who corresponded with the Catholic Emperor of Austria), and *Bishop John Fitzpatrick* (Boston) who toured Europe in 1862–63, but found most of his support in highly Catholic Belgium.

> Today . . . has been one of the happiest of my life—contrasting my present quiet with the experience of the army, where with some exceptions, everything corrupt, low vulgar and debasing in our corrupt nature is rampant. Would that I were out of it, but it cannot be yet. I may still do some good where I am and I will make the sacrifice of my feelings for that object.
>
> Fr. Joseph O'Hagan, Feb. 19, 1863 journal entry while on retreat

Unique Catholic chaplains

Some Catholic chaplains became well-known and nigh legendary for their work (William Corby, James Sheeran, Peter Cooney, Joseph O'Hagan, John Bannon and Abram Ryan, for example). Some were officially commissioned by their governments and served for either long or short periods of service. Others (perhaps an unknown number) were never officially commissioned, yet ministered as they could and as needed. But the wartime ministrations of some chaplains defy neat descriptions. The following three Catholic priests were never really formal chaplains, yet all made undeniable contributions in most unique ways.

Fr. Peter Whelan (1802–1871)—*Apostle to Andersonville*[18]
A native Irishman, Vicar General of the Savannah Diocese, and early-war chaplain at Fort Pulaski Georgia, Peter Whelan was serving the spiritual needs of all Confederate posts in Georgia when he was asked by Bishop Augustin Verot to minister at Andersonville prison. Whelan went there for four months (June-September 1864), writing later that he continually fell asleep exhausted, "full of sorrow for what he had seen all day." He was joined in ministry there for a short while by three other priests (Henry Clavrel, John Kirby and the multi-lingual Anselm Usannez SJ), all of whom worked only a few weeks before leaving.

Just before leaving Andersonville himself, Whelan borrowed money to purchase flour and bake bread for the remaining prisoners. This much-needed food became known as "Whelan's Bread" and lasted several weeks. Whelan returned to Savannah beset by a lung ailment and by invading Federal troops under Sherman in December 1864. After the war, he ministered to Henry Wirz (a Catholic) before his death, and visited Jefferson Davis at Ft. Monroe. Though he did become a post-war pastor in Savannah, his health was never the same, and Whelan died on Jan. 15, 1871. It is recorded that his funeral procession four days later was the longest ever seen, and that seldom was so large a gathering of people found in the streets of Savannah.[19]

Fr. Jeremiah Trecy (1825–??)—*Chaplain for both sides*[20]

Few chaplains could brag of acceptance by *both* Union and Confederacy, but such was Jeremiah Trecy. Born in Ireland, ordained in 1851, Trecy labored in Iowa and Nebraska before the war, establishing churches and representing area Indians on government business. In 1858, he went south for health reasons, doing missionary work in Alabama.

When Huntsville became a Confederate camp, Trecy volunteered his services to troops around Mobile Bay (Forts Gaines and Morgan). After Ft. Donelson, he was asked by a surgeon on the staff of Gen. A. S. Johnson to meet the spiritual needs of the hospitalized soldiers in Huntsville. He eventually got passes from generals of both sides to travel freely through Mississippi and Alabama, but after being stopped by one testy Union officer, he was brought before Union officers, including future Catholic convert Gen. David S. Stanley and Gen. William Rosecrans (whose brother Sylvester was a Catholic bishop).

Rosecrans would not permit him to return to Alabama (the Union army was then moving towards Iuka) so Trecy stayed with the Federals until after the battle of Iuka, working with Fr. John Ireland (5th MN), when he was permitted to return to Alabama. After the October 1862 battle of Corinth, Trecy got Rosecrans' permission to help the Southern wounded, but when Rosecrans was ordered to Cincinnati to take charge of the 14th Corps, he asked Trecy to accompany him.

Receiving authorization to visit the 14th Corps Catholic troops, Trecy traveled the Union camps freely, meeting Fr. Richard Christy (78th PA) with whom he became good friends. In April-May 1863, he requested to leave the army, as he had served without pay, but was convinced by Union officers to become chaplain of the 4th US Cavalry—a permission that was granted.

He remained with the army in Tennessee up to the battle of Chickamauga, where he "had many narrow escapes . . . three bullets passed through the cape of his great coat, and his vestments were captured but retaken. One Sunday his hat was blown off by a solid shot while attending a patient."[21] After Chickamauga, again Trecy was almost killed. While preparing a dying man, "a sharpshooter took accurate aim and put a bullet through the breast of his coat. The priest hurriedly mounted his horse, but as he did so, a perfect shower of bullets rained around him but he miraculously escaped with a few slight scratches on his horse."[22]

Trecy remained with the 4th Cavalry through the Atlanta Campaign, then followed Thomas' army to Nashville and Franklin, where he stood right beside Gen. Stanley as the general narrowly missed death when a bullet grazed his neck, cutting the string of his Catholic scapular. When the war was done, Trecy resigned his commission and returned to his mission at Huntsville, later pastoring as well in Bayou de Batre, Louisiana.

Fr. Joseph Bixio S.J. (1819–1898)—*Union or Confederate?*

Few Catholic chaplain stories are as colorful or checkered as that of this native Italian. Described by one as a sly and devious trickster "of unfailing chicanery and competence who spent an inordinate amount of time slipping back and forth across the Federal lines,"[23] Bixio was the brother of a famous Italian general, Nino Bixio, who was Garibaldi's right hand man in the struggle for Italian unification.

He entered the Jesuits in Italy, came to the United States in the late 1850s, and was in a parish that bordered both Virginia and Maryland as the war broke out. Unable to return to the northern side of his parish during the battle of Manassas,[24] Bixio volunteered as a Confederate chaplain. But by the spring of 1862, his true deviousness had emerged.

A Union chaplain wrote that Bixio had been in Federal camps "where he had gained the hearts of both officers and men," but by the summer he had turned up in Richmond. Then, in September 1864, Confederate chaplain Fr. James Sheeran (14th LA) noted that Bixio was again "now playing Yankee chaplain and drawing federal rations" while posing as northern Franciscan Fr. Leo Rizzo de Saracena.

Apparently, Bixio had slipped into the sick Fr. Rizzo's tent and stolen his chaplaincy credential and uniform. In this disguise he conned Gen. Phil Sheridan into giving up cartloads of Union supplies, an action that Sheeran himself would suffer for by being thrown into prison and enduring Sheridan's displaced wrath! Bixio then received a "polite message" in Staunton, Virginia from an unidentified Union general (likely Gen. Benjamin Butler) that he would be hung if caught—but he never was.

After the war ended, Bixio traveled to Georgetown with a trunkful of useless Confederate script expecting to found a college there, but left the area afterward, working awhile in Australia before finally returning to work and die at Santa Clara, California. Even to the end, the Italian retained his cunning charisma—he charmed the bishop in California, became his trusted confidant, and even founded a number of parishes for him in area counties.[25]

While never considered an official chaplain, Bixio certainly had a colorful history, *whatever* his true nature and intentions! While fellow Jesuit and wartime chaplain Fr. Hippolyte Gache S.J. (10th LA) wrote rather generously that Bixio "seems quite successful in the various places where he serves", it was Gache's translator Cornelius Buckley who perhaps best captured this unique and curious priest when he called him "every bit as ingenious and resourceful as he was double-dealing and cunning." [26]

Further reading recommendations

Benjamin Blied. *Catholics and the Civil War.* Milwaukee: Bruce Publishing, 1945.

John W. Brinsfield, Jr., William C. Davis, Benedict Maryniak, and James I. Robertson, Jr. *Faith in the Fight—Civil War Chaplains.* Mechanicsburg, PA: Stackpole Books, 2003.

William Corby. *Memoirs of Chaplain Life—Three Years with the Irish brigade in the Army of the Potomac.* Edited by Lawrence Frederick Kohl. New York: Fordham University Press, 1992.

Louis Hippolyte Gache. *A Frenchman, a Chaplain, a Rebel—the Civil War Letters of Pere Louis Hippolyte Gache, SJ.* Edited by Cornelius Buckley. Chicago: Loyola University Press, 1981.

Aidan Germaine. *Catholic Military and Naval Chaplains—1776–1917.* Washington, DC: Catholic University of America, 1929.

James Hennesey. *American Catholics—A History of the Roman Catholic Community in the United States.* New York: Oxford University Press, 1981.

James B. Sheeran. *Confederate Chaplain—A Military Journal.* Edited by Joseph T. Durkin. Milwaukee: Bruce Publishing, 1960.

Notes

1. Cf. James Moorhead, *American Apocalypse: Yankee Protestants and the Civil War, 1860–1869* (New Haven, CT: Yale University Press, 1978); and also Gardiner Shattuck, *A Shield and a Hiding Place: The Religious Life of Civil War Armies* (Macon, Ga.: Mercer University Press, 1987). For many guiding insights in this chapter, I am indebted to Randall Miller's excellent essay "Catholic Religion, Irish Ethnicity and the Civil War" in *Religion and the American Civil War,* edited by Randall M. Miller, Harry S. Stout, and Charles R. Wilson (New York: Oxford University Press, 1998), 261–296.

2. Fr. Richard C. Christie, elected as chaplain by the overwhelmingly Protestant 78th PA, was one such situation, however.

3. Miller, *op. cit.,* 265.

4. These numbers are my own, based upon research into and compilation of the best available current Catholic chaplain records. I used the two standard Catholic chaplain listings of Benjamin Blied, *Catholics and the Civil War,* (Milwaukee: Bruce Publishing Company, 1945), and Aidan Germaine, *Catholic Military and Naval Chaplains—1776–1917* (Washington, DC: Catholic University of America, 1929). Newer numbers and additional names have been added from John Brinsfield, Benedict Maryniak, William C. Davis, James I. Robertson, Jr., *Faith in the Fight* (Mechanicsburg, PA: Stackpole Books, 2003).

5. For general insights and perspective on Catholic chaplains, cf. James Hennesey, *American Catholics—A History of the Roman Catholic Community in the United States* (New York: Oxford University Press, 1981); also Aidan Germaine, *op. cit.*; and Benjamin Blied, *op. cit.* These last two books, despite their age, are the standard Catholic texts in outlining and understanding the role of Catholic Civil War chaplains.

6. Aidan Germain comments about the hardship placed on bishops in allowing their priests to volunteer as chaplains during the war. "Since immigration was practically unimpeded . . . the Catholic population of all states grew constantly and the need of priests to minister to them increased in proportion. It was next to impossible to determine in advance with what regiments the Catholic soldiers were most numerous, and thus it chanced that now and then a Catholic chaplain was, like Fr. Gombattelli, assigned to a regiment having very few Catholics. Again, as Fr. Ireland experienced, battle losses and expiration of enlistments diminished the Catholic soldiers of a given regiment to a comparative handful, which made it desirable that the services of chaplains be utilized in spheres of greater need." Cf. Germain, *op. cit.*, 71.

7. Miller, *op. cit.*, 265, 293. The Irish made up 11% of the Union Army, and Germans some 12%.

8. *Der Wahrheitsfreund*, as cited in Benjamin Blied, *op. cit.*, 112–13.

9. William Corby, *Memoirs of Chaplain Life—Three Years with the Irish brigade in the Army of the Potomac*, edited by Lawrence Frederick Kohl (New York: Fordham University Press, 1992), 207. Cf. also Randall Miller, *op. cit.*, 267.

10. Cf. Germaine, *op. cit.*, 46–48 for a fuller discussion of this issue.

11. As cited in John Brinsfield, Jr., Benedict Maryniak, William C. Davis and James I. Robertson, Jr.; *Faith in the Fight—Civil War Chaplains*; (Mechanicsburg, PA: Stackpole Books, 2003), 123–4.

12. Hennessey, *op. cit.*, 156.

13. Lincoln also wrote that "I intend to recommend in the most appropriate way I can that the Pope appoint Archbishop Hughes a cardinal, and so far interfere in the ecclesiastical affairs of the church." In retrospect, Bishop Hughes (a friend of William H. Seward) felt the government was complimenting him by making the request it did, and that this was a subtle condemnation of the "know-nothings" who had attempted to brand Catholics as disloyal.

14. Pope Pius IX expressed to the American minister to the Vatican, Alexander Randall, that they were "justly proud" of Hughes being entrusted with this emissarial responsibility.

15. Bishops Lynch and Hughes engaged in a public disagreement regarding slavery and the Southern cause in a series of letters written between themselves in 1861. After Lynch had outlined his views in an August 1861 letter, Hughes took the unusual step of publishing his response through his own newspaper. Lynch then published the full version of his own previous letter. The exchange attracted much public attention, but actually reflected how calm and tempered some religious leaders could be (in contrast to the fiery disagreements of other denominations) over these difficult sectional issues. Cf. John Tracy Ellis, *Documents of American Catholic History* (Milwaukee, WI: Bruce Publishing, 1956), 356–365.

16. Bannon remained in Ireland, joined the Jesuit order, and became a prominent preacher and pastor there. Cf. Blied, *op. cit.*, 91–93; and also the excellent biography of Bannon written by William Faherty, *Exile in Erin* (St. Louis, MO: Missouri Historical Society Press, 2002).

17. Domenec was in Rome for the canonization of the Japanese martyrs, and had audiences with the Spanish queen and her ministers, which (according to Archbishop John Hughes at least) went very successfully. Hughes wrote that "Bishop Domenec, of all those who had been sent by the government to arrange these matters, is the only one who ever really succeeded in his mission." However, the national archives in Washington are silent about any long-term influence Domenec might have had. Cf. Blied, *op. cit.*, 93.

18. Information taken from a marvelous booklet on Whelan by Peter J. Meaney OSB, "Father Whelan of Fort Pulaski and Andersonville," reprinted from the *GA Historical Quarterly*, vol. 71, no. 1, Spring 1987. Cf. also Brinsfield et al., *op. cit.*, 253; Blied *op. cit.*, 123; Germain, *op. cit.*, 133–34; and also Michael V. Gannon, *Rebel Bishop—The Life and Era of Augustin Verot* (Milwaukee: Bruce Publishing Company, 1964), 93–106 for an excellent history on Whelan and Andersonville as well.

19. Some post war unofficial sources indicated that Whelan was "Chaplain-in-Chief" of all the Catholic chaplains in the service of the Confederacy," but that this assertion cannot be established from any official records. Cf. Germain, *op. cit.*, 134.

20. I am indebted here to the unpublished manuscript of David Power Conyngham entitled *The Soldiers of the Cross; or Nuns and Priests of the Battlefield*, which is presently in the Conyngham Papers in the Archives of Notre Dame University.

21. Conyngham, *op. cit.*, 45.

22. *Ibid.*, 46.

23. Hippolyte Gache, *A Frenchman, A Chaplain, A Rebel—The War Letters of Pere Louis-Hippolyte Gache, SJ* (Chicago: Loyola University Press, 1981), 98.

24. In writing about the battle of Manassas, an anonymous Englishman who fought with the Confederacy said that "it is to the foresight and judgment of one (Jesuit) that Beauregard and Johnston escaped death or capture at Manassas, for had they not met one of these missionaries during the heat of the conflict, and heeded his modest advice, one or another of these calamities must have inevitably ensued." Seeing as there were no other Jesuit chaplains in Virginia in July 1861, it was undoubtably Joseph Bixio he was referring to. Cf. Gache, *op. cit.*, 97.

25. Gache, *op. cit.*, 98–99.

26. Gache, *op. cit.*, 97.

Chapter Twelve

RELIGIOUS REVIVALS

> Most chaplains who left records agreed that [revivals] were the most amazing display of spiritual power ever witnessed among fighting men on the American continent.
>
> John W. Brinsfield, Jr. *The Spirit Divided* (2006)

War-weary soldiers seek the Lord

By January 1863, the Civil War had killed hundreds of thousands, tearing apart the hearts and hopes of North and South alike. Soldiers from both sides, so ignorant of war and naively confident in 1861, had now confronted horrors no person could have prepared them for. Death had become horrifyingly real, touching nearly every American family and village in the states who sent troops to the fronts. Shiloh, the Seven Days Campaign, Second Manassas, Antietam, Corinth, Fredericksburg. Such appalling battles had shaken the hearts and souls of the most hardened skeptics. What increased the anxiety and stress even more was the dreadful realization that no end was in sight, and that come spring of 1863, the horrible conflict would begin all over again. So, in retrospect, what began to happen (and indeed had already begun in places) should not have been surprising—for the nature of religious "conversion" experiences is that they frequently follow times of great stress, trauma and personal struggle. As the World War II saying phrased it well, "There are no atheists in foxholes."

Beginning roughly in 1863, the response of hundreds of thousands of soldiers (even entire armies) to the death and horrors around them was a remarkable wave of *religious revival*. Starting in a noticeable way first in the Confederate Army of Northern Virginia, but spreading to other Northern and Southern armies in both theaters of the war, an outpouring of deep religious fervor and intensity began unmatched perhaps even to the present time. The Great Revival which began in the late fall of 1863 ebbed and fell in intensity and location, but remained strong and continuous until the end of the Civil War. In fact, as Stephen Woodworth remarks,

> such a thing never occurred in any other American war . . . Though is was customary to refer to what happened in the armies as a series of revivals, it is really more accurate to think of it as a single large revival, approximately two and a half years long, occasionally interrupted by military operations.[1]

These army revivals did not spring up in isolation from America's recent religious patterns. In the early nineteenth century, the Second Great Awakening had rolled across America, leaving a predominance of Baptist and Methodist converts in its wake. In 1857–1858, a so-called "businessman's revival" arose in many major cities and then spread throughout the country just prior to the war. These latter revivals set the tone for what happened in the Civil War, as they were "ecumenical and lay in emphasis, affecting all classes and regions." Lay spiritual leadership was important in Civil War armies because of the relative lack of clergy or formal chaplains, and "the belief that traditional ecclesiastical distinctions were without justification in the informal setting of camp life." The religious revivals of the Civil War were "quintessentially American, laying stress more on participation and practicality than on contemplation and speculation. The leaders of the revivals were concerned more with results than with process."[2]

We held three meetings a day—a morning and afternoon prayer meeting, and a preaching service at night . . . Our sanctuary has always been crowded . . . Loud, animated singing always hailed our approach to the house of God . . . the entire altar could scarcely accommodate the supplicants.

Confederate chaplain Rev. J.D. Stiles

Revivalism—North and South

We have already seen[3] how the North and South were two different places religiously before the war, so it should not be a surprise that the wartime revivals were affected by this as well. While wartime revival experiences were generally driven by the "lowest common denominator" of basic evangelical beliefs and doctrine (generally without regard to denominational differences), still the motives for, and the tone that revivals took, had subtle shades of difference between North and South.[4]

Beginning first in late 1862 with Lee's Army of Northern Virginia (Pryor's and Barksdale's Brigades) and the Army of Tennessee, the revival Spirit among Confederate troops was fanned into full flame by late 1863 after the battles of Antietam, Gettysburg and Chickamauga-Chattanooga. Historian Gardiner Shattuck notes that "according to reports, approximately 7,000 men (10% of Lee's soldiers) were converted in that period, and at least thirty-two of the thirty-eight infantry brigades were touched by the revivals."

In the West as well, reports noted that "at least eleven of the twenty-eight brigades of the Army of Tennessee" were touched by revival, and "the largeness of the means of grace proved gratifying to the clergymen who worked among the troops."[5] The winter of 1863-1864 at Dalton was an especially powerful religious time, with long prayer meetings and numerous conversions in nearly every brigade.[6] One soldier wrote that "nearly all our first Generals have joined the Church and the army is fast becoming . . . a God-fearing soldiery."[7] (Ironically, the Holy Spirit of revival was also touching *Union* troops across the lines at Ringgold at the same time!)

For the deeply evangelical South, the "Great Revival"[8] was best documented by Rev. J. William Jones (*Christ in Camp*) and Rev. William Bennett (*Narrative of the Great Revival*) for Lee's Army in Northern Virginia.[9] Though both writers had their own motives for promoting Southern wartime religiosity, without a doubt they did capture the intense and emotional revivalist Spirit that flowed through the heavily Baptist and Methodist Confederate troops. Several historians have noticed that revivals and religious enthusiasm seemed to break out more among Southern troops following their defeats and failures in battle.[10] As the war wore on, the difficult implications of these Southern defeats seemed to "shift the reliance they put on God— trusting him no longer as the giver of worldly success, but as a guarantor of spiritual victory instead."[11] George Cary Eggleston's *Rebel Recollections* notes that "a sort of religious ecstasy took possession of the army" in the last year of the war. Soldiers ceased to rely on their military leaders, looking instead "for a miraculous interposition of supernatural power" on their behalf.

For the larger, more culturally diverse Union troops, revivalism was more gradual and steady, perhaps less "explosive" than the South.[12] While the reality and proximity of death did motivate them, revivalism seemed more connected to the overall progress they were making in the war, giving them the encouragement needed to continue the war efforts. "The revivals gained force as the war's tempo accelerated and the soldiers felt themselves carried toward victory, and thus they tapped into the greater reservoir of emotions that the conflict inspired."[13] James McPherson adds a motivational rationale for the spiritual outpouring, remarking that "Union soldiers became more religious as death grew even more manifest. With the approach of the spring of 1864, men on both sides recognized that the forthcoming military campaigns would be more terrible than anything before."[14]

As with the South, scattered revivals among Union troops began sporadically in 1862,[15] grew rapidly throughout 1863, and reached a high in the winter of 1863-1864. Northern soldiers who had earlier dealt with a "tide of irreligion" (in the words of Gen. Robert McAllister), now seemed to adopt a more reflective and religious attitude, seeking further strengthening (spiritually and materially) for the battles ahead.[16] The religious enthusiasm of the Army of the Potomac led them to build many chapels and hold frequent prayer meetings. Black troops in the Atlantic coast garrisons also experienced a surge of spiritual fervor.

Perhaps one of the greatest revivals occurred among the Western troops in fall 1863 after their surprising victory at Missionary Ridge, seen by many as an act of God—including Gen. John Geary (fighting at Lookout Mountain) who said "I have been the instrument of Almighty God." Union troops camped at Ringgold baptized hundreds in Chickamauga Creek, the river becoming now not just a symbol of previous death, but new Life in Jesus Christ. Halted temporarily by the Wilderness Campaign,[17] religious interest rose again when Eastern troops settled into their Richmond entrenchments. Sherman's Western troops maintained a remarkable religious enthusiasm throughout their march through Georgia and the Carolinas. The black troops who entered Charleston, South Carolina did so "singing Methodist hymns" and having camp meetings which created "tremendous excitement."[18]

On the evening of Sept. 29, 1863, after the battle of Chickamauga, Union Lt. Chesley Mosman heard two preachers expounding at the same time—one in Confederate lines, and the other on the Union side. He related that he stood there for some time listening to two sermons in two hostile camps from the one and same Bible.

Steven Woodworth, *While God is Marching On* (2001)

The revival experience

While many soldiers felt the Spirit of revival for the first time, numerous soldiers were already believers and supported the army's religious revival. In the North, Gen. *George McClellan* mandated early in the war that worship services should be held in camp every Sunday morning, a decision Gen. *Oliver O. Howard* (a former divinity student who often officiated at services) certainly appreciated and supported. Gen. *William Rosecrans* was a devout Catholic who increased the number of chaplains, making it a policy never to fight on Sundays (as he chose not to do at Stones River in 1862).[19] While the North's most prominent soldiers were not particularly religious (*Grant, Sherman* and *Sheridan*), the same could not be said for the South's leading warriors. Generals *Lee, Jackson, Pendleton* and *Polk* (a pre-war Bishop) have always stood out for their religiosity.

During the height of the revival, even prominent military leaders were affected and drawn closer to God. During the Atlanta campaign of May-June 1864, Confederate Generals *Joseph E. Johnson* and *John Bell Hood* were among those baptized. They were brought to the "living waters" by Bishop Leonidas Polk before his own unfortunate 1864 meeting with a cannonball. Other prominent conversions included *Dorsey Pender,*[20] *Richard Ewell,*[21] *"Dick" Anderson, Robert Rodes,*[22] *Stephen D.*

Lee,[23] *Braxton Bragg,*[24] and *George B. McClellan* (who converted in 1861). Some of these seem to prove an old dictum that Wisdom in religious matters does necessarily not equate to wisdom in other matters—in this case, military!

The journal entries of a Methodist chaplain (5th NY Cavalry) Louis Beaudry, provide an interesting portrait inside the wartime revival experience. As 1864 begins, there is no mention of any special revival; in fact his ministry seemed slow and routine. But by April 24, 1864, things had changed—his evening Chapel services were jammed, and "many who came were not able to get in . . . the number is increasing daily of such as 'shall be saved.'" On April 28, 1864, Beaudry writes that "we had an interesting prayer meeting. Quite a number of new men are enlisting in the Army of Christ. The interest in religion is widening and deepening. Three young men entered the ranks of Christ tonite for the first time."[25] Then, on April 29th, Beaudry writes this inspiring account:

> as dark came on, the men of their own accord began to assemble at my tent . . . As the numbers increased, we began to sing and soon the tent was crowded full and a circle was formed of men sitting on the grass in front. Assembled thus, without appointment, but by an inner impulse, by the influence of the Spirit of Him who said "where 2 or 3 are gathered in my name etc." it may be expected that we had a season of prayer and conference full of melting interest and lasting profit. I never attended a better meeting. Such scenes make wonderful impressions.[26]

Another author captures poignantly the religious outpouring that ran through A.P. Hill's 3d Corps in the middle of 1863:

> There was a widespread surge in religious fervor. The hitherto perfunctory attendance of battle-jaded veterans towards religious observances was now supplanted by genuine interest and concern in spiritual matters. Even the dullest preachers drew large, attentive congregations in crude chapels built by the men. Services were held almost every day followed at night by hymn-singing and prayer services. Professions of faith increased as did formal church membership. . . .[27]

On the way home we kneeled and prayed that God bless our Regiment. The next week six met for prayer, and last week about thirty . . . [then] nearly every officer and man of our Regiment had come into the grove where the Christians were meeting. I never saw such a prayer meeting before, and I know the Spirit of the Lord was with us.

Elisha Hunt Rhodes, *All for the Union* (1985)

Results of revivals

Through the years, there has been much debate about the extent and ultimate impact of Civil War revivals. The revivals were probably more dramatic in the Confederacy, but were certainly no less pervasive in the Union—where the Christian influence was probably more widespread at the outset of the war in first place.[28] The long-term results of the Great Revival in both Northern and Southern armies are certainly impressive spiritually, but hard to measure with great accuracy.

However counted, it is obvious that such a "large a body [of Christians] had to be a conspicuous presence in the camps."[29] Rev. J. William Jones estimated that 150,000 soldiers converted during the war, a figure also used by Rev. William W. Bennett, who served as a missionary in the Army of Northern Virginia and later studied the Confederate revivals. Bennett remarks that "fully one-third of all the soldiers in the field were praying men and members of some branch of the Christian Church."[30]

Contemporary authors offer different numbers, allowing that *"at least 100,000 were converted"* in the Confederate armies.[31] Woodworth mentions that conversions in the Union armies were even more numerous, with estimates ranging from 100,000–200,000 (which would be some 5–10% of all Union troops). Gardiner Shattuck supports these numbers, adding that these were only the conversions, not the involvement of men who were already Christian or interested spectators at the revivals.

In summary, whatever the numbers of war-time conversions, two statements accurately capture the remarkable revival Spirit that touched Civil War armies, for "by any standard, the religious happenings of those four years were remarkable."[32] *First*, Steven Woodworth concisely summarizes this entire issue when he writes that

> a significant minority of soldiers went right on gambling, drinking, cursing and wenching. Another large segment of soldiers would have voiced a general agreement with the Christian worldview and given at least a nod to Christian morals, but did not personally embrace the faith themselves. Those who did openly profess and live the Christian faith probably numbered somewhat *under half of the total number of soldiers*. For those men, *perhaps well over a million in number*, the great army revival of the Civil War was the most vital part of their experience in the camps, and the source of their strength in facing the hardships and dangers of war.[33]

Finally, to anyone who might question the impact or power of such religious revivalism upon the fighting capacity of the soldiers, one need only reflect upon the conclusions of James McPherson in his excellent study of Civil War soldiers, *For Cause and Comrades*.

The Confederate revivals had gone a long way towards raising morale in Southern armies from its low point at the end of 1863. Heightened religiosity helped prevent the collapse of both armies during the terrible carnage of 1864, but was a particularly potent force in the Confederacy. It may not be an exaggeration to say that the revivals of 1863-1864 enabled Confederate armies to prolong the war into 1865. [34]

Further reading recommendations

William Bennett. *Narrative of the Great Revival in the Southern Armies During the Late Civil War between the States of the Federal Union.* Harrisonburg, VA: Sprinkle Publications, 1989.

John William Jones. *Christ in Camp—The True Story of the Great Revival during the War Between the States.* Harrisonburg, VA: Sprinkle Publications, 1986.

Phillip Shaw Paludan. Pp. 339–374 of *A People's Contest—The Union and the Civil War, 1861–1865.* New York: Harper and Row, 1988.

Sidney J. Romero. *Religion in the Rebel Ranks.* Lanham, MD: University Press of America, 1983.

Gardiner H. Shattuck. *A Shield and a Hiding Place.* Macon, GA: Mercer University Press, 1987.

Steven E. Woodworth. *While God is Marching On—The Religious World of Civil War Soldiers.* Lawrence: University Press of Kansas, 2001.

Notes

1. Steven E. Woodworth, *While God is Marching On—The Religious World of Civil War Soldiers* (Lawrence: University Press of Kansas, 2001), 253.
2. Gardiner H. Shattuck, *A Shield and a Hiding Place* (Macon, GA: Mercer University Press, 1987), 83–84. I am greatly indebted in this chapter to Shattuck for his fine insights of the differences in revivalism between North and South.
3. In chapter 6, "Religious differences between North and South."
4. The Catholic version of "revival" was called a "parish mission". In the mid-late nineteenth century, and well into the twentieth, such missions were extremely popular renewal tools, as well as powerful and often emotionally moving events. One order prominent in mission preaching in these centuries was the Redemptorists (Congregation of the Most Holy Redeemer). They held a November 1860 mission in Richmond which even the *Richmond Daily Dispatch* mentioned highly, as it doubled the number of communicants there from their previous mission. Cf. Harry S. Stout and Christopher Grasso, "Civil War, Religion and

Communications," in *Religion and the American Civil War*, edited by Randall M. Miller, Harry S. Stout, and Charles R. Wilson, (New York: Oxford University Press, 1998), 356, footnote 72.

5. Shattuck, *op, cit.*, 99–101.

6. The diary of Rev. Edward Wiatt, chaplain of the 26th VA, contains an interesting day-by-day account of the revival that went through his troops during July through August 1863. Cf. Alex Wiatt, *Confederate Chaplain William Edward Wiatt—An Annotated Diary* (Lynchburg, VA: The Virginia Civil War Battles & Leaders Series, 1994).

7. Shattuck, *op. cit.*, 102.

8. Southern churchmen later used this phrase when speaking of the revivalist enthusiasm which ran through the Southern armies in the Civil War years.

9. The two classic works on the revival in the Army of Northern Virginia are J. William Jones, *Christ in Camp*, originally published in 1887, and William Bennett, *The Great Revival Which Prevailed in the Southern Armies*, published in 1877.

10. Kurt O. Berends is one who would dissent from this opinion, remarking that "if there is a consistent pattern to the revivals, I have not been able to locate it." He feels that reports of the greatest revivals coming after defeats are not substantiated. Kurt O. Berends, "Wholesome Reading Purifies and Elevates the Man," in *Religion in the American Civil War, op. cit.*, 157, footnote #11.

11. Shattuck, *op. cit.*, 101–02.

12. Beginning in the second half of 1863, the Union army was forced to deal with large numbers of conscripts and replacements coming into their ranks—many of whom were drawn from what Woodworth calls "the absolute dregs of Northern industrial society, the most debauched and spiritually hardened class of people on the continent." Still, Union soldiers and volunteers built chapels, chaplains held services and preached, believers sang and "found the Lord" in great numbers. Cf. Woodworth, *op. cit.*, 227.

13. Shattuck, *op. cit.*, 92–93.

14. James McPherson, *For Cause and Comrades* (New York: Oxford University Press, 1997), 75.

15. They began in the large Union encampments where troops were gathering and training at Washington, Chicago and St. Louis. The United States Christian Commission *Annual Report* 1 (1862) reports this on pp. 96–99.

16. Shattuck, *op. cit.*, 78–79.

17. Maintaining the revival spirit was always difficult when troops were marching or in campaigns. The soldiers and chaplains had little opportunity to organize large-scale religious activities until they could again return to more settled and less bellicose living arrangements.

18. Shattuck, *op. cit.*, 81–82, 88–89.

19. In a heavily Protestant and evangelical nation, William Rosecrans' fervent Catholicity seems to have only added to the fire created when his military failures led to removal from command. Charles A. Dana, upon visiting Rosecrans in the field, supposedly commented that "I knew we were in trouble when he made the sign of the cross." His report was highly critical of the Catholic general, whose brother Sylvester was a bishop in the Midwest.

20. A Division Commander in the Army of Northern Virginia during 1862–1863, Pender was baptized before his troops, confirmed by a Virginia Episcopal bishop, mortally wounded at Gettysburg, and met his Maker in Staunton, Virginia on July 18, 1863. Cf. Shattuck, *op. cit.*, 98.

21. He entered the church at time of the revivals. Cf. Herman Norton, "Revivalism in the Confederate Armies," *Civil War History* 6, no.4 (1960), 424.

22. Charles F. Pitts, *Chaplains in Gray* (Concord, VA: R.M.J.C. Publications, 2003), 60.

23. Although Lee was not baptized until 1868, he traced his religious interests back to 1862, remembering that "his first mature thoughts about religion occurred while gazing at the Union charge against his guns at Second Manassas." Cf. Shattuck, *op. cit.*, 98.

24. Bragg was convinced to accept God into his life by the doctor/chaplain Charles Todd Quintard during a revival in the Army of Tennessee, being baptized and confirmed in June 1863.

25. Louis N. Beaudry, *War Journal of Louis N. Beaudry, Fifth New York Cavalry*, edited by Richard E. Beaudry (Jefferson, NC: McFarland and Company Publishers, 1996), 109. It should be noted that Methodists, who did not require profession of faith as a prerequisite for admission, often had "seekers" in their churches in order to help them along to conversion. The term occurs frequently in the journals of war-time chaplains like Beaudry.

26. Beaudry, *ibid.*, 109–10.

27. William Woods Hassler, *A.P. Hill—Lee's Forgotten General* (Chapel Hill: University of North Carolina Press, 1957), 172.

28. Woodworth, *op. cit.*, 230. "Only about 25% of CSA soldiers were church-members at beginning of war." Another 25% of the Confederate fighting troops were barely literate, and had trouble reading Scripture for themselves.

29. Shattuck, *op. cit.*, 92.

30. W.W. Bennett, *Narrative of the Great Revival* (Harrisonburg, Va.: Sprinkle Publications, 1989), 413.

31. Shattuck, *op. cit.*, 92.

32. Woodworth, *op. cit.*, 246.

33. Steven Woodworth, "The Meaning of Life in the Valley of Death," *Civil War Times Illustrated*, December 2003; 55–58. Drew Gilpin Faust, in "Christian Soldiers: The Meaning of Revivalism in the Confederate Army," *Journal of Southern History* 53, no.1 (February 1987); 63–90 also speaks of how Southern revivalism helped Confederate soldiers in both personal spirituality and in the larger understanding of God's plan for them in the midst of destruction and defeat.

34. McPherson, *op. cit.*, 75. In his book *Goodmen*, analyzing the character and values of Civil War soldiers, Michael Barton offers an interesting insight into the significance of these wartime revivals. Barton discovered that more than three-quarters of the men in the sample he surveyed referred to religion as an important factor in their lives—thus ranking it *third* on a list of *fifteen* significant "core values" on which soldiers of this period based their behavior. Another factor in his survey covered what he called "moralism"; and from both of these factors, Barton suggests that spiritual and moral questions were a notable concern of those men who commented on their experiences in the army. Cf. Michael Barton, *Goodmen: The Character of Civil War Soldiers* (University Park, PA: Pennsylvania State University Press, 1981).

Chapter Thirteen

THROUGH A MORAL LENS—DARKLY

> If only it were all so simple! If only there were evil people somewhere insidiously committing evil deeds, and it were necessary only to separate them from the rest of us and destroy them. But the line dividing good and evil cuts through the heart of every human being. And who is willing to destroy a piece of his own heart?
>
> Alexander Solzhenitsyn, *The Gulag Archipelago* (1973)

"The light of a higher morality"

On April 12, 1864, Nathan Bedford Forrest's Confederate cavalry killed dozens of unarmed black troops who had already surrendered at Fort Pillow, TN. In February 1865, Sherman's marauding Union armies rampaged through South Carolina, wreaking horrible revenge upon the "birthplace of the Confederacy." In 1856, a "guerilla war" murdered hundreds of people and transformed a calm Western territory into "Bloody Kansas." By 1865, over one hundred Union soldiers were dying nearly daily at Andersonville, a prison designed to hold 10,000 but crammed eventually with 33,000 men.

Civil War devotees quickly recognize these well-known names and events, because they are part of most standard war-time histories. But viewed together as a whole, they expose another religious aspect of the war—a darker and far less righteous perspective which slowly filters into focus through the rarely used lens of *morality and ethics*. What was the moral appropriateness or rightness of actions such as these? Who if anyone was ethically responsible for these (and even worse) wartime actions? Is everything justified at a time of war? What ethical questions are raised by the war itself as well as how it came to be prosecuted by both sides?

This is a perspective on the Civil War which has virtually never been dealt with, most likely because it is loaded with unanswered questions and ominous implications, and complicated by near insoluble moral paradoxes. Unlike unit histories, campaign summaries or wartime diaries, this frame of reference is not neat or clear cut, neither cleanly delineated nor easily encapsulated. It is not an area popular to the hordes of avid Civil War readers—who generally want valiant (if flawed) heroes and heroic battles. More often than not, as William Dean Howells noted, "what the American public always wants is a tragedy with a happy ending."[1]

And yet the Civil War was a tragedy fought because of intrinsic moral differences surrounding race-based slavery. It was waged by religious soldiers who believed in personal moral principles active in their individual lives. It was a war which began with medieval chivalric ideals and ended in pyrrhic Union victory more resembling twentieth century total war. Morality and ethics dripped over every aspect of the war, like the lingering haze and smoke of a fifty-gun cannon barrage. Whether the politicians, generals, soldiers, civilians, theologians and pastors fully realized it, spoke of it or consciously wrestled with it—that is another story. But the moral issues and the ethical context were present. Harry Stout, in his recent provocative moral history of the War, maintains that the clergy of both sides *did* drop the ball in speaking out on the moral issues surrounding the conflict. Thus they became simple "moral cheerleaders" for the blind nationalism of cause and comrades, losing sight of the larger ethical issues involved.[2]

But because the War and its prosecution was permeated by issues of right and wrong, America's greatest conflict deserves to be raised for a moment onto the higher plane of analysis that is the proper domain of religion. The reason is simple—religion and faith *ask the difficult questions of Life.* A religion that is true to its Source is meant to be discomforting and challenging, to "comfort the disturbed and disturb the comfortable" as an old priest once told me.

But because antebellum religion became politicized and divisive, with clergy eventually acting more as cheerleaders than prophets, it lost some of its intrinsic capacity to perform this function, perhaps best described as a "prophetic" role—the "criticizing and judging the secular order in the light of a higher morality than can be found in the marketplace or in the corridors of power." In this chapter, I will lay out some moral perspectives and religious trajectories—to shine a moral Light upon some of the horrendously difficult decisions made both corporately and individually throughout the Civil War.[3]

As mentioned above, historian Harry Stout has already taken the first steps into this field with his latest project, described as a moral history of the war. In his introduction, Stout provides an insightful explanation of this concept which will help us delineate the parameters of the moral issues to follow: "Moral history imbues the present with a heightened sensitivity to what the actors *might* have done, what they *ought* to have done, and what, in fact, they *actually* did. It is in the distances between the oughts and the actualities that moral judgments emerge."[4]

Describing a skirmish, a 24th NY officer wrote "Uncle Levi took deliberate aim at one of the rebels at a distance so short he could have sent him to eternity in a second, but he could not fire on a man in that fashion, and he dropped his gun . . . I think he did right . . . in battle it would be different and I would be killing as many of them as possible.

Cited in James M. McPherson, *For Cause and Comrades* (1997)

A framework of moral values

A soldier in the 1st MN confessed that "I cant feel right to try to kill my brother man although I see no other way to settle this matter." Thousands of soldiers had learned at their mother's knee that killing was wrong. At its most elemental basis, war is always evil (*"hell"* was Sherman's purported postwar description)—as naïve 1861 soldiers would all too quickly discover. Since the moral prohibition against the taking of life is so obviously opposed to Biblical ideals, warfare has always presented an enormous moral problem for believers.

In the Christian tradition, war has never truly been "acceptable"—only tolerable as a "necessary evil", and justifiable by an appeal to the common good. For this reason, since the early Middle Ages, a "just-war theory" slowly developed in the Christian tradition—the purpose of which was not to rationalize violence, but to limit its scope and methods. "Such laws and rules transcend personal opinion or individual caprice. When particular battles and wars are laid alongside the laws of just war, judgments are called for that can be applied to all participants and to nations as a whole." [5]

The following ethical principles of the just-war theory provide a moral lens through which we are able to view the wartime actions and decisions of soldiers, generals and politicians. Through them we can begin to discern and articulate a plausible framework of moral values for two scenarios—when a war might justifiably be declared (traditionally known as *"jus ad bellum"*), and the guidelines for just and fair wartime conduct (*"jus in bello"*). Although this section must necessarily be brutally succinct in laying out these criteria, and contain no moral case studies as to their application, it is my hope that describing these foundational principles will suffice to perhaps stimulate within readers a moral reflection process upon our "beloved" Civil War events and people. (Further analysis may be found in the sources cited in the footnotes to this section.) The basic moral principles underlying the just-war theory are: [6]

(1) *War is declared by a legitimate authority.* Decisions to wage war must be made by those who are legally authorized to do so. Any organized society needs to regulate the use of force to protect its members. Thus, since war involves killing force, society needs to rest that authority in certain institutions and personnel. The constitutions and laws of nation-states specify who that is.

(2) *Wars may be fought only for a just cause, and as a last resort.* Traditional theory recognizes two such causes. (a) *To prevent or rectify unjust actions by another nation.* Included in here *could* be defending national territory, preventive attacks, rescuing captured nationals, deterring terrorism, rectifying economic injury, vindicating territorial claims. (b) *There should be a just proportion between the wrong to be prevented and the destruction the war will entail.* Despite this being a

subjective value judgment, there is an objective reference point—the cause's real worth in the scale of human values (casualties, costs).

Nations are not justified in resorting to war as long as they have a reasonable hope that other means may resolve the wrong. The key word here is *"reasonable"*— which negotiations might well be, *if* there is no ploy to delay or escape retaliation, and there exists a belief they will lead to correcting the wrong.

(3) *Secessionist wars.* Though not formally part of the theory, just-war theorists do "recognize the general right of the people of a given territory to decide how they will organize themselves as a community." This is based on the free nature and will of human beings, who can decide how their political community is organized. Regarding this self-determination and the secession of component states in a federal union, Richard Regan has four qualifiers. The secessionist and remaining "states" should (a) negotiate or arbitrate boundary disputes, (b) recognize and protect the civil rights of ethnic minorities, (c) compensate individuals for losses due to destruction and violence, and (d) negotiate or arbitrate apportioning any previous national debt.[7]

(4) *Right intentions are required.* This involves the intentionality, the "right moral reasoning," of war-decision makers. Objectively, the goal or end of the war must be justified in terms of the larger common good. (Non-valid ends would be national honor, commercial or national aggrandizement, weakening of an enemy regime.) Subjectively, one's motivations and intentions must be "in order"— inadmissible motives for war would be hatred, vengeance, desire for power/fame, material gain, etc.[8]

(5) *The conduct of war ("jus in bello").* Two primary principles govern ethical conduct during wartime. *Discrimination* prohibits acts of war that target ordinary civilians. Noncombatants are considered outside the field of war, thus it is considered unjust to attack them (or to utilize reprisals, hostage-taking or terrorism). Enemy personnel and even political leaders may be targeted, but civilians and the innocent are always to be protected.

The principle of *proportionality* requires that the damage/losses which will result are kept in perspective with the goals hoped to be achieved. Stout accurately captures this when he comments that "even granting that soldiers at some level give up their right to life by enlisting in the armed forces, principles of proportionality still invoke limits to the carnage."[9] At times civilians come into danger indirectly by being too close to the fighting (known today as "collateral damage"). But the doctrine of *"double effect"* justifies the attack if their deaths are not intended but accidental, and if the importance of the military target outweighs the resulting deaths.

> A crack shot in the 100th IN was once ordered to pick off the Confederate artillerymen ahead, who limbered up to move just as he prepared to shoot. "The rider was on the rear mule . . . Something seemed to say 'Don't kill the man, kill the mule' . . . He went down and that delayed them so much that we got the gun. I am glad that I shot the mule instead of the man."
>
> Cited in James M. McPherson, *For Cause and Comrades* (1997)

"Morality is messy"

While the abstract principles behind the just-war theory may be clear, their application to specific Civil War situations is not. Knowing the moral absolutes is one thing, but applying them to the horrors of the battlefield—where shock, fear, terror, rage and panic race through one's body—is quite another. As a friend of mine once said to me, "You know, Father, morality is messy sometimes!" At the risk of yielding to my own biases and values, I would like to suggest some incidents that "contextualize" some of these principles. As you read through them, you may well find yourself agreeing or disagreeing with my selections. But, if this section helps encourage *some* deeper level of moral reflection upon this War which has captivated so many, my ultimate purpose will have been accomplished.

"Secession ideology." With the November 1860 election of the "Rail-Splitter" Abraham Lincoln, the road to secession became an expressway. Southern leadership, especially in South Carolina, had wrestled with "secession ideology" for years. According to John C. Calhoun's arguments, the Constitution not only permitted slavery but also justified secession. By February 1861, seven states had left the Union—but did they even *have* a moral right to secede? Lincoln did not think so, feeling that "the Union embodied an idea and a rule of law that was unbreakable." In his First Inaugural, he clearly declared that "it follows from these views that no state, upon its own mere motion, can lawfully get out of the Union—that resolves and ordinances to that effect are legally void . . ."[10] It would take 620,000 deaths to resolve this Constitutional and moral issue in favor of the Union once and for all.

What actions did the Civil War justify? ("Jus in bello") Without getting into technical definitions of "total war," Civil War students know well that 1861's chivalric ideals rapidly morphed into a "total war" scenario in which noncombatants, their property and resources all become military targets.[11] As that began to slowly occur, it is safe to say that just-war principles were hardly high priorities for military on any level (though some valiantly tried to be just and fair). With often deadly consequences, traditional ethical values protecting civilians from harm, or restraining soldiers from excessive violence or cruelty, or refraining from downright immoral decisions, far too often were lost in the belligerent, vengeful heat of battle. Examples here are far too many.

- Grant at Cold Harbor in spring 1864. Grant's controversial final assault here truly cemented his reputation as a "butcher"—but solid arguments can also be made that Robert E. Lee sacrificed his troops even more than Grant.[12]
- The deadly conditions at prisoner-of-war camps like Elmira, Andersonville, Camp Douglas, Rock Island, etc.
- The Northern decision in 1863 not to continue the prisoner exchanges
- The outright post-battle massacres of black troops (Fort Pillow, Petersburg's "Crater," and others)
- The Union army's frequent use of captured Southern churches to stable and feed their horses.
- The February 1865 Union army violence and bedlam at Columbia SC, including the raping of numerous black women.[13]

Personal moral conflicts. If war usually intensifies religious convictions, it also tests and challenges them. Just how does a nineteenth century soldier raised to respect God, Bible, country and neighbor begin to deal with the morally difficult, sometimes instantaneous ethical decisions confronting him? Attend church on Sunday—and yet kill your neighbor? Follow your conscience—or follow your comrade's example or superior's orders? Each soldier had to wrestle in his own soul, as best he was able, about crucial moral decisions.

- The pious Stonewall Jackson believed far more in Old Testament vengeance than in New Testament love of neighbor.
- The Catholic William Rosecrans tried not to fight on Sunday (e.g. Stones River), while fellow Catholic Henry Wirz was later tried for war crimes for his command at Andersonville Prison
- Many soldiers ignored orders not to fraternize, exchanging items between lines, assisting wounded enemy soldiers; and opposing pickets often agreed not to shoot each other because "that would be murder"
- One wonders how many Civil War soldiers simply could not shoot at another human. Col. S.L.A. Marshall's controversial World War II study found that only 15% of trained riflemen on an average fired their weapons in battle[14]

Issues of moral ambiguity. The ultimate factor in discerning moral judgments is a person's own formed conscience. But some moral issues involving one's conscience contain immense ambiguity—either from conflicting moral options and/or personal issues. When looking backward into some Civil War events, making moral decisions becomes at times quite problematic—and a person's opinion (and moral perspective) often depends on which side of the battlefield you have chosen to stand on.

- Nathan Bedford Forrest, pre-war slaveowner and alleged post-war Klan leader, was pilloried by the North for the April 1864 massacre of black troops at Fort Pillow. But Forrest avoided later censure because "he neither ordered nor condoned the massacre."

- "Uncle Billy" Sherman's troops "made Georgia howl" with their depredations, yet he freed black men and women from slavery as they went. In contrast Robert E. Lee's Confederate troops marching into Pennsylvania returned blacks to slavery.[15]
- In July 1864, after not receiving an exorbitant ransom from Chambersburg, Pennsylvania, Jubal Early burned 400 buildings and caused $1.5 million in damages—all because he knew of Union Gen. David Hunter's destruction in Virginia and felt "it was time to try and stop this mode of warfare by some act of retaliation." [16]

> Criticized by Jefferson Davis as the "Attila of the American Continent," William Sherman deliberately devastated huge areas of the deep South, convinced that economic warfare was now as crucial as military warfare. "We are not only fighting hostile armies but a hostile people, and we must make old and young, rich and poor, feel the hard hand of war."
>
> William Tecumseh Sherman, *Memoirs* (1892)

Further reading recommendations

Liva Baker. "The Burning of Chambersburg." Pp. 165–173 in *The Civil War—The Best of American Heritage*. New York: American Heritage Press, 1991.

James M. McPherson. *The Negro's Civil War*. New York: Ballantine Books, 1991.

Harry S. Stout. *Upon the Altar of the Nation—A Moral History of the Civil War*. New York: Viking/Penguin, 2006.

John Howard Yoder. *When War is Unjust*. New York: Orbis Books, 1996.

Notes

1. As quoted in Allan Gurganis, *The Oldest Living Confederate Widow Tells All* (New York: Ivy Books, 1984), epigraph.

2. Harry S. Stout, *Upon the Altar of the Nation—A Moral History of the Civil War* (New York: Viking, 2006), xvii–xviii.

3. Cornell West, *Prophetic Fragments* (Grand Rapids, MI: Eerdmans Publishing Company, 1988), as cited in George M. Frederickson, "The Coming of the Lord—The Northern Protestant Clergy and the Civil War Crisis," in *Religion and the American Civil War*, edited by Randall M. Miller, Harry S. Stout, and Charles R. Wilson (New York: Oxford University Press, 1998), 111.

4. Harry S. Stout, *op. cit.,* xii.

5. Stout, *op. cit.,* xii. For information on the just-war theory, I am indebted to John Howard Yoder, *When War is Unjust* (New York: Orbis Books, 1996); Richard McBrien, *Catholicism* (Minneapolis: Winston Press, 1980), 1035–1042; and Richard J. Regan, *Just War—Principles and Cases* (Washington, DC: Catholic University, 1996). Just-war principles were first formulated by St. Augustine (d. 430), developed into a broader system of moral thought by St. Thomas Aquinas (d. 1274), and unfolded as a legal/moral system on its own by Francisco de Vitoria (d. 1546) and Francisco Suarez (d. 1617). Augustine regarded war as both the product of sin and a remedy for it. In a world corrupted by sin, the use of force by public authorities was a legitimate means of avenging evil. Thomas Aquinas carried Augustine's arguments further and was more specific about the criteria for a just war, elaborating a series of discerning principles.

The criteria of the just-war theory are today recognized as officially binding by many major Christians denominations including Lutherans, Presbyterians, Anglicans and Congregationalists. They are affirmed as being "standard principles" by denominations that have no formal creeds (e.g., Baptists). The 1st MN soldier's quote is cited in James M. McPherson, *For Cause and Comrade* (New York: Oxford University Press, 1997), 72.

6. I have borrowed here the categories of Richard J. Regan in *Just War—Principles and Cases, op. cit.,* 20–99.

7. Regan, *op. cit.,* 74–75.

8. These descriptions for "right intentions" are found in Yoder, *op. cit.,* 152.

9. Stout, *op. cit.,* xiv. It should be noted that "unconventional" or guerilla warfare raises the proportionality issue as well—namely, is the importance of the intended target compatible with the level of potential casualties and destruction (especially innocent civilians).

10. Stout, *op. cit.,* 12.

11. There is much discussion surrounding "total war," and many different dates given as to when it began in the Civil War. The dates probably most often used are the 1864 appointment of Ulysses Grant as commander of the Federal armies, and the subsequent campaigns of Grant and his subordinates (most notably William Sherman). Mark Grimsley marks the onset of "hard war" as 1864 in his *The Hard Hand of War: Union Military Policy toward Southern Civilians, 1861–1865* (Cambridge, MA: Cambridge University Press, 1995). Harry Stout chooses the July-August 1862 date on which General Orders No. 5 were issued, requiring that John Pope's Army of the Potomac should begin living off the land. The term "total war" seems to be easily used but seldom clearly defined—which pacifist theologian John Howard Yoder undertakes to do in Appendix II of his *When War is Unjust, op. cit.*

12. Three excellent books on this point are Grady McWhiney, *Attack and Die—Civil War Military Tactics and the Southern Heritage* (Tuscaloosa, AL: University of Alabama, 1982); Edward H. Bonekemper; *How Robert E. Lee Lost the Civil War* (Spotsylvania, VA: Sergeant Kirkland's Press, 1999) and Edward H. Bonekemper, *A Victor, Not a Butcher—Ulysses S. Grant's Overlooked Military Genius* (New York: Regnery Publishing Company, 2004).

13. This rampant sexual exploitation of colored women by Union officers and men also happened after Union troops took Port Royal SC in 1861. Cf. Thomas Wentworth Higginson, *Army Life in a Black Regiment and Other Writings* (New York: Penguin Books, 1977), xiii.

14. As cited in Gwynne Dyer, *War* (New York: Crown Publishers, 1985), 118; also in James McPherson, *op. cit.*, 72. It should be noted, however, that Marshall has been criticized for inadequate research on this point.

15. Reid Mitchell, *Civil War Soldiers* (New York: Penguin Books, 1988), 157.

16. Liva Baker, "The Burning of Chambersburg," in *The Civil War—The Best of American Heritage*, edited by Stephen Sears (New York: American Heritage Press, 1991), 165–173.

Section Four

CHURCHES AND RELIGION AFTER THE CIVIL WAR

What comes over us is no easy applicability, schematically perfect, to the occasion, but rather the tragic aura of the event. The tone is that of the end of Herman Melville's Supplement to *Battle Pieces*, his poems of the Civil War, issued in 1866: "Let us pray that this terrible historic tragedy of our time may not have been enacted without instructing our whole beloved country through pity and terror . . . ."

Robert Penn Warren, *The Legacy of the Civil War* (1961)

Chapter Fourteen

"LOST CAUSE" RELIGION

> The restoration of the Union led to a South more southern than before the war. Believing itself the sole practitioner of right and the chief speaker for God, the South froze its institutions against all change and closed its society to the outside. In the moment of death the Confederacy entered upon its immortality.
>
> Robert Penn Warren, *The Legacy of the Civil War* (1961)

"Southern by the grace of God"

It was the Southern churches who had laid the foundations for secession long before the Civil War ever started. During the War itself, the churches and clergy had been the strongest morale-building force in the Confederacy, sustaining both soldiers and civilians in the destructive conflict. When the horrible war had finally come to its painful end in 1865, the South was devastated in every way. The flower of Southern youth had been killed;[1] homes, churches, land and property were in ruins;[2] the political dream of independence had died. Southern whites struggled mightily to come to terms with their apparent defeat, to comprehend the painful reality that the "cause" seemed to have been lost. Depression and demoralization hung over the South like a pall of death—and indeed many thousands of Southerners would never recover from the shock of the War or defeat, remaining "unreconstructed" and defiant until their dying days.

But yet again, into this void stepped the South's churches, clergy and religion to help lead the way to an entirely new understanding of not only the War, but the very identity and mission of the South. The year after the war ended, Richmond editor Edward A. Pollard wrote a book summoning the South to a new ideological battle with the North, a "war of ideas" to retain the unique Southern identity. Pollard maintained that the South had heroes and memories worth celebrating; and that military losses had not destroyed the natural superiority of the Southern culture, but merely dealt it a temporary setback. The symbolic phrase he coined was the title of his 1866 book—*The Lost Cause: A New Southern History of the War of the Confederates*—and immediately it became a byword for those attempting to perpetuate the ideals of the Old South.[3]

143

In essence, Lost Cause mythology[4] stated that the Confederacy might have lost the war, but it held onto the belief that it had been the victor in God's eyes. The South may have lost the military victory, but they had "won" a moral and spiritual victory. The "cause" was lost at one level, but the Lost Cause became grand and triumphant deeper in the southern soul. This strong sense of a separate southern evangelical religious identity is one of most persistent legacies of the Old South even to this day. On a recent trip to visit the battlefield at Vicksburg, a car roared past me with a bumper sticker that indicated this spirit was still very much alive— "American by birth, Southern by the grace of God"!!

The historian who most powerfully captured the religious aspect of the Lost Cause is Charles Reagan Wilson in his 1980 work *Baptized in Blood—The Religion of the Lost Cause, 1865–1920*. In this fascinating work, Wilson captures succinctly the heart of what the "mythology" or "philosophy" of the Lost Cause became.

> The dream of a separate Southern identity did not die in 1865 . . . the cultural dream replaced the political dream: the South's kingdom was to be of culture, not of politics. Religion was at the heart of this dream, and the history of the attitude known as the Lost Cause was the story of the use of the past as the basis for a Southern religious-moral identity, an identity as a chosen people. The Lost Cause was therefore the story of the linking of two profound human forces, religion and history. [5]

Thus, the poignant mid-nineteenth century experiences of the white South (in both culture and war) evolved into a highly religious movement, albeit more in the anthropological sense of a Southern civil religion—with clear symbols, myths, rituals, theology and organization, all based upon Christianity and Southern regional history.[6]

That the Lost Cause did indeed manifest strong religious foundations can be seen in Samuel Hill's comparison of it to classic religious categories—creed, code, cult and community. *Creed*: there were clear beliefs and convictions about what was true, good and lasting. *Code*: a pattern of conduct exhibited by men and women of the Old South (especially the "war-years" heroes), which needed to continue on in postwar ethical living and virtue. *Cult*: ongoing personal and public reverence for the South, and for its cultural and wartime heritage. *Community*: Southerners were one people—they knew who they were, where they had come from; and even the slaves had a place. [7]

We had pride and patriotism to spare, but we couldn't feed the living, or raise again our dead.

John Deering, *Lee and His Cause* (1907)

The "celebrants" of the Lost Cause

It was the churches and clergy of the white South who were intimately involved in formation and dissemination of Lost Cause civil religion—just as they had always been the educators, moral voices and regular "gatherers" of Southern culture and people. Southern clergy were "honored figures at the center of the Southern community, and most of them had in some way been touched by the Confederate experience." Churches had always been deeply tied to Southern culture, as Donald Matthews has noted. "Religion became identified with a public reaffirmation of social solidarity. Going to church became not merely a religious act, but a civic responsibility."[8]

White Christian clergy were in many ways the primary "celebrants" of the religion of the Lost Cause. These ministers

> saw little difference between their religious and cultural values, and they promoted the link by constructing Lost Cause ritualistic forms that celebrated their regional mythology and theological beliefs. They used the Lost Cause to warn Southerners of their decline from past virtue, to promote moral reform, to encourage conversion to Christianity, and to educate the young in Southern traditions.

It was white Southern ministers who consistently "celebrated" Lost Cause principles through their pulpit preaching, keynote addresses, benedictions, religious journals, writings and teaching. Church buildings were heavily used for Lost Cause gatherings such as funerals and memorial celebrations. The most important organ of the Lost Cause, the *Confederate Veteran* magazine (founded in 1893), not only had its offices in, but was published by the Southern Methodist church in Nashville, Tennessee. Richmond itself was a center of religious postwar publishing—with the Episcopalians, Methodists, Baptists and Presbyterians all having periodicals based out of that city. These denominational writings always supported Lost Cause in their fund-raising and publicity efforts, and recommended Confederate writings.[9]

"Evangelical" Protestant denominations led the Lost Cause charge—Baptists, Methodists and Presbyterians. It was an evangelical post-war culture in which Calvinist theology dominated, and these three denominations had an overwhelming percentage of Southern church members (94%).[10] However, Episcopalians also played an important role in the Southern public religion, helping make the Lost Cause a defense of aristocratic Southern values. The Episcopal Church had always played a large leadership role in the South—from wartime convert Jefferson Davis to Robert E. Lee, Bishops/Generals Leonidas Polk and Ellison Capers. Because of their more ritualized worship, Wilson comments that they "may have been a logical choice for preeminence in the highly ritualized religion of the Lost Cause."[11]

But, in the end the "roll call" of ministers who were preeminent in promoting the Lost Cause was truly ecumenical. The list includes men like Moses Drury Hoge (Presbyterian), Robert Lewis Dabney (Presbyterian), William N. Pendleton, (Episcopal) J. William Jones (Baptist), Mark P. Lowry (Baptist), Sam Jones (Methodist), Albert Taylor Bledsoe (Episcopal), Randolph McKim (Episcopal) and Fr. Abram Ryan (Catholic).

The "Poet Priest of the Lost Cause"

Fr. Abram J. Ryan was born Feb. 2, 1838 in Hagerstown MD. He was ordained in 1860 (St. Louis), and worked in Illinois and New York before his Confederate brother David was killed in 1863. Ryan then left the North, walking into the Confederate camp at Chattanooga three days before the battle of Missionary Ridge. He fought in the army and served as chaplain, founded a rabidly pro-Southern newspaper, and ministered in Georgia and Alabama after the war. But Fr. Ryan became best known for melancholic post-war poems celebrating the "Lost Cause." Ryan's most famous were "The Conquered Banner" and "Prayer of the South", but one of his final poems ("Reunited") marked a late-life attitude change—when the generosity of Northerners during a Southern yellow-fever epidemic finally "converted" him from his earlier virulently anti-Northern bias.

Southern identity

A major key to understanding why the Lost Cause became a religious experience is examining how Southerners viewed themselves. The white South underwent a deep and profound self-examination after their devastating Confederate experiences. They gradually came to understand that their unique background, including the Civil War, had truly given them a very different history than the North. The unique story of the South centered on their strong and pure Anglo-Saxon heritage, their well-ordered society, and their evangelical religious heritage. This unique Southern story included the founding of colonial Virginia, their role in the American Revolution, and the myths of the Old South and Reconstruction.

All these aspects eventually melded together to become part of the Lost Cause religion. It also seemed to affirm their unique identity as a *divinely* blessed people, indeed as God's specially chosen people (like the Israelites of old)—called and chosen, tested by fire, set apart for a unique Southern mission to the country and even the world. Because they feared their war-time defeat might erase this national identity, white Southerners reasserted this newly emerging sense of covenanted identity with a vengeance in the postwar years.

Charles Reagan Wilson states the point clearly. "The South's religious leaders and laymen defined this identity in terms of morality and religion: in short, Southerners were a virtuous people. Clergymen preached that Southerners were the chosen people, peculiarly blessed by God." Samuel Hill, another leading historian of Southern religion, writes that many southern whites regarded their society as God's most favored. To a greater degree than any other, theirs approximates the ideals the Almighty has in mind for mankind everywhere ... the religion of the southern people and their culture have been linked by the tightest bonds. That culture, particularly in its moral aspects, could not have survived without the legitimizing impetus provided by religion.[12]

As the late nineteenth century passed, organized Southern religion and churches continued to trumpet the themes of a special Southern mission and identity. Preachers promoted the special link between the Confederacy and Christianity not just in their pulpits, but in their journals, books and newly formed educational institutions. They wanted to ensure that not just the present generation, but all future generations would be taught the "correct" interpretations of Southern history and identity.[13]

Another stream that made up Southern post-war identity was a bold confidence in Southern superiority. A Baptist preacher named Victor Masters spoke of this when he said that from defeat in war, and humiliation in Reconstruction, Southerners had now developed "a great gentleness of spirit which was worth more than all the billions we have now gained." Thus, the South had a "peculiar responsibility"—to demonstrate to the entire nation its moral and spiritual superiority. If Southerners succeeded in this quest, they could vindicate their past, by drawing upon it for inspiration in the modern day struggles against the introduction into the weakened South of Northern economic and social structures, especially materialism.[14]

The North as well played a major role in helping define post-war Southern identity. The white "Lost Cause South" nurtured a self-perception of major philosophic, religious and regional differences from the North—with the one consistent theme being the wickedness and evil nature of Yankees. Indeed, a key part of the South's identity lay in being different from (and superior to) the North. By maintaining their traditional virtue and unique Christian culture, the South could serve as an example and a model to the corrupt North.

One of the bitterest Lost Cause advocates of the "old ways," Presbyterian minister Robert Lewis Dabney, gave an 1882 commencement talk in which he warned that the North stood as a fearful warning to a South on the precipice of change. He cautioned Southerners against thinking that "the surest way to retrieve your prosperity will be to become like the conquerors." Dabney predicted that the North faced "an approaching retribution" and he admonished Southerners not to "share for a few deceitful days, the victors' gains of oppression."[15] Other post-war ministers would as well consistently warn about Northern attempts to corrupt Southern principles by bringing material prosperity to the South.

Confederate chaplain and later apologist Rev. J. William Jones once offered this post-war prayer: "Lord we acknowledge Thee as the all-wise author of every good and perfect gift. We recognize thy presence and wisdom in the healing shower. We acknowledge Thou had a plan when Thou made the rattlesnake, as well as the song bird, and this was without help from Charles Darwin. But we believe Thou will admit the grave mistake in giving the decision to the wrong side in eighteen hundred and sixty-five."

Charles Reagan Wilson, *Baptized in Blood* (1980)

Rituals, myths and theology

Every religion has its rituals and theology because, as one writer says, it is "out of the context of concrete acts of religious observance that religious conviction emerges on the human plane." [16] The value of rituals is that they provide an external "vessel" or human structure for relating to the powerful sacred forces involved in religion. As a civil religion, the Lost Cause gradually developed certain ritualistic expressions that captured its basic underlying "theology"—a focus on virtue and an ordered society, the upholding of traditional Southern values, the wickedness of the North, the framing of Confederate soldiers as high moral examples, and an underlying but unstated white Anglo-Saxon supremacy. Again, Charles Reagan Wilson captures the essence of this point:

> The Confederate myth reached its true fulfillment after the Civil War in a ritualistic structure of activities that represented a religious commemoration and celebration of the Confederacy. One part of the ritualistic liturgy focused on the religious figures of the Lost Cause . . . Robert E. Lee, Jefferson Davis, Stonewall Jackson and others. [17]

In *Baptized in Blood*, Wilson lists the four major ritualistic expressions of the Lost Cause that emerged in post-war years:

(1) *Special days* appointed by denominations or states for humiliation, fasting, prayer or thanksgiving;
(2) *Confederate Memorial Day* celebrations (begun in Georgia in 1866 by a Confederate widow Mrs. Charles Williams, and eventually designated as June 3 each year)
(3) *Funerals* of Confederate veterans (always attended by veterans in their gray uniforms, and done ritualistically according to the standard "Confederate Veteran's Burial Ritual")

(4) *Monument-making*—described by Wilson as truly "an obsession," with Richmond leading the way, thus cementing its place as "the capitol of the Lost Cause."[18] Wilson cites the Oct. 27, 1875 dedication of Stonewall Jackson's Richmond statue as an example, calling it a "creation myth" (an attempt to create a Southern nation). According to a 1914 edition of the *Confederate Veteran,* there were over 1000 monuments being set aside as pilgrimage sites with "holy shrines."

Another religious ritualistic linkage in Lost Cause theology were the *stained-glass windows* placed in many Southern churches to commemorate Confederate wartime sacrifices. St. Paul's Episcopal (Richmond, Virginia) established a Lee Memorial Window highlighting an Egyptian scene, thus making an Old Testament connection with the Confederacy. While Federal troops still occupied the town, Trinity Church (Portsmouth, Virginia) put a new window in featuring a weeping Rachel at a tomb with names of all its parish members killed in the war.[19]

After the War, a black Presbyterian church in Roanoke, Virginia dedicated a special stained glass window to Stonewall Jackson. The pastor had been a pupil of Jackson's Sunday school in prewar Lexington.

Not surprisingly, *Confederate wartime artifacts* came to have a sacred near sacramental quality about them, and were often used and displayed in various near-sacred forms after the war. For example, when a torn overcoat belonged to the "martyred" Sam Davis was suddenly discovered in 1897, the United Daughters of the Confederacy present (who took an especially assertive role in preserving records and history of the Southern past) responded with "sacred silence", and then deep weeping.[20] Museums became holy sanctuaries consecrating such "holy relics" of battle as medals, flags, uniforms, weapons and Bibles.

The Lost Cause religion even had its favorite *hymns*—"Nearer my God to Thee", "Praise God from whom all blessings flow" and "Let us Pass over the river and rest in the shade of the trees"(officially adopted by the Southern Methodists), but the favorite of all was "How Firm a Foundation." This latter hymn was sung at Stonewall Jackson's funeral and at every funeral of the Jefferson Davis family as well after the war. It was the "official hymn" in the United Daughters of the Confederacy's book of rituals.

Lastly, the Lost Cause religion even had its "structural-functional aspect," that is, institutions which directed its operations, and provided ongoing leadership and institutional encouragement. The first of these two "organizing institutions" were the *Confederate veteran's groups*, not only various local and regional groups (which dominated in the 1870-1880s), but pre-eminently the 1889 established

United Confederate Veterans and their later 1896 heirs the *United Sons of Confederate Veterans*. Outdoing both these groups for religious intensity, however, were the *United Daughters of the Confederacy* (1894), who brought an unmatched zeal and enthusiasm to the Lost Cause and especially preservation of Confederate traditions and Southern society.

The second group who provided institutional encouragement to the Lost Cause religion were the Southern *Christian churches*. These two entities shared similar moral and social values, many Lost Cause "heroes" did have strong personal faith backgrounds, and of course the God invoked in Lost Cause rituals was distinctly Biblical and transcendent. Church buildings were also the most frequently used temples for Memorial Day activities, veteran's funerals and memorial meetings held when prominent Confederates died. [21]

> In the south, the war is what A.D. is elsewhere: they date from it.
>
> Mark Twain, American writer

The post-war South

There is little doubt that in the postwar white South, Christianity and the civil religion of the Lost Cause strongly supported each other. Preachers like ex-soldier and postwar Lee champion Randolph McKim, Baptist evangelist Sam Jones and Lost Cause evangelist J. William Jones, among others, were certainly rarely ambivalent about the connection. At one gathering, Jones in benediction appealed to "the 'God of Israel, God of the centuries, God of our forefathers, God of Jefferson Davis and Sidney Johnston and Robert E. Lee, and Stonewall Jackson, God of the Southern Confederacy!'" [22] The God who was invoked in Lost Cause events only added to the glory of the South.

However, Charles Wilson makes a telling point in summing up the civil religion that was the Lost Cause: "Unfortunately, the self-image of a chosen people leaves little room for self-criticism. This deficiency has led to the greatest evils of the religion-culture link in the South." [23] David Blight states the problem succinctly, remarking in his Race and Reunion, that "as the sections reconciled, by and large, the races divided."[24] Thus, quoting Thucydides, as "the people made their recollections fit in with their sufferings," another darker process was also at work in the Lost Cause—"the denigration of black dignity and the attempted erasure of emancipation from the national narrative of what the war had been about."[25]

White supremacy was simply taken for granted in the post-War South (being seen as almost synonymous with Southern culture), and Lost Cause religion simply lacked the "prophetic, ethical dimension" needed to honestly speak to or judge their society's racial patterns. "If there has ever been a single constant in the American experience, it has been that where a racial factor is present, the values of 'forgiveness, reconciliation, and love' have been largely impotent—even in church—to resolve conflict and stave off strife."[26]

Thus, the absolute core Christian ethic of love was never prophetically applied to the race issue, and the Lost Cause sadly ended up providing a model for the segregation that replaced slavery—a model the white Southern churches were all too complicit with. Ultimately the darker implications of the Lost Cause on racial relations would lead to a truly deadly extreme—the Ku Klux Klan, which linked the Confederacy to white supremacist philosophy in a way no one could forget, and became the epitome of using the Confederate experience for destructive purposes.

I will leave the final words of this chapter to the historian who best summarized and understood Lost Cause religion:

> The lesson of the ministers who constructed a religion of the Confederate past is perhaps that they should have paid more attention to human weakness and vice, to the moral ambiguities and uncertainties of life, to the possibility that their society ... might not be virtue incarnate. Southerners made an attempt to utilize the spiritual resources of their historical perspective, but, as in all things human, they fell short of perfection.[27]

Further reading recommendations

David W. Blight. *Race and Reunion.* Cambridge, MA: Belknap Press, 2001.

Eric Foner. *Reconstruction, 1863-1877—America's Unfinished Revolution.* New York: Harper and Row, 1988.

Samuel S. Hill, "Religion and the Results of the Civil War." Pp. 360–384 in *Religion and the American Civil War*, edited by Randall Miller, Harry Stout, and Charles R. Wilson, New York: Oxford University Press, 1998.

Charles Reagan Wilson. *Baptized in Blood—The Religion of the Lost Cause, 1865–1920.* Athens: University of Georgia Press, 1980.

Notes

1. Of the one million men who served in the Confederate Army, at least one-quarter died in battle or disease. Many more were incapacitated and unable to support their families. Cf. Samuel Hill, "Religion and the Results of the Civil War," in *Religion and the American Civil War*, edited by Randall M. Miller, Harry S. Stout, and Charles R. Wilson (New York: Oxford University Press, 1998), 381.

2. Samuel Hill, Jr., details one historian's description of the severe destruction to church buildings, finances, educational institutions, etc. Samuel Hill, Jr., *op. cit.*, 366–67.

3. Gordon Shattuck, *A Shield and a Hiding Place—The Religious Life of Civil War Armies* (Macon, GA: Mercer University Press, 1987), 111.

4. Please note that the use of the word "mythology" here is not intended to be pejorative or judgmental, because it does not refer to something that is false or untrue, but rather is a technical term denoting a system of historic beliefs, traditions and legends which comprise larger philosophical or spiritual reality.

5. Charles Reagan Wilson, *Baptized in Blood—The Religion of the Lost Cause, 1865–1920* (Athens: University of Georgia Press, 1980), 1.

6. Wilson goes into great detail about the anthropological and historical bases for judging the Lost Cause civil religion as a truly authentic religious experience. Though his entire book makes that point, it is well summarized on pages 10–17. A further fine analysis of the Lost Cause is chapter eight of David Blight's *Race and Reunion* ("The Lost Cause and Causes Not Lost"), though he does not analyze the religious factor as does Wilson.

7. These categories were formulated by Joachim Wach, and are outlined in Samuel Hill, "Religion and the Results of the Civil War," in *Religion and the Civil War*, *op. cit.*, 363.

8. Wilson, *op. cit.*, p. 11. The second quote is cited in Samuel Hill, "Introduction," *The South and North in American Religion* (Athens: University of Georgia Press, 1980), 6. Also see Samuel Hill, "Epilogue," in *Churches in Cultural Captivity: A History of the Social Attitudes of Southern Baptists,* edited by John Lee Eighmy (Knoxville: University of Tennessee Press, 1972), 202.

9. Wilson, *op. cit.*, 11 and 34.

10. C.C. Goen, *Broken Churches, Broken Nation* (Macon, GA: Mercer University Press, 1985), 54.

11. Wilson, *op. cit.,* 36.

12. Wilson, *op. cit.,* 7.

13. Cf. chapter 7 of *Baptized in Blood,* entitled "Schooled in Tradition—A Lost Cause Education," pp. 138–160, for an in-depth study of how Southern educational institutions promoted "correct" Southern history and education.

14. Wilson, *op. cit.,* 98.

15. Wilson, *op. cit.,* 86.

16. Clifford Geertz, "Religion as a Cultural System," in *Anthropological Approaches to the Study of Religion,* edited by Michael P. Banton (London: Tavistock Publications, 1968), 4, 8–12, 14, 23, and 28.

17. Wilson, *op. cit.,* 25.

18. Wilson, *op. cit.* 18–23.

19. Wilson, *op. cit.,* 25.

20. Wilson, *op. cit.,* 26.

21. Wilson, *op. cit.*, 30–33.
22. *Ibid.*
23. Wilson, *op. cit.*, 7.
24. David Blight, *Race and Reunion* (Cambridge, MA: Belknap Press, 2001), 4.
25. Blight, *op. cit.*, 5.
26. Goen, *op. cit.*, 11.
27. Wilson, *op. cit.*, 16–17.

Chapter Fifteen

PUTTING A MISCONCEPTION TO DEATH?

> I charge the historian of these times . . . to tell the future ages that the Southern soldier was a Christian warrior, and that he was brave, he was irresistible, because his faith was in God and in the justice of his cause.
>
> Rev. H. Melville Jackson, 1887

"Holier, braver, purer, nobler, tougher, and a better shot"

When the Civil War ended, the re-visioning work of Lost Cause began. The Confederate army played a significant role in the postwar drama of shaping the Confederate experience as a religious-moral crusade. Southern clergy and orators portrayed the Confederate army as "a carrier of the contagion of morality and of evangelical Christianity." In story after story, the intense, pure, faith-focused fervor of the Southern Christian warrior was consistently contrasted with the impersonal, machine-like, evil Yankees, "who won by overwhelming numbers rather than righteous purpose or character."

Thus, one of the most enduring images of the Civil War was born—the Confederate Christian soldier, the "Christian warrior . . . brave [and] irresistable, because his faith was in God and in the justice of his cause" (in the 1887 words of Rev. H. Melville Jackson). The Southern soldier was the Yankee's superior in faith, piety and about every other way. As Steven Woodworth remarks, "the Southern soldier was braver, purer, nobler, tougher and a better shot than his Yankee counterpart. In short, he was the bluecoat's superior in everything except cleanliness, and that he could not help, because the army was short of soap and new uniforms."[1]

The "Confederate Christian soldier" became a foundational part of Lost Cause mythology primarily because of two men, both Southern clergy. In 1877, *Rev. William W. Bennett D.D.* wrote *A Narrative of the Great Revival Which Prevailed in the Southern Armies* to talk "about what extent religion prevailed among the soldiers of the South." The words of his introduction gave a hint of his own leanings—"To thousands in the North, this book will appear an enigma." The *Rev. Mr. John William Jones*, a Virginia Baptist, was a soldier and chaplain in the Army of Northern Virginia, and published his famous *Christ in Camp* (or *Religion in Lee's Army*) in 1887, which proved to be extremely influential, touching off other reminiscences. Reid Mitchell comments on Jones in humorous style, remarking that "Stonewall Jackson alone provided Jones enough grace to redeem the entire Confederacy."[2]

Both authors used firsthand information on religion in the southern armies obtained from fellow preachers, newspapers and anecdotal material. Both claimed religion's greatest role was raising the morale of the soldiers, and both contrasted Southern armies with the English Puritan forces of Oliver Cromwell. Both writers claimed that the Confederate army was the most Christian army in the history of the world, with the Union army "not even in the running for the title 'Most Christian Ever'" since comparisons were generally made with Cromwell's army! However, of the overall purpose and general scholarship that went into these books, Steven Woodworth makes a telling point. "The factual information they gathered was sound, but the goal in compiling it was to support a false claim that the South had been more devoted to God and therefore must have been right in the cause for which it fought."

Charles Reagan Wilson ties what happened in this entire process into larger Southern fears.

> The defeat of the Confederates created such chaos, especially in values, and for ministers it activated the fear of even greater moral anarchy if traditional Southern values died. The myth of the Crusading Christian Confederates enabled the clergy to assert that the Confederacy's values survived the war and would be a stable basis for Southern society. [3]

The books of Jones and Bennett (and the further works they inspired) contributed enormously to the postwar attitude of Southern spiritual superiority. For their part, Northern spiritual leaders after the war seemed to cede the entire issue to their Southern cousins, no longer feeling the need to prove their superiority in such "moral worthiness" quarrels, as they moved onto other Social Gospel issues. Thus the "mantle of Christianity" became part and parcel of Lost Cause mythology and religion.[4] But as a result, the misconception remains with us even to the present day.

Some twentieth century historians have continued on in the same vein. The preeminent social historian Bell Irvin Wiley clearly contends in his books *The Life of Billy Yank* and *The Life of Johnny Reb* that Confederate soldiers were more religious than Union soldiers. Gardiner Shattuck, Jr., echoes the same sentiment with a 1994 book review statement that "southern soldiers were generally more pious than their northern counterparts." Gerald Linderman describes religion as "pervasive in the Confederate armies" and "less conspicuous" in the Union.[5]

> The Southern army is pervaded with the sense of dependence upon God. Every soldier is taught to feel that the cause in which he contends is one that God approves, that if he is faithful to God, his Almighty arm will protect, and his infinite strength ensure success. Thus believing that God's eye of approval is upon him, and that God's arm of protection is thrown around him, and that God's banner of love is over him, the Southern soldier enters the field of battle nerved with a power of endurance and a fearlessness of death which nothing else can give.
>
> William W. Bennett, *The Great Revival* (1877)

Going after the "high ground"

It is well past the time to question this long-held Lost Cause belief. As Reid Mitchell remarks, "Confederate chaplains and southern ministers have held the high ground long enough." Mitchell and historians like Steven Woodworth have recently begun to contend that religious activity among Union soldiers was just as strong as among Confederate, and that it is a misconception to portray Confederate armies as more religious than their Northern counterparts. Woodworth maintains that "the degree of Christian belief and activity was about the same on both sides," but because Northern writers did not feel the need to do the "revisionist" publishing that Jones and Bennett did, "the faith of the Union soldiers has remained relatively invisible down to the present day." He writes that "in fact the religious awakenings occurred about equally on both sides of the lines, and the average Union soldier was at least as devout as his Confederate counterpart, if not more so." [6]

Reid Mitchell takes on the principal evidence used by Jones, Bennett and others to establish Southern spiritual superiority—namely, the greater frequency of and evangelical fervor for revivals held in the Southern army. Bell Wiley worked from soldiers' letters and diaries for his books, but in regard to his conclusions "Wiley argued the superior religiosity of Confederate soldiers from the large-scale revivals that spread through the Confederate armies." While agreeing that large-scale revivals happened, that they were powerful events, well documented by preachers and newspapers (to help rebuke flagging morale at home), Mitchell makes the point that extensive revivals hardly proves that the Confederate army was more religious than the Union army.

Mitchell reflects that if the emphasis of revivalism is *conversion*, then this begs the questions of why so many southern soldiers *needed* to be converted! It seems historically that "army revivals . . . often attracted more backsliders than believers," which means that if all those saved in revivals were "backsliders" (previously saved but fallen away), it appears missionaries would have less to brag about than they wanted. Mitchell concludes by remarking "the principal difference between Union and Confederate revivals may have been that Confederate revivals had better post-war publicists."[7]

Mitchell also makes a very significant point about Jones and Bennett both having ulterior motives in touting Southern conversions and spiritual fervor. For Jones especially, the overall post-war promotion of Christianity (especially Southern-style) was at stake; and a more extensive Christianity for the Confederacy meant a greater moral superiority for the Confederacy itself. Mitchell writes that "The Christian Confederate stood near the center of Lost Cause theology. Proponents of the cause argued that ultimately God would vindicate the South." Furthermore, this "southern strategy of making sweeping religious claims was not limited to discussions of the Confederate army . . . southern churches became accustomed to grandiose bragging."

Samuel S. Hill has written in this vein as well, remarking that

> from Reconstruction forward, ecclesiastics compared the religious situation of the South with that prevailing elsewhere—itself a startling disposition and always to the South's advantage. From many quarters came assessments of the superior purity of regional Methodism, Presbyterianism, or Baptist life, with the implication or even the assertion that their brand was the hope of the world.[8]

A final ulterior motive of J. William Jones was his linking of Christianity with Southern manhood. In the preface of the 1904 edition of *Christ in Camp*, Jones states that "this book is sent out with the fervent prayer that . . . it may prove useful in showing our young people the power of religion to promote real manhood." Jones was not just highlighting faith-filled Southern Christian men, but also those strong and virile male chaplains who took risks and endured hardships side by side with them (and himself). In doing this, Jones was actually part of a much larger societal process—a mid-nineteenth-century trend to "masculinize" spirituality and the Christian message. We shall speak more of this process in the final chapter of this book.

> I yield to no one precedence in love for the South. But because I love the South, I rejoice in the failure of the Confederacy.
>
> Woodrow Wilson, as a law student at UVA, 1880

Religion and Faith were now becoming intimately connected to very manly images—honor, duty, courage, bravery and the "heroic spirit of men." The war had brought a deep masculine camaraderie, almost a sense of "community," which flowed naturally from being with one's fellow male soldiers. A new image thus emerged of the good soldier who was also a manly Christian. It was in the postwar era that one of the most famous of all Protestant hymns became the immortal "Onward Christian Soldiers." This religious aspect of the Civil War I will speak to in a later chapter; but for the present, it is worth noting that for Jones, the image of Southern Christianity (and its heroic male faith) was at stake as well the moral superiority of the Southern soldier.

> One Southern preacher is supposed to have presented a revolver to a Confederate soldier before his departure into the war, with the following injunction—"If you get into a tight place and have to use it, ask God's blessing if you have time, but be sure and not let the enemy get the start of you. You can say amen after you shoot!"
>
> James Silver, *Confederate Morale & Church Propaganda* (1957)

"Missing" Southern soldiers

Finally, it seems that the proponents of a "superior Southern spiritual army" have omitted some soldiers from their analysis. The misconception of southern spiritual superiority conveniently leaves out soldiers from several religious denominations which did not fit Lost Cause religious "ideals"—namely Roman Catholics, blacks and smaller groups like Jewish believers. Because of the innate prejudice against these groups in the late nineteenth and early twentieth centuries, the faith lives of Catholics and blacks were completely ignored in post-war Lost Cause writing. Here again is where the underlying evangelical bias of Southern society and religion becomes the gist of the problem. As one writer says aptly, "in the nineteenth century, to be blunt, when Americans often said 'Christian,' they meant 'Protestant.'"

Reid Mitchell deals with the issue directly in his article "Christian Soldiers?" in "Religion and the American Civil War."

> The standard of the Christian soldier by which the Confederates usually were measured was Protestant—Cromwell, Havelock, Gustavus Adolphus, and Lee and Jackson themselves. Furthermore, Wiley, by using revivalism as his principal index of Christianity . . . assured that Catholics, who did "not pretend to come to our meetings" would be ignored. If conversion experiences and river baptisms are the principal index of Christianity, the nonrevivalist Catholics, as well as more liturgical Lutherans and other Protestant denominations, will not register as Christian.[9]

Thus, the evangelical Protestant bias of Southern religion conveniently over-looked the not insignificant presence of large numbers of religious believers whose theology did not fit the "Christian soldier" mythology. This fact necessarily affects any assessment and analysis of the effect of religion and faith on Civil War soldiers.

Granted, in the Southern armies, non-evangelical soldiers were a minority, as were true foreign-born Confederate soldiers. Irish Catholics were few in number and scattered mostly in individual companies, except for the 10th TN "Sons of Erin" (from four Tennessee towns).[10] Likewise, about 3000 Jews fought for the Confederacy, with some 7000 fighting for the North.[11] In May 1865, the Confederacy did authorize the recruiting of 300,000 black troops with some actually being raised, but their numbers are of little significance for our purposes. But in the Northern armies, non-Protestant believers need to be considered as a significant factor in reflecting upon the religiosity of the soldiers or army. James I. Robertson's research in *Soldiers Blue and Gray* indicates that one of every four Union soldiers was a 1st or 2nd generation immigrant.[12] Randall Miller estimates that about 145,000 Irish Catholics served in the Union army. With black soldiers comprising nearly 10% of Union troops by war's end, to not consider their strong religious and spiritual tendencies would be a major oversight.[13]

> We don't know any black men here, they're all soldiers.
>
> White Union soldier after July 1863 attack on Ft. Wagner

However, in the highly prejudiced society of the time, there was simply little if any tolerance for those who didn't "fit the mold" either religiously or culturally. The Irish Catholic immigrants who fought in the War had a double strike against them—many were reviled as foreigners, and ignored because of their "popery" and moral inferiority. William Bennett encapsulated the religious attitudes of many regarding immigrants of both Irish and other extractions who served in Northern armies. He boasted that "there were but a few thousand foreigners at any time in Confederate ranks. There was but little of the beastliness and brutality displayed which marked the foreign mercenaries of the opposing armies."[14] Being ministers of the Gospel, it is most curious how Bennett, Jones and others subsequently forgot to mention that the Lord and Savior that the Catholics in the 63d NY (Irish Brigade) prayed to on September 17, 1862 in the Bloody Lane at Antietam, was the same God that their Christian opponents from Wright's Brigade of R.H. Anderson's Division were praying to at the same time.

Black soldiers of course, had unique societal challenges different than white Americans, North or South. Aside from near universal racism, many Christians refused or were unable to take black religion seriously, as indicated in numerous diary entries of the time. But many who could see past the external cultural, racial and societal differences, like Thomas Wentworth Higginson (commander of the First SC Volunteers) came to have great respect for black Christianity. In a highly ironic statement, what Higginson wrote of his black troops echoed *exactly* what Southern Lost Cause writers were saying about white Confederate soldiers. "It used to seem to me that never, since Cromwell's time, had there been soldiers in whom the religious element held such a place. 'A religious army,' 'a Gospel army' were their frequent phrases."[15] Thus, the racial biases of Lost Cause superior spirituality ignored black soldiers' spirituality as much as it did their overall status in society. The black soldier, like the immigrant Irish Catholic, was simply part of the alien "scum" and "hirelings" with whom nearly all white southerners contrasted their own highly virtuous soldiery.

In conclusion, Southern spiritual superiority was a highly consoling myth for the South (and perhaps some in the North as well)—but it seems time to put it to rest. Confederate armies were no more or less religious than their Northern counterparts—they simply seem to have had better press and writers who wrote from motives of their own. As Reid Mitchell summarizes, "claiming more extensive Christianity for the Confederate army became one way of claiming moral superiority for the Confederacy itself, just as the faith of Lee and Jackson was used to justify the Lost Cause." The sentiments of Union soldier William H. Walling could have been echoed by all soldiers of whatever denomination who ever saw the need to reach out for a Higher Power. "He who numbers the very hairs of our head and notes even the fall of the sparrow shielded me in the hour when bullets rained like hail around me."[16]

> While the southern people bow in submission to the will of God in their defeat . . . the spirit of the old South—all that was best and truest purged from the dross of it—has survived the dark days of defeat and is still moving on from victory to victory.
>
> H.D.C. Maclachlan, *Confederate Veteran* (1917)

Chapter Fifteen

Further reading recommendations

Eric Ethier. "Who Was the Common Soldier of the Civil War?" *Civil War Times* 42, no. 5 (December 2003): 52–53.

Reid Mitchell. "Christian Soldiers? Perfecting the Confederacy." Pp. 297–309 in *Religion and the American Civil War*, edited by Randall Miller, Harry Stout, and Charles R. Wilson. New York: Oxford University Press, 1998.

James Silver. *Confederate Morale and Church Propaganda.* Tuscaloosa, AL: Confederate Publishing Company, 1957.

Steven Woodworth. "The meaning of life in the valley of death." *Civil War Times* 42, no. 5 (December 2003): 55–88.

Notes

1. Cf. Charles Reagan Wilson, *Baptized in Blood* (Athens, GA: University of Georgia, 1980), 43; Randall Miller, "Introduction," in *Religion and the American Civil War*, edited by Randall M. Miller, Harry S. Stout, and Charles R. Wilson (New York: Oxford University Press, 1998), 15; and Steven Woodworth, *While God is Marching On* (Lawrence: University Press of Kansas, 2001), 290–1.

2. Cf. William W. Bennett, *A Narrative of the Great Revival Which Prevailed in the Southern Armies* (Harrisonburg, VA: Sprinkle Publications, 1989), iv; and Reid Mitchell, "Christian Soldiers?" in *Religion and the American Civil War, op. cit.*, 299.

3. Cf. Steven Woodworth, *op. cit.*, 290; Reid Mitchell, "Christian Soldiers? Perfecting the Confederacy" in *Religion and the American Civil War, op. cit.*, 298; Charles Reagan Wilson, *Baptized in Blood, op. cit.*, 38, 43–44.

4 Robert Penn Warren phrased it this way. "The North imagined they had gained an inexhaustible "Treasury of Virtue" in the conflict. Success had made the Northerners complacent, and complacency allowed them to be magnanimous to the South." (Cf. Robert Penn Warren, *The Legacy of the Civil War: Meditations on the Centennial* (New York: Random House, 1961), 59.

5. Gardiner Shattuck Jr., a review of "The Confederacy's Fighting Chaplain," in *Journal of South History*, #60 (Feb. 1994), 149. Cf. also Gerald F. Linderman, *Embattled Courage: The Experience of Combat in the American Civil War* (New York: Simon and Schuster, 1987), 102.

6. Cf. Steven Woodworth, "The meaning of life in the valley of death" in *Civil War Times* 42, no. 5, (December 2003), 88; also Woodworth, *While God is Marching On, op. cit.*, 291 and Reid Mitchell, *op. cit.*

7. Mitchell, *op. cit.* 299.

162

8. Samuel S. Hill, Jr., *Religion and the Solid South* (Nashville, TN: Abingdon Press, 1972), 42–43.

9. Mitchell, *op. cit.,* 304.

10. The most notable Irish Catholic Confederates were the 10th TN "Sons of Erin", composed of mostly Irish immigrants and Irish Americans from four heavily Irish Tennessee towns (Nashville, Pulaski, Clarksville, McEwen). They were commanded by Col. Randal McGavock, a Scotch-Irish Presbyterian who had connections to Catholicism in Tennessee. Two priests were chaplains of the 10th TN: Fr Henry Osbourne OP, and then Fr. Emmeran Bliemel, a German Benedictine who was killed by a cannonball on August 31, 1864 at Jonesborough. Only 35 of the original 714 soldiers were still left in the regiment by the end of war. Other Southern Catholic Confederates were found in individual companies in the 2nd and 21st TN, the 4th KY, with scattered Catholics in the West from St. Louis and New Orleans. Cf. Edward Gleeson, *Erin Go Gray,* (Carmel, IN: Guild Press of Indiana, 1997), 111–113 and 126–7; also Gleeson, *Rebel Sons of Erin—A Civil War Unit History of the 10th TN Irish Infantry, CSA Volunteers,* Carmel, IN: Guild Press of Indiana, 1993), 21.

11. Eric Ethier, "Who was the common soldier of the Civil War?" in *Civil War Times* 42, no. 5, (December 2003), 52–53.

12. Robertson's statistics about Union troops are as follows: 200,000 soldiers were German (ten New York regiments were nearly all German); 180,000 were black (comprising roughly 10% of the army by 1865, with one-third of them dying in wartime); and 150,000 were Irish (with twenty regiments nearly all Irish). James I. Robertson, Jr., *Soldiers Blue and Gray* (Columbia: University of South Carolina Press, 1988), 27–35.

13. But of black Christian faith, Reid Mitchell writes that "certainly the tenth of the Union army that was black was largely Christian. Black soldiers practiced an African-American Christianity that had its origins in the same eighteenth-century evangelical movement as white Southern Protestantism." Mitchell, *op. cit.,* 304.

14. William Bennett, *The Great Revival in the Southern Armies* (Harrisonburg, VA: Sprinkle Publications, 1989), 23.

15. Thomas Wentworth Higginson, *Army Life in a Black Regiment and Other Writings* (New York: Penguin Books, 1997), 197.

16. Cf. Mitchell, *op. cit.,* 301, and Woodworth, "The meaning of life in the valley of death," *op. cit.,* 59.

Chapter Sixteen

THE GREATEST
WARTIME THEOLOGIAN

> I do not believe that any royalty, princely, or republican state document of recent times can be compared to this inaugural address for genuine Christian wisdom and gentleness.
>
> Author Philip Schaff (Berlin, 1866)

The religion of Abraham Lincoln

"The greatest theologian of the war years . . . [whose] religious convictions were superior in depth and purity to those held by the religious as well as the political leaders of his day." Why would twentieth century Christian theologian Reinhold Niebuhr write this of a layman with no standing in any church and no formal training as a theologian—a layman who just happened to be the sixteenth President of the United States? One of the great theological puzzles of the entire Civil War is how Abraham Lincoln could (in Mark Noll's words) propound "a thick, complex view of God's rule over the world and a morally nuanced picture of America's destiny" when the theologians of the time could only present a "morally juvenile view of the world and its fate."[1]

Abraham Lincoln's faith life has been a much-speculated enigma ever since his death. He has been described as a "biblical Christian,"[2] a "religious fatalist like his mother,"[3] as "unique, nonsectarian, undenominational," and as "the least orthodox yet the most religious" of all the Presidents.[4] Biographers and historians over time have variously described him as an "atheist, agnostic, deist, fatalist, spiritualist, and Christian."[5] Not being a Lincoln scholar, I will not wade into this fray with any attempt at new insights into Lincoln's spirituality; however, from my research, two clear facts have emerged which form solid starting points for reflecting upon Lincoln's religion and faith.

First, although certainly not an externally "religious" man regarding piety or church attendance, Lincoln was undoubtedly a faith-filled man who acknowledged the important role of God and the Word in his life, and who appeared to become both more highly religious and faith-motivated in his Presidential years. An insightful anecdote supporting this is an 1864 meeting Lincoln had with his best friend Joshua Speed at the Soldiers Home north of Washington, where the Lincolns stayed many nights during the sweltering Washington summers. Speed found Lincoln reading the Bible and commented "Well, if you have recovered from your skepticism, I am sorry to say that I have not." Lincoln stood, placed his hand on Speed's shoulder, and said "You are wrong, Speed. Take all of this book upon reason that you can and the balance upon faith, and you will live and die a happier and better man." Given a personal Oxford Bible as a much-appreciated gift in mid-1841 by Lucy Speed, many people have reported that Lincoln read the Bible frequently during his Presidential years, and had memorized whole chapters of the New Testament, as well as many passages from Isaiah and the Psalms.[6]

Rebecca Pomeroy, a nurse at the White House, recalled that Lincoln liked to recline on the couch while waiting for lunch, reading from his mother's old worn-out Bible. When Lincoln asked her what book she liked best, she responded "the Psalms." Lincoln said, "Yes, they are the best, for I find in them something for every day of the week."

Rebecca Pomeroy, *What His Nurse Knew*

Lincoln also became more regular in his church attendance in Washington, and had frequent interchanges with Rev. Phineas Gurley, an "Old School" Presbyterian pastor[7] who preached to Lincoln, officiated at Willie's funeral, prayed beside the dying Lincoln and preached the funeral sermon for the martyred President at the Executive Mansion.[8] Lincoln had grown up rather wary of emotion, embracing instead the powers of logic and reason. Thus he always appreciated pastors like Gurley whose sermons were thoughtful and reasonable in their approach towards Faith. Lincoln's own "spirituality" was based upon an opposition to mere individualistic, isolated private faith. For Lincoln, reaching out to others (i.e., communitarian religion) was the necessary essential for true faith. Religion had to be about ethics, and specifically the ethics of Love, not just mere emotion or theological jargon. Lincoln said he was ready to join any church that would inscribe above its altar as the sole qualification for membership the Great Commandment of Love (love of God, neighbor and self).[9]

But, just as with countless soldiers of both sides, it was the devastating impact of the War itself which drew Lincoln deeper into religion and faith, forcing him into wrestling with the religious and philosophical implications of the horrendous conflict. It was this spiritual and personal "wrestling match" between God's ways of providence (a classic Calvinist theme) and human fallibility (the "offense" of slavery, the "scourge of war") which brought Lincoln to a highly developed sense of spiritual maturity despite his outer lack of formal religiosity. Lincoln came to a balance of strong personal faith convictions with realistic reservations about the limitations of "religion." He could appreciate the power of Faith to anchor men's spirits in crisis, yet also criticize "the religion that sets men to rebel and fight against their own government."

It is upon this point that the second insight into Lincoln's religion and faith becomes applicable. His greatest speech, the Second Inaugural Address, is the visible fruit of Lincoln's personal, philosophical and spiritual struggles to make sense out of the war that was tearing America in two. This Address is perhaps the finest single presentation of the relationship between religion and the Civil War found anywhere in American theology or history. It is to this very day, in the words of Mark Noll, "among the handful of semi-sacred texts by which Americans conceive their place in the world."[10]

> Frederick Douglass offered this impression of Lincoln upon meeting him for the first time in August 1863. "I never met a man, who, on the first blush, impressed me more entirely with his sincerity, with his devotion to the country, and with his determination to save it at all hazards." Though he disagreed with Lincoln on some issues, Douglass knew he could work with him to promote the role of black soldiers in the Union army.

The Second Inaugural Address

By 1865, the fruit of Lincoln's inner philosophic and religious struggles had become ripe in his marvelous Second Inaugural Address, where he seems to have become resigned to the mysterious reality that "the Almighty has his own purposes." Delivered on March 4, 1865, this Address is inspirational and insightful—a meditation both on the ultimate purposes and reasons for the War, as well as on God's actions in history and on America's place in that history. Frederick Douglass called it "more a sermon than a state paper" and "a truly sacred effort." Ronald White, Jr., calls it "the finest presentation of the relationship between religion and the Civil War." Sidney Ahlstom wrote that

> By a general consensus the Gettysburg Address and the Second Inaugural are Lincoln's supreme statements on the meaning of the war. We can appreciate even in these few words the astounding profundity of this self-educated child of the frontier, this son of a hard-shell Baptist who never lost hold of the proposition that nations and men are instruments of the Almighty.[11]

The 701-word address (the second shortest inaugural in history[12]) contained only twenty-five sentences, and took barely six or seven minutes to deliver. The African-Americans who were in attendance (estimated by one paper to be half the crowd) routinely cried out *"Bless the Lord!"* at the end of nearly every sentence.

The "unusually" high theological and religious content of his talk would be criticized by some people afterward.[13] But now, some 140 years later, Lincoln's Second Inaugural Address still remains an object of fascination, study and admiration. While it is beyond the scope of this book to go into specific analysis of this fascinating speech, it is important to point out several key insights which highlight the extraordinary nature of this speech.

The Address is amazingly religious in tone

While every previous President had cited God (the Deity) somewhere in their inaugurals, Lincoln mentions God or Lord fourteen times. He moved into totally new territory by quoting Scripture directly four times (Gen. 3:19; Matt 7:1; Matt 18:7 and Ps 19:9);[14] then refers to prayer three times as well. In the last half of the speech, virtually every phrase and sentence springs from Judeo-Christian Scriptural foundations. Standard Presbyterian themes that Lincoln would have heard often from preachers like Phineas Gurley (Washington DC) and James Smith (Springfield, Illinois) are reflected in the Address—as he speaks of the "divine attributes of God," of slavery as an "offense," and the "Providence of God" (versus mere fatalism).[15]

Lastly, several historians have seen shades of an old preaching device called a *"jeremiad"* in this Address—a classic Puritan sermon form combining *criticism* (the judgment due because of sin or failure) and *reaffirmation* (coming from repentance, forgiveness and reform). Lincoln deftly combines *social criticism* (the "offense of slavery" which deserves judgment) and the *promise of reconciliation* ("malice towards none, with charity towards all . . . a lasting peace among selves & with all nations").[16]

One Northern preacher wrote Lincoln to reassure him that God was on the Northern side. The president responded to his letter by saying that his own prayer went the other way—he hoped the Union would be on God's side.

Philip S. Paludan, *A People's Contest* (1988)

Lincoln did not presume the North had "moral high ground"

His Address was a challenge to many "religious" people, denominations and churches alike—so many of whom believed that God was on "their side." In this inaugural, Lincoln confronted the moral pretentiousness of many abolitionists, as well as the self-righteousness of individual churches. He speculated very clearly that "the Almighty has his own purposes" in allowing the war to continue as long as it did—which humans could never discern, whether from a Northern or Southern perspective. Lincoln actually linked the North with their "enemy" under a divine judgment which focused on *both* sections of the country.

> If the Almighty shall have ordained that the war continue until all the wealth amassed by the bondsman's two hundred and fifty years of unrequited toil be sunk and every drop of blood drawn with the lash be atoned with another drawn with the sword, as was said three thousand years ago, so still it must be said, 'The judgments of the Lord are true and righteous altogether.

Lincoln expressed remarkable charity to his enemy

Very much against expectations of people at that time, Lincoln refused to offer victorious words over a soon-to-be-vanquished foe. Lincoln's magnanimity towards the South flew in the face of what many expected. Ronald White says "the speech caught most of his hearers by surprise by offering a benediction more than a renewed call to arms."[17] The year 1865 seemed to be a time for vindication, great triumph, and soaring rhetoric that lifted and inspired people. Some expected words of celebration for the recent great military victories, and others looked for words indicating what his post-war public policy would be. But Lincoln took a different tact—in the line of what could be called "traditional" Christian virtues of charity, forbearance and generosity of spirit. "Both read the same Bible and pray to the same God . . . It may seem strange that any men should dare ask a just God's assistance in wringing their bread from the sweat of other men's faces, but let us judge not, that we be not be judged."

Ten days after his Second Inaugural, Lincoln reiterated his basic themes in a letter to Thurlow Weed. "Men are not flattered by being shown that there has been a difference of purpose between the Almighty and them. To deny it however, in this case, is to deny that there is a God governing the world. It is a truth that I thought needed to be told . . . ."

Harold Holzer, *Dear Mr. Lincoln:*
Letters to the President (2006)

Religious themes in the Address

The Second Inaugural Address showcased Lincoln's central philosophic, national and theological convictions—the Union, the nation under God, with a moral purpose, the great testing of America by an ordeal of blood, and the way of charity to a new birth. This speech, which Lincoln regarded as his best, was "a prism through which he refracted his understanding of the involvement of God in history."[18] The religious themes underpinning the Address remain insightful to this very day in the unique global and national challenges that America faces. Let us review a few of the major spiritual themes underlying this Address, all of which were tightly interwoven and flowed into each other.

The finitude of human judgment

Lincoln's theological thoughts truly begin in the third paragraph of the inaugural where he offers an assessment of human behavior. He points up the shallowness of human pretensions by reflecting that it was "strange that any men should dare to ask a just God's assistance in wringing their bread from the sweat of other men's faces." For the President, Biblically sanctioned slavery was "the ultimate pretension," but he would not limit judgment to the South, and, in the words of Reinold Niebuhr, went on to "cast doubt on the intentions of both sides."[19] Using Scripture for the second time, he offered religious reservations about the "partiality" of making any judgments—*"but let us judge not, that we be not judged."* The irony was that both sides failed to understand adequately both the cause and result of the conflict. "Both read the same Bible, and pray to the same God; and each invokes His aid against the other . . . The prayers of both could not be answered. That of neither has been answered fully." Justice for Lincoln was evenhanded—not only for Southern Biblically sanctioned slavery, but so also for the Northern spirit of self-righteousness and vengeance.[20]

"The Almighty has his own purposes"

Lincoln's central issue in this Address was *who was responsible for this war.* Through four long, wearying and discouraging years, the President had reflected philosophically on where God was in the public realm while death and defeat inextricably rolled on. He ended up resolving the conundrum in a metaphysical and spiritual way, with an unexpected answer—*God was the primary actor in this drama!* Using the passive voice in speaking, Lincoln initially directed the remarks away from himself, leading to the conclusion that the country was being acted *upon* rather than being an active participant in these terrible years. "The Almighty has his own purposes . . . He gives to both North and South this terrible war . . . Yet, if God wills that it continue . . ." Actually, Lincoln had already begun to arrive at these conclusions as early as 1862, with his private *"*Meditation on the Divine Will."

But in this 1865 Address, called by one theologian the "most remarkable theological commentary of the war," Lincoln moved to more clearly redefine what "Divine providence" could mean. "The will of God prevails. In great contests each party claims to act in accordance with the will of God. Both *may* be, and one *must* be wrong. In the present civil war, it is quite possible that God's purpose is something different from the purpose of either party."[21]

> In September 1862, a discouraged Lincoln wrote a private spiritual "meditation on the Divine Will" not discovered until after his death. In it, one can see Lincoln already beginning to try to understand God's purposes in the struggle and issues of the Civil War. "God cannot be for, and against the same thing at the same time . . . it is quite possible that God's purpose is something different from the purpose of either party . . . I am almost ready to say that . . . God wills this contest, and wills that it not end yet."

The "offence" of American slavery

The third Scripture Lincoln used was Matthew 18:7, *"woe to the man by whom the offence comes."* Interestingly, the Greek word *"skandalon"* used here could mean "stumbling block"—the reference is part of a larger context of Jesus urging protection for His "little ones." In this context, Lincoln clearly states that the *"offence"* against God here is "American slavery"—an Evil that brings a judgment upon the Land, and which was the cause of the war "somehow." Thus, there are moral consequences to this offense, which all of America is guilty of. While Lincoln clearly assigned the leadership of the South the blame for starting the war, still both parts of the country must own the offense. Slavery had run its appointed course in American history. Now judgment had to follow—a "mighty scourge of war . . . every drop of blood shed by the lash shall be paid by another drawn with the sword."

The Second Inaugural ends in hope, with an appeal for healing, and the proclamation of a promise of reconciliation. "With malice towards none; with charity for all . . . let us strive now to finish the work we are in: to bind up the nation's wounds; to care for him who shall have borne the battle." These words quickly became the most repeated and remembered words of the speech—"with malice towards none; with charity for all." Just days later, he would be assassinated by a man in attendance at that Address, and these words would come to represent Lincoln's legacy, his last will and testament to the entire American people.[22]

In summary then, Lincoln's Second Inaugural was perhaps the most spiritual political address ever given by an American President. The "fruits" of his crisis-inspired conclusions were more distinctly theological, succinctly phrased and overtly religious than most other religious thinkers of the day were able to produce. In his award-winning book, *America's God*, Mark Noll emphasizes the theological uniqueness of this remarkable speech.

> Lincoln's conception of God's rule over the world set him apart from the recognized theologians of his day. None probed so profoundly the ways of God or the response of humans to the divine constitution of the world. None penetrated so deeply into the nature of providence. None . . . mustered the theological power so economically expressed by Lincoln.[23]

How ironic, and yet how symbolically and spiritually appropriate it is for America's unique religious heritage, that a man untrained in theology, committed to no official denominational membership, should offer the most succinct, theological and spiritual reflection on America's most bloody conflict. He truly was a "man for the ages."

Further reading recommendations

Richard Carwardine. *Lincoln.* New York: Longman Press, 2003.

William E. Gienapp. *Abraham Lincoln and Civil War America.* New York: Oxford University Press, 2002.

Reinhold Niebuhr. "The Religion of Abraham Lincoln." Pp. 172–175 in *The Christian Century*, Feb. 10, 1965.

Ronald White. "Lincoln's Sermon on the Mount." Pp. 208–228 in *Religion and the American Civil War,* edited by Randall M. Miller, Harry S. Stout, and Charles R. Wilson, New York: Oxford University Press, 1998.

Ronald White. *Lincoln's Greatest Speech.* New York: Simon & Schuster, 2002.

Abraham Lincoln's Second Inaugural Address

This great amalgam of religion, faith and history was delivered on Saturday, March 4, 1865. Weeks of wet weather preceding Lincoln's second inauguration had caused Pennsylvania Avenue to become a sea of mud and standing water, but thousands of spectators stood in that thick mud at the Capitol grounds to hear the President. As he stood on the East Portico to take the executive oath, the completed Capitol dome over President Abraham Lincoln's head was a physical reminder of the resolve of his Administration throughout the years of civil war. Chief Justice Salmon Chase administered the oath of office. In little more than a month, the President would be assassinated. By this time of the war, Lincoln was a "tired man," admitting after this speech that "sometimes I think I am the most tired man on earth." These were his words.

Fellow-Countrymen: At this second appearing to take the oath of the Presidential office there is less occasion for an extended address than there was at the first. Then a statement somewhat in detail of a course to be pursued seemed fitting and proper. Now, at the expiration of four years, during which public declarations have been constantly called forth on every point and phase of the great contest which still absorbs the attention and engrosses the energies of the nation, little that is new could be presented. The progress of our arms, upon which all else chiefly depends, is as well known to the public as to myself, and it is, I trust, reasonably satisfactory and encouraging to all. With high hope for the future, no prediction in regard to it is ventured.

On the occasion corresponding to this four years ago all thoughts were anxiously directed to an impending civil war. All dreaded it, all sought to avert it. While the inaugural address was being delivered from this place, devoted altogether to saving the Union without war, urgent agents were in the city seeking to destroy it without war—seeking to dissolve the Union and divide effects by negotiation. Both parties deprecated war, but one of them would make war rather than let the nation survive, and the other would accept war rather than let it perish, and the war came.

One-eighth of the whole population were colored slaves, not distributed generally over the Union, but localized in the southern part of it. These slaves constituted a peculiar and powerful interest. All knew that this interest was somehow the cause of the war. To strengthen, perpetuate, and extend this interest was the object for which the insurgents would rend the Union even by war, while the Government claimed no right to do more than to restrict the territorial enlargement of it.

Neither party expected for the war the magnitude or the duration which it has already attained. Neither anticipated that the cause of the conflict might cease with or even before the conflict itself should cease. Each looked for an easier triumph, and a result less fundamental and astounding. Both read the same Bible and pray to the same God, and each invokes His aid against the other. It may seem strange that any men should dare to ask a just God's assistance in wringing their bread from the sweat of other men's faces, but let us judge not, that we be not judged. The prayers of both could not be answered. That of neither has been answered fully. The Almighty has His own purposes. "Woe unto the world because of offenses; for it must needs be that offenses come, but woe to that man by whom the offense cometh." If we shall suppose that American slavery is one of those offenses which, in the providence of God, must needs come, but which, having continued through His appointed time, He now wills to remove, and that He gives to both North and South this terrible war as the woe due to those by whom the offense came, shall we discern therein any departure from those divine attributes which the believers in a living God always ascribe to Him?

Fondly do we hope, fervently do we pray, that this mighty scourge of war may speedily pass away. Yet, if God wills that it continue until all the wealth piled by the bondsman's two hundred and fifty years of unrequited toil shall be sunk, and until every drop of blood drawn with the lash shall be paid by another drawn with the sword, as was said three thousand years ago, so still it must be said "the judgments of the Lord are true and righteous altogether."

With malice toward none, with charity for all, with firmness in the right as God gives us to see the right, let us strive on to finish the work we are in, to bind up the nation's wounds, to care for him who shall have borne the battle and for his widow and his orphan, to do all which may achieve and cherish a just and lasting peace among ourselves and with all nations.

Notes

1. Cf. Reinhold Niebuhr, "The Religion of Abraham Lincoln," *The Christian Century*, Feb. 10, 1965; 172–175, and Mark A. Noll, *America's God* (New York: Oxford University Press, 2002), 434.

2. William Clebsch, Review of "The Religion of Abraham Lincoln," in *Church History* 33, No. 4, (Dec. 1964), 501–502.

3. In Stephen Oates' 1977 biography, *With Malice Towards None: A Life of Abraham Lincoln* (New York: Harper and Row, 1977).

4. William W. Sweet, Review of "Lincoln and the Preachers," in *Mississippi Valley Historical Review* 36, no. 1 (June 1949), 145–146.

5. Ronald White, "Lincoln's Sermon on the Mount," in *Religion and the American Civil War*, edited by Randall M. Miller, Harry S. Stout, and Charles R. Wilson (New York: Oxford University Press, 1998), 217.

6. I am indebted here and elsewhere in this book to Ronald White for his excellent insights into Lincoln's faith. Cf. his marvelous book, *Lincoln's Greatest Speech* (New York: Simon & Schuster, 2002), 110–11.

7. The "Old School" of American Presbyterian thought grew out of sixteenth century Reformed or Calvinist theology, and balanced a high view of God (the primary actor of history) with a low view of humanity. While believing strongly in the sinfulness of human beings, Old School Presbyterians were confident that in God's sovereign rule human beings were instruments of divine purpose. Central to this American Reformed tradition was the concept of providence—which Lincoln heard emphasized often in Gurley's homilies. Cf. White, *ibid.,*132–141.

8. White, *ibid.*, 132, 138–139. When Lincoln was asked about Gurley and his sermons, he is reported to have responded, "I like Gurley. He don't preach politics. I get enough of that through the week, and when I go to church, I like to hear the gospel."

9. This "communitarian focus" of Lincoln's religious experience is made by Ronald White in "Lincoln's Sermon on the Mount," *op. cit.*, 221.

10. Cf. White, Ronald; *Lincoln's Greatest Speech; op. cit.*, 67, 97, 109–11, and Mark A. Noll, *op. cit.*, 426.

11. Sidney Ahlstrom, *Religious History of the American People* (New Haven, CT: Yale University Press, 1972), 686-687.

12. George Washington's 1793 address was only 135 words.

13. White, *Lincoln's Greatest Speech, op. cit.*, 194.

14. Only John Quincy Adams had quoted Scripture previously in an inaugural, and then only once. Philip Shaw Paludan points out the Biblical language and imagery that also permeated Lincoln's Gettysburg Address— from the opening "four score and seven years ago," to the image of a birth that would have meaning for all people on earth, to the idea that death could consecrate the ground on which they stood, to the final image of a *"nation under God"* that could have a rebirth because of the deaths that had occurred. Cf. Philip S. Paludan, *A People's Contest* (New York: Harper and Row, 1988), 371.

15. See pp. 141–149 of Ronald White, *Lincoln's Greatest Speech, op. cit.* for a more indepth analysis of these key "Old School" Presbyterian theological principles.

16. White, *ibid.,* 151-163.

17. White, "Lincoln's Sermon on the Mount," *op. cit.*, 211.

18. *Ibid.*, 208–9.

19. Niebuhr, *op. cit.*, 173.

20. White, "Lincoln's Sermon on the Mount," *op. cit.*,214; and *Lincoln's Greatest Speech, op. cit.*, 118–20.

21. Mark Noll offers a fine elaboration on how Lincoln redefined the classical Calvinist theme of "providence" in this "Meditation" (Noll, *America's God, op. cit.*, 430 31). Cf. also White, *Lincoln's Greatest Speech, op. cit.*, 122.

22. White, *Lincoln's Greatest Speech, op. cit.*, 122.

23. Noll, *op. cit.*, 426.

Chapter Seventeen

RELIGIOUS CONSEQUENCES OF THE CIVIL WAR

> The Civil War was the crimson baptismal lever of our nationalism, and so it continues to enjoy a mythic transcendence not unlike the significance of Eucharist for Christian believers . . . Just as Christians believe that 'without the shedding of blood there can be no remission for sins,' so Americans in the North and South came to believe that their bloodletting had to contain a profound religious meaning for their collective life as nations.
>
> Harry S. Stout, in *Books and Culture,* July/August 2003

What was it all for?

In 1865, the great War ended—concluding with poignant drama at Appomattox Court House on April 9th, followed by an anti-climatic spasm in the Carolinas on April 26th, and a sputtering last gasp at Palmito Ranch, Texas on May 12–13th. So, what was it all for? Why did soldiers fight and die, slaves dream and rejoice, preachers theologize, politicians scheme, and everyone suffer? What were the ultimate results of the Civil War—the consequences of these four historic years that have marked a watershed in American history?

Certainly *death*—some 620,000 were dead, with an estimated 30% of the Confederate army dead from wounds or disease.[1] Certainly *destruction*—the South was devastated in property, buildings, politics, economy and social structure, and would take decades to recover. Certainly *political and military defeat*—one side finally surrendered, the side that had been in rebellion, supporting states rights and institution of race-based slavery. Civil War students and historians could certainly list far more than these. But, in final corroboration of why a book on this topic has long been needed, the religious consequences of the Civil War for the American people have also been far less well known and discussed—even for avid students of mid-nineteenth century American history.[2]

We have already spoken of several religiously-connected ramifications of the Civil War—the religion of the Lost Cause, the related "saintly status" of the Confederate warrior, and Lincoln's theological and national masterpiece—the Second Inaugural Address. We could explore still more—the massive and seemingly deliberate destruction of southern churches and property by Union soldiers, the enormous devastation wrought on southern educational institutions (including seminaries) and church finances, the religious ramifications of changes in women's roles, the ramifications for the human soul of George Frederickson's "inner Civil War" reflections, trends towards "modernization" in church organizations (including the "social Gospel"). But perhaps the best general summary belongs to W. Harrison Daniel. "The social instability of a people at war, the absence of clergymen, the scattered nature of many congregations, the destruction wrought by the invaders, and a preoccupation with matters of war had a debilitating influence upon the [southern] church."[3]

In this final chapter, I would like to conclude with three specific religious ramifications of the Civil War upon our culture which merit special remembering. All of these had special long-range implications for the United States, and in some ways have left their fingerprints even upon our twenty-first century generation.

Hymns written during the Civil War

"Battle Hymn of the Republic"   (Juliet Ward Howe in 1861)
"Hold the Fort, I am Coming"   (Phillip Paul Bliss, inspired by
                                               the Battle of Allatoona Pass on Oct. 4, 1864)
"Onward Christian Soldiers"   (Sabine Baring-Gould in 1864)

"Under their own vine and fig tree"

When asked about results of the Civil War, some would immediately say "Well, it ended slavery." But anyone aware of American history from about 1877 to 1950 would have to answer in a far more nuanced fashion. The institution of southern race-based slavery put to death by the Civil War unfortunately only gave way to a different version of America's Great Paradox—a deeply-entrenched racism which "birthed" Jim Crow segregationist laws, Ku Klux Klan lynching and vigilante violence, and paramilitary "White Leagues" intent on securing white rule. What the Civil War did achieve regarding "slavery" and black Americans was the passage of three Amendments to the Constitution and a Civil Rights Act—all of which would be used 100 years later in a "second Reconstruction" to truly bring full freedoms to black Americans through legislation like the 1964 Civil Rights Bill.[4]

However, there was one clear religious consequence of the War affecting black Americans which was of paramount importance. The single most long-lasting result of the Civil War was *black religious self-determination*—the literal and meteoric rise of independent black churches, schools and religious institutions. As Samuel Hill remarks, "all things considered, the formation of independent black congregations and denominations . . . proved to be the most profound religious change brought on by the Civil War."[5]

Statistics from that era bear this out. In 1860, there were about 400,000 total black church members (mostly Baptist and Methodist); but by 1900 this had swelled to 2.7 million church members (out of a total black population 8.3 million). This is even more impressive when considering that this only considers *formal* church affiliation—many more black Americans were informally affiliated in looser ways with their churches.[6] Many historic black colleges began at this time, some funded by idealistic Northern-educated ministers—Morehouse (Atlanta), Spelman (Atlanta), Tougaloo (Mississippi), Fisk (Nashville), and Morgan State (Baltimore) are examples. The Methodists alone are connected to beginnings of no fewer than eleven historically black colleges.

> I want to be able to read the Bible before I die.
>
> Anonymous black man's 1861 words

With the war ended, the "invisible institution" of slave religion now exploded forth in new church organizations and increased religious activity. New church meetings sprang up regularly, with thousands of blacks beginning to organize their own autonomous congregations (again, mostly Baptist and Methodist). Many Northern ministers, teachers and social workers (black and white) came South to assist as they could in promoting educational and religious development (some said the place was "teeming" with Yankees!).

Biracial churches nearly all disappeared—because freed blacks could now sing, dance, preach, pray, shout and fellowship in their own company, and in their own unique African-American manner. For the first time, no one else would be in the building or the fields with them, and no one would supervise their every action or word. Indeed, simply taking fellowship together was almost as important as worshiping together. "The people needed each other for laughing, talking, shouting and planning—for caring for one another during a cataclysmic period. They relished being 'under their own vine and fig tree' [Micah 4:4]"[7]

While northern and southern denominations did offer independent black churches organization and material assistance in their efforts (the era generally saw both competition and cooperation between these three groups), still what black church goers accomplished after the Civil War was truly remarkable. Never before had southern blacks *ever* been able to take part in public activities or agencies where their voices would be heard and respected. Only rarely were there viable opportunities to learn about forming or guiding social institutions—certainly not from business or government ventures, and only in a few voluntary societies.

So, as Samuel Hill points out, after emancipation, the black community literally received "in-service training"—that is, they learned to organize by doing organizing themselves. Southern ex-slaves successfully confronted enormous challenges of illiteracy and unfamiliarity in constituting local church governments, of getting preachers licensed and ordained, of acquiring buildings to worship in, and of creating educational structures for themselves and their children. In wrestling with these areas, they slowly grew into the self-determining, autonomous, prophetic voice that became the backbone of the twentieth century African-American community.[8]

They would need all of that and more in the dark Jim Crow decades ahead—for the example of their churches and of 179,000 black Union soldiers had not persuaded the country of the justice of black citizenship. Black Americans had crossed the wilderness of slavery and passed through the Red Sea of church organizing—but the Promised Land of freedom and the Jordan River of full civil rights were still a long way off.

> The Negro Church . . . was usually a plain, ramshackle structure serving a small neighborhood in the Southern countryside . . . [It was usually] led by a very modestly educated minister. In most cases he had no more than elementary schooling. Yet as a member of the only profession open to a Negro, in charge of the blacks' only free institution, he was a very important man, "the greatest single influence among the colored people of the United States."
>
> Sydney Ahlstrom, *Religious History of American People* (1972)

The masculizing of Christianity

With the general antebellum belief "that the church was a woman's place," it is not a shock to realize that pre-war church membership was generally dominated by females. Donald Matthews points out that sixty-five women filled church pews for every thirty-five men present—despite men outnumbering women in the general population 51.5% to 48.5%. James McPherson mentions that, although the Great Awakening had brought many more to faith, still two-thirds of the members of Protestant churches in 1860 were female.

Influenced by beliefs such as southern notions of honor and manliness, typical pre-war portrayals of religion tended to emphasize Christian women as "gentle, soothing, pure, virtuous and sensitive," Christianity as feminine, gentle and pure, and Faith as requiring patience, meekness and resignation. So when thousands of males gathered at campsites preparing for battle with their fellow men, many coming to deeply personal religious convictions by war's end, many pre-war male religious attitudes necessarily underwent major transformation.[9]

The revivalism and religion of the Civil War helped transform pre-war spiritual stereotypes. The horrific carnage and destruction that was "male-only" warfare demanded different images of Faith than previously experienced.[10] Men hardened by all-male camp environments, facing temptations and allurements rarely seen, shaken to the core by death, maiming and destruction—all this demanded a Faith far tougher and more "real" than the gentle, virginal sentiments of women back home. But in the War years, if they wanted it, soldiers had opportunities to experience a masculine brand of Faith in ways they would never again find.

Bible messages were made clear, basic and simple by preachers who (by war's end at least) had often themselves experienced the same privations as their audiences. Sermons were frequently given in outdoor settings, or in chapels hand-made by soldiers themselves. The religious messages preached were quintessentially American—focusing on *results* more than on *process*, stressing more *participation and practicality* than *contemplation and speculation*. The best preaching was generally done in tones of urgent unexpectedness ("no one knows the day nor the hour"), with blunt overtones of what needed to be done immediately. Countless personal witness stories stood all around them—comrades fallen in battle, the narrow escape of friends, brothers kneeling before a preacher in prayer. It was an energetic, virile, "muscular" Christianity and Faith that emerged from the Civil War.

> "Such was the war. It was not a quadrille in a ball-room. Its interior history will not only never be written—its practicality, minutiae of deeds and passions, will never be written."
>
> Walt Whitman

"Religion is what makes brave soldiers." These well-chosen words of one Pennsylvania soldier hint at some of the "masculizing" effects of religion that occurred in those men who discovered a deeper "battle-tested" faith. It affected *self-images*. As men watched other men die, and wondered about their own bravery, a new ideal emerged—the brave soldier who was also a manly Christian, fortified by faith. Spirituality became intimately connected to manly faith images—honor, duty, courage, bravery and heroic faithfulness.

It affected *attitudes towards fellow soldiers*. The war brought that unique male bonding that only intense shared trauma can—there was a deep masculine camaraderie, almost a "spiritual communing", which flowed naturally from having endured the crucible of war together. It affected *attitudes toward death*. Strong, courageous faith helped men face death bravely. A strong personal belief in God could empower soldiers with confidence to face any foe without flinching, imparting a manly courage that all (especially fellow warriors) could admire. As one Confederate said,

"Christians make the best soldiers, as they would not fear the consequences after death as others would."

As James McPherson notes, this topic of war-time masculinization of Christianity needs much more study. The long-term post-war effects, as well as the nature and dimensions of this phenomenon, would benefit greatly by such analysis. But without a doubt, it can be said that the religious images and attitudes of Civil War soldiers received a serious war-inspired makeover. One religious Northern officer, Newton Martin Curtis, wrote of the war's positive influences on the personalities of the majority of the men who fought in it. Despite the arguments of a few who said that war made men more brutish, Curtis thought that battle had actually "refined" and "brightened" the natures of most Civil War soldiers.

Post-war authors like Lost Cause advocate J. William Jones repeatedly emphasized the spiritually edifying power of Civil War Religion, noting in a 1904 preface to his classic work *Christ in Camp* that he hoped his book would "prove useful in showing our young people the power of religion to promote real manhood." But perhaps no one captured the simple but profound changes that war had made upon men than the 2nd IA corporal who simply said "I am not the Same Man, Spiritually, as I was. . . ." He spoke for many more soldiers than he could know.[11]

> It was after the War that "Onward Christian Soldiers" became one of the most famous Protestant hymns of all times, the staple song of Sunday schools for many generations to come. It perfectly reflects the "martial" masculine tone of war-time religion. "Onward Christian soldiers, marching as to war./ With the cross of Jesus, going on before! / Christ the Royal Master, leads against the foe. / Forward into battle, see his banner go!"

An American "civil religion"

After his death, William Herndon remarked that Abraham Lincoln had been "the noblest and loveliest character since Jesus Christ . . . God's chosen one."[12] It was an amazing transformation for the simple Illinois rail-splitter—from a despised pre-war fool into God's divinely chosen vessel. This was made possible through the onset of one of the most profound Civil War legacies: the creation of an *American civil religion* in which Abraham Lincoln was "messiah," and the new "deity" was national Union. The sectarian divisions which had for generations ripped America asunder were slowly transformed into a near-mystical national Union enduring to this very day. "Death gave birth as northern and southern whites learned that they were all Americans—or, more accurately, that all *white* folk were Americans." Thus the Civil War in essence was the true birth of modern America.[13]

I spoke earlier about how early American history was dominated by the traditional denominations which found fertile ground on the new soil of freedom. In G.K. Chesterton's words, America was "the nation with the soul of a church", and that religious soul (an evangelical one) reigned with powerful moral influence over every aspect of society. Traditional faith language and cadences sounded everywhere. America was the "new Israel," and its colonists "chosen people." Churches of all denominations proliferated. The Scripture was the country's most popular book. Churchmen exerted powerful sway over people and politics—and had ample opportunity to steer a course away from War.

Yet, as Richard Carwardine indicates, by about 1850 it seems the "high water mark" had been reached of "clerical power and voluntarism independent of the state." Having inspired their churches and led their people to the brink of division, America's traditional churches now became loud but increasingly impotent voices in a rapidly changing country.[14]

As the Civil War surged across America, clergy were themselves caught up in the raging flood—and then washed away by patriotism and rhetoric. "Northern churches willingly—even enthusiastically—became subjugated to government priorities, and clergy gave way to politicians. The same was true of the Confederacy." As Americans groaned in agony trying to understand the bloodletting, the War itself became slowly recast as a sacred event, elevated to a cosmic spiritual plane. "War became worship; presidents became prophets; soldiers became saints; the nation's clergy became cheerleaders; and blood became baptismal water." The American churches, unable to bring the nation any unity in its greatest moral conflict, would now see national unity emerging in an entirely different way. The *traditional religion* that birthed the country now gave way symbolically to a *civil religion* that could finally unify the country.[15]

[The Civil War] created in this country what had never existed before—a national consciousness. It was not the salvation of the Union, it was the rebirth of the Union.

Woodrow Wilson, Memorial Day 1915

The concept of "civil religion" in America has its origin in Robert N. Bellah's 1967 essay, but Harry Stout has recently fleshed out the War's role in leading America to remember religion "differently than its traditional associations with Christian and Jewish faiths." Because of the immense "blood sacrifice" made by both sides, "something transformative took place that would render the war *the* defining phenomenon in American history. Patriotism itself became sacralized to the point that it enjoyed equal or even superior status to conventional denominational beliefs."

The "civil religion" that flowed from this (and which exists alongside our traditional religious faiths to this very day) Stout describes as "nation worship—a form of patriotism that trumps morality and spirituality in times of crisis and violent upheaval." New spiritual symbols have emerged to engage America's soul—images whose archetypal religious origins would henceforth now carry broader republican and national symbolism. These symbols and rituals borrow from the language of traditional religion, but spring more from our country's informal folk traditions, national rituals and patriotic myths:[16]

- Sacred *monuments* like the Lincoln Memorial, Washington Monument and Statue of Liberty evoke reverential awe.
- *Texts* such as the Declaration of Independence, the Constitution and Lincoln's speeches provide today's "sacred" Words.
- America's *"holy days"* were fast/thanksgiving days, and are now Memorial Day, Independence Day, Veterans' Day, Presidents' Day, Martin Luther King Day, Inauguration Day, etc. Nonsectarian prayers begin most of these days.
- The *American flag* is a sacred symbol—meriting massive patriotic displays, a Pledge of Allegiance, military flag-covered coffins, songs about "Old Glory" and even "desecration" charges for trampling upon it.
- *Presidents* are the traditional prophets and priests of this civil religion, and the State is its locus—both using the sacred symbols of the nation for their own purposes and perpetuation.

Thus, even after the bloody Civil War concluded, religion and faith in a myriad of non-intentioned forms continued to play a significant role in shaping America. The War between the States was the defining moral crisis of the United States. The country could never again be the same—and indeed it has never been. Whereas America's religious traditions chose to play a central role in dividing and sundering national bonds before the War, now it would be forced into a strangely influential yet significantly lessened national role in unifying the country after the war.

After a war that traditional churches helped facilitate, a new post-war religion would unite and encourage black Americans, spiritualize the men of America, and bind a diverse country together. In a strongly Christian nation, the blood of Jesus Christ has always had enormous unifying significance for believers. But in that "holy blood" of our Civil War, we racially and culturally Americans of today have gained a new national bond—one that invests us with a collective spiritual Unity, and offers us a doorway to transcend our many differences. "Both pray to the same God . . . both read the same book."[17]

I think the damned old cuss of a Preacher lied like Dixie for he sayed that God has fought our battles and won our victorys. Now if he has done all that why is it not in the papers, and why has he not been promoted.

Sgt. Albinus Fell (6th OH Cav) at war's end

Further reading recommendations

These articles in the periodical *Books and Culture—A Christian Review* 9, no. 4, (July/August 2003):

    Allen C. Guelzo, "Free to Do What? Emancipation Reconsidered"

    Mark A. Noll, "Getting it Half-Right"

    David Rolfs, "'When Thou Goest out to Battle'—The religious world of
        Civil War Soldiers"

    Harry S. Stout, "Baptism in Blood"

Robert N. Bellah, "Civil Religion in America." Pp. 21–44 in *American Civil Religion*, edited by Russell E. Richey and Donald G. Jones, New York: Harper Forum Books, 1974.

Kurt O. Berends, "Wholesome Reading Purifies and Elevates the Man." Pp. 131–166 in *Religion and the American Civil War*, edited by Randall Miller, Harry Stout, and Charles R. Wilson, New York: Oxford University Press, 1998.

Samuel S. Hill, "Religion and the Results of the Civil War." Pp. 360–384 in *Religion and the American Civil War*, edited by Randall Miller, Harry Stout, and Charles R. Wilson, New York: Oxford University Press, 1998.

Sidney E. Mead, "The 'Nation with the Soul of a Church.'" Pp. 45–75 in *American Civil Religion*, edited by Russell E. Richey and Donald G. Jones. New York: Harper Forum Books, 1974.

William H. Montgomery. *Under Their Own Vine and Fig tree: The African-American Church in the South, 1865–1900*. Baton Rouge: Louisiana State University Press, 1992.

Harry S. Stout. *Upon the Altar of the Nation—A Moral History of the Civil War*. New York: Viking/Penguin, 2006.

Robert Penn Warren. *The Legacy of the Civil War*. Lincoln: University of Nebraska Press, 1961.

Notes

1. This percentage is derived from James Pherson's estimations of approximately 850,000 total Confederate armed forces and 258,000 Confederate dead.

2. A classic and profound look at the effects of how the Civil War changed the American republic forever is Robert Penn Warren's *The Legacy of the Civil War*, (Lincoln: University of Nebraska Press, 1961). A distinguished poet, novelist, historian and Pulitzer-Prize winner, Robert Warren's centennial analysis of the Northern "Treasury of Virtue" and the Southern "Great Alibi" is stimulating and thought-provoking.

3. W. Harrison Daniel, "The Effects of the Civil War on Southern Protestantism," in the *Maryland Historical Magazine*, 69 (1974), 47–48. This article is excellent for a detailed description of the destruction wrought upon southern church buildings, property, finances and more during the war. George Frederickson's book is entitled *The Inner Civil War— Northern Intellectuals and the Crisis of the Union* (New York: Harper and Row, 1965). In general terms, it focuses on an 1880-1890s dimension of the war's effect on the inner man— on the human psyche, spirit and mentality; an effect which introduced into the American sensibility such "spiritual" traits as courage, resolution to endure, action, the strenuous life, etc. Harry Stout's article in *Books and Culture* July/August 2003 lists three well-stated "*consequences for the nation and the world*" of the Civil War: (1) the destruction of slavery, (2) the elimination of secession as a sectional option, and (3) the central place of the Civil War in nineteenth century world history. He speaks also of the "tragedy" and "epiphany" of the war—namely, the failure to counter racism, and the rise of an American civil religion. (Cf. Harry S. Stout, "Baptism in Blood," in the periodical *Books and Culture*, July/August 2003, 16–17).

4. The three post-war Amendments were the *Thirteenth* (1865) abolishing slavery, the *Fourteenth* (1868) extending privileges of the Bill of Rights to former slaves (i.e., civil rights), and the *Fifteenth* (1870) granting black men the right to vote (i.e., political rights). The Civil Rights Act of 1866 made blacks citizens of the United States and states in which they lived, granting them the same rights as held by whites. But following a disputed 1876 Presidential election between Rutherford B. Hayes and Samuel Tilden, weakened Republicans promised non-interference in southern affairs in exchange for granting Hayes the election. This decision, known as the *Compromise of 1877*, in effect ended Reconstruction and overturned the short-lived freedoms won for southern black Americans. Southern state legislatures slowly passed harsh laws restricting the activities of freeman, and used the courts to nullify the effects of previous legislations like the above Amendments, with legislation like "Jim Crow laws" coming into effect (which enforced segregation in places of business and on public transportation). Finally, the 1896 Supreme Court decision *Plessy v. Ferguson* affirmed as constitutional those southern laws allowing segregation on public conveyances, as long as "separate but equal" facilities were in place for both blacks and whites.

5. Samuel S. Hill, "Religion and the Results of the Civil War," in *Religion and the American Civil War,* edited by Randall M. Miller, Harry S. Stout, and Charles R. Wilson (New York: Oxford University Press, 1998), 366.

6. Sydney Ahlstrom, *A Religious History of the American People* (New Haven, CT: Yale University Press, 1972), 709; and Samuel S. Hill, *op. cit.*, 364. Ahlstrom breaks out the 400,000 black pre-war Christians into about 225,000 Methodists and 175,000 Baptists. Georgia provides a representative example of the massive growth in black religion after emancipation. In 1860, the Georgia Conference of the Methodist Episcopal Church (South) reported 27,371 members—but only one decade later, the five Methodists denominations of Georgia reported over 68,000 black members (an increase of 150%). Georgia Baptist churches reported 26,192 black members in 1860—and by 1870, the six black Baptist associations had 38,878 members (an increase of 48%). By 1877, when better records were kept, they reported 91,868 members—three and a half times the number of 1860. Cf. Daniel,W. Stowell, "Crossing Jordan: The Black Quest for Religious Autonomy," part of the *American Society of Church History Papers*, presented on January 4–7, 1996; on microfiche in the Notre Dame Library Archives.

7. Hill, *op. cit.*, 364–65. As mentioned, Baptists and Methodists had the largest attraction among blacks after the war, with Baptists becoming the largest post-war southern denomination. The Baptists had earlier increased greatly in the black community because the slaves found that theology and worship to their liking. The National Baptist Convention was organized in 1895 (culminating thirty years moving toward such independence), giving blacks even more self-government in issues like sponsoring their own missionary societies, Sunday school programs, publishing, schools and colleges. In 1866, the Southern Methodist church released its black members so that in 1870 a Colored Methodist Episcopal church could form (the name was changed in 1954 to "Christian" Methodist). However, there were also post-war church representatives in the south from the two northern African Methodist Episcopal denominations as well (founded in 1816 and 1821 respectively). In 1880, AME membership reached 400,000 because of its rapid spread south of the Mason-Dixon line.

8. Hill, *op. cit.*, 364. A further excellent book on the topic of post-war southern black church development is William H. Montgomery, *Under Their Own Vine and Fig Tree: The African-American Church in the South, 1865–1900* (Baton Rouge, LA: Louisiana State University Press, 1992).

9. The statistics from Donald Matthews and James McPherson can be found in *Religion and the American Civil War, op. cit.*, 97 and 409. Cf. also Kurt O. Berends, "Wholesome Reading Purifies and Elevates the Man," in *Religion and the American Civil War, op. cit.*, 136, 141. Berends also contends that the experience of baptismal immersion (done especially by the Baptists) was a specifically and truly *masculine* action—and it symbolically contrasted with the "nurturing feminine symbols" of sprinkling practiced by other denominations (like the Presbyterians, who had focused on "sacramentality" as opposed to the masculine "ordinance" terminology of Baptists).

10. In using the phrase "male-only warfare," I certainly do not demean the fact that research now reveals that a significant number of women fought in the Civil War as well. For the purposes of this issue, however, I think the reader will understand the larger point being made about male soldiers, their all-male living and fighting environments, and the uniquely male religious themes that the war produced.

11. Cf. Shattuck, *op. cit.*, 84–7 passim. Also McPherson, "Afterword," in *Religion and the American Civil War, op cit.*, 409–10.

12. Quoted in Sherwood Eddy, *The Kingdom of God and the American Dream* (New York: Harper and Bros., 1941), 162.

13. Edward J. Blum, "Review of *Grapes of Wrath*," in *Books and Culture*, March/April 2006, 15.

14. Richard J. Carwardine, *Evangelicals and Politics in Antebellum America* (New Haven, CT: Yale University Press, 1993); Harry Stout, "Baptism in Blood," *op. cit.*, 17.

15. Harry Stout, *ibid.*; and Edward J. Blum, *op. cit.*, 15.

16. Harry S. Stout, *Upon the Altar of the Nation—A Moral History of the Civil War* (New York: Viking/Penguin, 2006), xvii; and Harry Stout, "Baptism in Blood," *op. cit.*, 17. For Robert Bellah's original article on civil religion, as well as an excellent discussion of the topic from a variety of areas, cf. Russell E. Richey and Donald G. Jones, *American Civil Religion* (New York: Harper and Row, 1974).

17. Harry Stout, *Upon the Altar of a Nation, op. cit.*, xvi–xxii. Cf. also two articles in *American Civil Religion*—Robert Bellah's "Civil Religion in America," and Sidney E. Mead's "The 'Nation with the Soul of a Church.'"

Appendix

Author's Note on the Appendix

The following Appendix is a random, scattered "snapshot" of the denominational affiliations of some prominent Civil War figures, drawn from the comments of historians and authors who have written about them. These reflections are the result of "incidental information" discovered while researching this book.

However, in no way do I wish to represent this as a meticulously researched or thorough in-depth and accurate analysis of these individual religious affiliations. The people selected here were purely the result of my personal choice and/or the specific material available to me at the time. Occasionally the religious records conflicted, while others were silent about religion, with some information simply being unavailable. I chose to enclose this Appendix purely because I found this information rather fascinating and informative, it adds an interesting and relevant element to this book, and on the whole it simply is kind of nice to know!

Finally, there is one note about sources used for this Appendix. The predominant source for Confederate religious affiliation is Jon Wakelyn's short, several page listing in his *Biographical Dictionary of the Confederacy*. Though I found that the religious information in this 1977 work occasionally conflicted with later individual biographers, I cite him because of his foundational information. Because of its frequent use, I chose not to repeatedly make his book a formal endnote but only a one-word reference after the individual's religious affiliation.

I also heartily welcome additional insights, comments and information by those who may have access to further accurate specific data on religious affiliation. The author may be contacted at civilwarreligion@mac.com. Enjoy!

RELIGIOUS AFFILIATIONS

Adams, John. This Irish Tennessee-born Confederate general, who fell at Franklin atop the Uautonion works after being struck nine times, has a disputed religious background. According to one he was a Catholic, but according to the biography of Charles Todd Quintard (probably a more reliable source), Adams was Episcopal. Whatever the case, Adams' last words at Franklin reportedly were "it is the fate of a soldier to die for his country."[1]

Alexander, E. Porter. Son of a prominent Georgia plantation owner and a mother who taught Sunday School to slaves, Alexander's religious affiliation is unclear. Jon Wakelyn calls him a Presbyterian—but whatever his denomination (if any), Alexander was skeptical of excessive Confederate "reliance" on Divine Providence during the War. After the war, he wrote

> I think it was a serious incubus upon us that during the whole war our president and many of our generals really and actually believed that there *was* this mysterious Providence always hovering over the field & ready to interfere on one side or the other, & that prayers & piety might win its favor from day to day. It was a weakness to imagine that victory could ever come in even the slightest degree from anything except our own exertions.[2]

Anderson, Richard. Confederate general, Episcopalian   (Wakelyn)

Archer, James. Confederate general, Presbyterian   (Wakelyn)

Armistead, Lewis A. Confederate general, Episcopalian   (Wakelyn)

Baker, Alpheus. This Confederate General was one of two Roman Catholic generals from Alabama in the Civil War (Raphael Semmes was the other). [3]

Banks, Nathaniel P. Union General, politician. Episcopalian [4]

Barksdale, William. Confederate general, Baptist (Wakelyn)

Beauregard, Pierre G. T. Louisiana-born Confederate general, Catholic[5]

Beecher, Catharine Esther. At odds with her father's stern Calvinist beliefs, Catharine transferred her membership from the Congregationalist to the Episcopal Church. Though a physically frail woman, she became an indefatigable warrior for reform on women's issues, as a school teacher and popular writer.

Beecher, Henry Ward. A Congregational pastor who gained fame as one of America's most renowned mid-nineteenth century preacher. The boxes of Sharps rifles his Brooklyn NY church sent to 1854 "bleeding Kansas" became known as "Beecher's Bibles."

Beecher, Lyman. This stern Calvinist reformer was a Yale graduate, a Presbyterian minister, a Second Awakening revivalist preacher. After pastoring a Boston Congregational Church from 1826 on, he returned to the Presbyterian denomination, and in 1832 moved to Cincinnati OH to become president of Lane Theological Seminary.[6]

Benjamin, Judah P. This foreign-born lawyer was a prewar United States Senator from Louisiana and a notary in New Orleans. He became a three-time Confederate Cabinet member and a good friend of Jefferson Davis. Benjamin was a southern Sephardic Jew, though essentially a non-practicing one.

Bickerdyke, Mary Ann. "Mother Bickerdyke" went to the Civil War to make sure sick and wounded soldiers got the food and supplies they needed. She served as a nurse and hospital matron at many Union hospitals, including those at Cairo (IL), Shiloh and Chattanooga. Called by one living historian the "Cyclone in Calico," she was a member of Dr. Edward Beecher's Congregational church, but once told a journalist "I worship with the Methodists, the Congregationalists, or the Episcopals, as I happen to light on 'em."[7]

Bragg, Braxton. Baptized and confirmed in the Episcopal tradition on June 2, 1863 in Shelbyville TN by Bishop Stephen Elliot. Charles Quintard seems to have been primarily responsible for Bragg's baptism, as he relates in his journal.

> I was resolved to see the General, no matter what happened, so I said [to the sentry] "It is a matter of death and life." The sentry returned and said: "You can see the General, but I advise you to be brief. He is not in a good humor." He met me with: "Well, Dr. Quintard, what can I do for you? I am quite busy, as you can see." I was very much frightened, but I asked the General to be seated, and then, fixing my eyes upon a knot-hole in the pine board floor of the tent, talked about our Blessed Lord and about the responsibilities of a man in the General's position. When I looked up after a while I saw tears in the General's eyes, and took courage to ask him to be confirmed. At last he came to me, took both my hands in his and said: "I have been waiting for twenty years to have some one say this to me, and I thank you from my heart. Certainly I shall be confirmed if you will give me the necessary instruction."

Quintard mentions that Bragg's "life subsequent to the war was quiet. He was a God-fearing man in peace and in war."[8]

Branch, Lawrence O'Brien. Confederate general, Catholic[9]

Breckinridge, John C. This Confederate statesman and general was a Calvinist Presbyterian. As a boy Breckinridge had two uncles who were ministers. He grew up at Cabell's Dale (his grandfather's house) where the Mount Horeb Presbyterian Church was founded in 1827 in the drawing room. Breckinridge was tutored in the bible as well as church dogma. He attended Kentucky Academy, a church boarding school, and Danville's Centre College (Presbyterian) before attending Princeton.[10]

Brown, John. Born in Connecticut with a Calvinist upbringing by his devout abolitionist father, Brown grew up in a strong religious environment, with Scripture reading and prayer being a daily occurrence. Dedicated to doing God's will, he became a determined foe of slavery at an early age. No less than Frederick Douglass said that he had never been in the presence of a stronger religious influence than Brown.[11]

Brownlow, William. This Southern Methodist newspaperman and circuit-riding preacher championed the South in the most famous pre-war debates between northern and southern ministers about the morality of slavery. He became troubled by the rush to secession, however, and took a Unionist stance in Tennessee in 1861. Brownlow loathed abolitionism but rejected secession, vowing he would fight it "until Hell freezes over." He proposed hanging people who opposed the Northern cause, and eventually was sent north by an angry mob. He became a popular speaker, wartime Reconstruction governor of Tennessee, and post-war United States Senator.

Buckner, Simon B. Confederate general, Episcopalian (Wakelyn)

Butler, Benjamin F. Union general, politician and Presbyterian[12]

Chamberlain, Joshua L. Chamberlain's prominent war and political career was marked by a long and deep connection to the Congregationalist Church. At age sixteen he joined the Church, and feeling a calling to preach in foreign lands, he chose against going to West Point, opting instead for Bangor Theological Seminary (described as a bastion of Congregationalism). While in seminary, he gave up his dream of going to the foreign missions, concentrating instead on preaching to a congregation, but left seminary before ordination. Although he later became licensed to preach, he never became an ordained minister due to his future wife Fannie's lack of support—she "didn't want to be a minister's wife." He never lost his personal "belief in a spiritually directed destiny."

Chesnut, Mary. The famous Richmond VA diarist was an Episcopalian. She was in St. Paul's Episcopal Church (Richmond) with Jefferson Davis on Sunday, April 2, 1865 when couriers from Lee's Army broke into the service to inform them that Richmond's defenses had been breached, and they would have to flee.

Clay, Henry. This famous politician was not a practicing Christian most of his life, but joined the Episcopal Church five years before his death. He was greatly disturbed by the church divisions on 1844–1845, remarking that "the sundering of the religious ties which have bound our people together, I consider the greatest source of danger to our country. If our religious men cannot live together in peace, what can be expected of our politicians, very few of whom profess to be governed by the principles of love."[13]

Cleburne, Patrick. One of the more well-known non-Catholic native Irishmen, Cleburne was born on St. Patrick's Day, the son of a Protestant physician with a large (and often uncompensated) practice among poor Catholics. Raised Episcopalian, he came to America in 1849, becoming a Mason and vestryman of the Episcopal Church in Helena, Arkansas. Quintard wrote that shortly before his death at Franklin, while Cleburne rode with him past the consecrated ground of St. John's Church in Ashwood, Tennessee, Cleburne remarked that he would like to be buried there. After his death, Quintard had Cleburne and four others disinterred from the places they had been buried, and moved to the beautiful Ashwood Church yard which Cleburne had spoken of.[14]

Cooper, Samuel. Confederate general, Episcopalian (Wakelyn)

Corse, Montgomery D. This Virginia-born Confederate general was an Episcopalian. (Wakelyn)

Crenshaw, William G. Confederate general, Episcopalian (Wakelyn)

Custer, George A. This famed Union general was nominally a Methodist, while his wife Elizabeth (Libby) was Presbyterian. They were married in February 1864 at the First Presbyterian Church in Monroe, Michigan.[15]

Dabney, Robert Lewis. A pre-war Presbyterian pastor in Richmond VA, Dabney was Stonewall Jackson's chief-of-staff for three months in 1862. As moderator of the Presbyterian Synod of Virginia, he had initially counseled moderation and the need for prayer in the prevailing crisis, but after Lincoln's election he had a change of heart, and by March 1861 was calling for voters to take VA out of the Union. After the war Dabney became an embittered and outspoken champion of Confederate nationalism.[16]

Davis, Jefferson. As a boy, Davis was raised Baptist, but had a Catholic early education with Dominican priests near Springfield, Kentucky. He became a member of the Episcopal Church in 1862, being baptized and confirmed at St. Paul's Episcopal (Richmond), where he worshiped regularly. Davis was there at Sunday worship on April 2, 1865 when the order came that Lee was evacuating Richmond. Not all saw Davis' conversion and his renewed religious interest as beneficial to the Southern war effort. Mary Chesnut (in attendance at the same April 2, 1865 service) commented huffily in her diary about "how less piety and more drilling of commands would suit the times better." Edward Ruffin wrote how the "morbid tenderness of conscience" of Davis negatively affected him. Ruffin believed that the sensibilities that had led Davis to become "engaged in seeking to save his own soul" also prevented him from giving appropriate attention to prosecuting the war against the enemies of the South.[17]

Davis, Varina Howell. Jefferson Davis' wife was an Episcopalian, recognized for her strong religious convictions. According to the biography of Confederate chaplain Fr. Hippolyte Gache, it was she who persuaded her husband to be baptized Episcopalian. She had a penchant for employing Catholic nurses for her children, and both she and her husband were quite favorable to Catholics throughout their lives.[18]

DeLeon, David C. This South Carolina native was Jewish—a pre-war surgeon who became head of the medical department of the Confederacy. (Wakelyn)

Dix, Dorothea Lynde. Dix was the often difficult superintendent of northern Civil War nurses (although not a nurse herself), and a Unitarian by denomination. She had the power to rule on the acceptability of all nurse applicants for service with the army. Among those who ran across her prejudices were Catholic nuns—for in Dix' eyes, only Protestants were acceptable as nurses.[19]

Douglass, Frederick. The son of a slave mother and a white father, he was sent by his father at age eight to Baltimore to work as a servant. After escaping to New York at age twenty-one, he changed his last name, sent for a free black woman named Anna Murray, whom he married and had five children with. Upon freedom, he became a licensed preacher in the African Methodist Episcopal Zion Church, and began his career as an abolitionist lecturer. Despite being mentored by William Lloyd Harrison, Douglass grew troubled by his disdain for violence, party politics and the Constitution, and he began to distance himself from Garrison. At the outbreak of the war, he helped recruit troops for the 54th Massachusetts, enrolling two of his own sons. A friend of Abraham Lincoln, Douglass held post-war positions under two Presidents. After his wife died, he married a white woman (Helene Pitts), which generated much criticism—but he saw the marriage as a blow against racism.[20]

Du Pont, Samuel Francis. Union Admiral, Episcopalian. He was a respected member of the church hierarchy and attended the general convention of the Protestant Episcopal Church in Richmond in 1859 as one of the delegates.[21]

Early, Jubal. Confederate general, Episcopalian (Wakelyn)

Ewell, Richard S. Although designated as Episcopalian by several authors (e.g., Wakelyn, McPherson), others call Ewell "an agnostic at best" (James Robertson, E.M. Boswell). According to yet another source, he "joined the church during the revivals which ran through the Southern armies."[22] As with several other wives of prominent Southern generals (e.g., Varina Howell and Lydia McClane Johnston) Ewell's wife did have a very religious background. Confederate chaplain Fr. James Sheeran remarks that she was "a lady of more than ordinary intellectual powers, well educated . . . a rigid Episcopalian, somewhat fond of discussing religious subjects, but very respectful when speaking of Catholic dogmas." Quite familiar with the famous 14th LA chaplain, General Ewell once complained to Sheeran that "you have never called on Mrs. Ewell, notwithstanding her many invitations." Sheerhan obediently did so that very afternoon![23]

Ewing, Thomas. This Ohio-born Union general, along with his two brothers Charles and Hugh (also generals), were foster brothers to William T. Sherman, and were Catholics.[24]

Evans, Clement Anselm. Brigadier General in the CSA. After the war, he became a Methodist minister, trustee of three colleges, and editor of the 12-volume *Confederate Military History*. He preached at many of the major Confederate funerals after the war. He is buried at Oakland Cemetery in Atlanta.

Fish, Hamilton. This prewar United States Senator and postwar Secretary of State (1869–1877) was a prominent Episcopal layman.[25]

Forrest, Nathan Bedford. Considered by Jon Wakelyn to be Presbyterian, supposedly the enigmatic Forrest had a religious conversion experience towards the end of his life. One night in December 1864, Forrest and Confederate chaplain Charles Quintard shared a bed together, bringing about the quip that this was truly "the lion and the lamb lying down together." Quintard later remarked about Forrest that "he is certainly an uncut diamond—of remarkable appearance and great native vigor of thought and expression."[26]

Fremont, John C. Union general and politician, Episcopalian[27]

Fuller, Richard. This South Carolina native was a Harvard graduate, a Baptist convert, and later president of the Southern Baptist Convention. He defended slaveholding yet was troubled by the growing national sectionalism and rabid proslavery agitation. He quietly advocated both the colonization of blacks to Africa and Unionism. Fuller moved to Baltimore for the last years of his life, and became reviled in South Carolina.[28]

Garesche, Julius P. This Union officer, West Point graduate and chief of staff for William Rosecrans, was a strong and fervent Catholic, and had a brother who was a priest. He died at Stones River on the last day of 1862.[29]

Garfield, James A. This Ohio politician, Union general and future President was a member of the Disciples of Christ. He wrote during the war that "one of the painful facts of the Rebellion" was that "nearly all the cultivated and enlightened people . . . are on the side of the Rebellion"—even his fellow Disciples of Christ. He attributed this to the leadership of the Southern aristocracy in secession.[30]

Garrison, William Lloyd. Unitarian. Born in 1805 into indentured servitude, and trained as a printer. A radical abolitionist, Garrison in 1831 founded the newspaper *The Liberator* attacking slavery. He accumulated a large following of mostly Quaker and Puritan followers, but gradually grew more and more militant in his beliefs, and less willing to compromise on abolitionism. Garrison's anger and arrogance hurt the abolition cause; however it was an 1839 Garrison speech that inspired a recently freed Frederick Douglass to become active in public speaking.

Gist, States Rights. Confederate general, Methodist (Wakelyn)

Gordon, John B. This Confederate general was a Baptist known for his outstanding piety. After the war, he became the first commander of the United Confederate Veterans, a group which helped formulate and promote the ideology of the Lost Cause.[31]

Gorgas, Josiah. Head of the Confederate Ordinance Bureau, he was a convert to the Episcopal Church during the Civil War. He interpreted the Confederate losses at Gettysburg and Vicksburg as a sign of God's possible anger with the South. He also expressed his worry that "the sins of the people of Charleston" and the "rottenness" of that city would bring about its fall to the Union forces that were attacking it."[32]

Granbury, Hiram. Although one author considered this Texas lawyer one of the Confederate "fighting preachers", Charles Quintard remarked simply that "of General Granbury, I have no knowledge of his religious views."[33]

Grant, Ulysses S. According to Gordon Shattuck, Grant "mainly involved himself with military matters [and] evinced little interest in cultivating any spiritual sensitivity during the war." Others remark that although Grant was the leading Union general and a later President, he certainly was no saint. The Grant family pew sits in the United Methodist Church at Galena, Illinois—which testifies to his religious roots, but finding evidence of faith in Grant's adult life is far more difficult. He had complained at West Point that the academy was trying to mold cadets into gentlemanly Episcopalians—and he resisted. His wife Julia was a devout Methodist, and throughout their marriage it rankled her that Grant never became a churchgoer. However, at his deathbed, after a long battle with throat cancer, Grant was re-baptized at the insistence of his friends.[34]

Greenhow, Rose O. One of the most renowned Confederate spies, Greenhow ("Little Rose") was Catholic. She drowned in 1864 while returning from England, being dragged down by the weight of the gold she had received in royalties for her book.[35]

Gregg, Maxcy. Confederate general, Episcopalian (Wakelyn)

Hampton, Wade. Confederate general, Episcopalian (Wakelyn)

Hancock, Winfield S. This Union general and Gettysburg hero was a Baptist.[36]

Hardee, William J. An early Episcopalian who later converted to Catholicism, this prominent Confederate general asked Bishop Polk to baptize him during the 1864 Georgia campaign.[37]

Harrison, Benjamin. The 23d President of the United States was a lawyer by profession, and a Presbyterian by denomination. He enlisted in the Union army in July 1862 as a Second Lieutenant and later helped form Indiana's 70th Regiment. After the Atlanta Campaign battle of Peach Tree Creek, Harrison won a promotion to brevetted Brigadier General, at the recommendation of Gen. Joe Hooker. Harrison was active throughout his life as a Presbyterian, being elected deacon in 1857 at the First Presbyterian Church in Indianapolis, and an Elder of that church in 1861. He held the position of Elder until his death in 1901.

Heth, Henry. Confederate general, Episcopalian (Wakelyn)

Higginson, Thomas W. A pre-war Massachusetts Unitarian pastor, this ardent abolitionist and well-known writer was appointed colonel of the First South Carolina Volunteers, which became the basis for his classic work *Army Life in a Black Regiment*. His correspondence with the reclusive Emily Dickinson eventually resulted in the posthumous publication of her poems.

Hill, Ambrose Powell. Born in Culpepper, Virginia, Hill was married in 1859 in an Episcopal service. Hassler's biography describes Hill as an "undemonstrative, highly principled Episcopalian who confined the outward observance of his faith to Sunday worship. His wife averred that before the war he never missed a service and during the conflict he attended church whenever possible."[38]

Hill, Daniel H. According to Gordon Shattuck, Hill was "celebrated for his outstanding piety". A prominent Presbyterian layman, after the war Hill edited the short-lived journal *The Land We Love*, which became one of the principal organs for promoting the Lost Cause. The publication frequently contained articles about the religious life of the Confederate armies, and linked the supposed superiority of the South to its fighting men.[39]

Hoke, Robert F. Confederate general, Episcopalian (Wakelyn)

Hood, John Bell. Along with Gen. Joseph Johnston, Hood was baptized by Episcopal Bishop Leonidas Polk in the fall of 1864, during the Atlanta Campaign, during the great revival which had broken out among the Confederate army. The Episcopal bishop of Arkansas, Henry Lay (a missionary in the army in Georgia) movingly described Hood's baptism. Amidst the explosions of shells around them, Hood's soldiers watched as their leader was baptized. Crippled by his wounds, Hood "was unable to kneel," but "supported himself on his crutch and staff, and with bowed head received the benediction." Hood's baptism seemed to symbolize the quest of all Southern soldiers for the only realistic support still left them—the spiritual strength of their God.[40]

Holmes, Oliver W. Holmes openly denied the major truths of Christianity, which put him in a small minority in the mid-nineteenth century. The son of a Boston Brahmin, Holmes left Harvard in his senior year to join the 20th MA Volunteers as a private, and was wounded three times in the War. After his 1861 Ball's Bluff wound, thinking he was dying, Holmes rejected the Deity with succinct finality, and a witness records him saying, "Well, I'm dying, but I'll be God-damned if I know where I'm going."

After witnessing fearful losses, doubting that any decisive contest would take place, Holmes was exhausted mentally and physically. He resigned in July 1864, returning to Harvard to study law. His famous 1881 book *The Common Law*, led to a Harvard professorship and later the Mississippi and United States Supreme Court. He also wrote of "The Soldier's Faith," but his vision of faith was purely existential, and God was gone from that faith. "That faith is true and adorable which leads a soldier to throw away his life in obedience to a blindly accepted duty, in a cause which he little understands, in a plan of campaign of which he has no notion, under tactics of which he does not see the use."

In a little known incident, when Jubal Early's Confederates threatened Washington, DC, in the summer of 1864, President Lincoln himself went out to Fort Stephens to see the action. While standing there, a nearby onlooker was hit by a bullet, and it was Oliver Wendall Holmes who caught sight of the tall stranger standing in the line of fire, and yelled out "Get down, you damn fool, before you get shot!" The chastened President immediately got down.[41]

Hotchkiss, Jedediah. A transplanted New Yorker who settled in Virginia, Hotchkiss was Presbyterian, becoming the most famous of Confederate cartographers. (Wakelyn)

Howard, Oliver O. James McPherson remarks that one could assign almost any mainstream Protestant denomination to the general known as the "*Christian General*" and "*old prayer book*" because of his strong faith beliefs. Howard became a Methodist through a religious conversion at age twenty, but later at West Point he and his wife decided to become Episcopalian, yet never joined any church. Then, during Reconstruction he was close to the American Missionary Association (Congregational), and taking the lead in founding Howard University. In the 1880's Howard belonged to Tabernacle Church in New York City, a rather interdenominational church that leaned Congregational.

Whatever he saw himself as, Howard was an abolitionist who never smoke, drank or swore. He lost his right arm at the battle of Seven Pines, and hence became known as the "*one wing devil*" because he seemed to desire his army to become Protestant crusaders! As a brigade commander, Howard made sure his regiments held services on Sunday, and if no chaplain was present, often preached himself. One soldier who heard him preach commented favorably on this, and was gratified to know that Howard "though he ranked high among men . . . humbled himself before God." He later served as chairman of the American Tract Society and superintendent of West Point, beginning there in 1869 a practice that continues to this day—presenting Bibles to all incoming West Point cadets.[42]

Hunt, Henry Jackson. This Michigan-born Union general, chief of artillery for much of the war, was a Catholic.[43]

Iverson, Alfred. Confederate general, Presbyterian (Wakelyn).

Jackson, Thomas J. Even as a teen, the legendary Jackson was interested in faith—at age sixteen he would walk three miles to church to hear a sermon. He began pursuing faith more seriously while in the Mexican War, finding the Catholic religion quite impressive, although personally desiring a more simple faith. On Sunday, April 29, 1848, Jackson publicly declared his faith and was baptized at St. John's Episcopal Church in New York City. But when he became a teacher at Virginia Military Institute in Lexington, Virginia, Jackson joined the Lexington Presbyterian Church, after being assured by the pastor that he did not have to accept all the points of Presbyterian theology!

He became a deacon, a student of theology, and taught a Sunday School that included black children (causing no little controversy later on). Indeed for the rest of his life, he was often referred to as "Deacon Jackson." His two wives were both daughters of Presbyterian ministers (Elinor Junkin in 1853, and Mary Anna Morrison in 1857). Jackson always regarded the ministry as life's highest calling. During the war, he would often invite pastors and chaplains of nearby churches to debates and discussions on religion and theology. He was instrumental in establishing a Chaplain's Association to work with the troops, naming Rev. Beverly T. Lacy as Second Corps chaplain, who reported to him regularly the "spiritual progress" being made.

As is his public image even today, Jackson was strict, stern, unrelenting and severe in his beliefs, actions and demeanor, always remaining opposed to both Sunday mail and fighting, as well as dancing, theater-going, card-playing, smoking or drinking. He was faithful church attender, even spending much of his leisure moments in prayer and meditation, although he was known to fall asleep during services! One member of the Rockbridge Artillery wrote that he saw Jackson many times come quietly in among the soldiers and occupy a camp stool or modest seat and listen reverently to the singing and sermons. The often loud troops would quiet immediately if someone raised a hand and said "Sh-h-h! Keep quiet! Old Stonewall is praying for you."[44]

Jenkins, Albert. This Virginia-born Confederate general, who died on May 21, 1864 after the Battle of Cloyd's Mountain, was a Catholic.[45]

Jenkins, Micah. Confederate general, Episcopalian (Wakelyn)

Johnson, Bushrod R. Confederate general, Quaker (Wakelyn).

Johnston, Albert S. Confederate general, Episcopalian (Wakelyn)

Johnston, Joseph E. Episcopalian (Wakelyn). Along with John Bell Hood, he was baptized by Bishop Leonidas Polk during the 1864 Atlanta Campaign, during the great religious revival which had broken out amidst the Confederate army. Quintard has the following glowing description of Johnson in his journals.

> I found General Johnston a charming man. He was of perfectly good manners, of easy and graceful carriage and a good conversationalist . . . Afterwards in command of the Army of Tennessee, no man enjoyed greater popularity than he did. Soldiers and citizens alike recognized that General Johnston possessed a solid judgment, invincible firmness, imperturbable self-reliance and a perseverance which no difficulties could subdue. It was my privilege to be frequently

with the General after the war and more and more he entered into the religious life, illustrating in his daily walk and conversation the highest type of Christian gentleman.[46]

Kershaw, Joseph B. Kershaw was an Episcopal Church warden (1851–1894), a Confederate Brigadier General and a post-war state senator from South Carolina. Despite being buried in the Old Quaker Cemetery in Camden, South Carolina, he was not a Quaker (as mistakenly noted by Jon Wakelyn).[47]

Lane, James Henry. This Virginia university professor and Confederate general was Episcopalian, and curiously lived at the same time as another man of the exact same name—who was an anti-slavery advocate, U.S. Army general, and Kansas senator! [48]

Law, Evander. Confederate general, Presbyterian (Wakelyn)

Lee, Fitzhugh. Another of the distinguished lineage of Virginia Lee's, Fitzhugh was a Confederate major general, a postwar consul general in Havana, and an Episcopalian. (Wakelyn)

Lee, Robert Edward. A practicing Episcopalian, Lee was a highly devout and pious man in both formal religion and personal faith. He regularly attended Christ Church in Alexandria, a historic church pastored by Bishop William Meade (which still maintained George Washington's pew) and used his Bible for public Scripture reading. Lee loved Scripture, leading his family in daily devotions when able, and reading it daily himself when away. After the war, Lee served as president of the Rockbridge County Bible Society, which had as its sole purpose "assisting in extending the inestimable knowledge of the priceless truths of the Bible."

Lee's faith was humble, sincere, heartfelt and never disrespectful even of his enemy. His sense of duty and personal moral character was beyond reproach, as Alexander Stevens noted when he wrote "Lee used no stimulants, was free from even the use of tobacco, and was absolutely stainless in his personal life." The renowned Army of Northern Virginia chaplain Rev. J. William Jones tells the story in his diary about the time he and Rev. B.T. Lacy (Jackson's chaplain) called on Lee to tell him all the chaplains were praying for him. Lee's eyes filled with tears, Jones said, and he said "Please thank them for that, sir—I deeply appreciate it. And, I can only say that I am nothing but a poor sinner, trusting in Christ alone for salvation, and in need of all the prayers they can offer me."[49]

Lee, Stephen D. Lee was the postwar chairman of deacons and the building committee of the First Baptist Church of Columbus, MS. He was yet another prominent soldier who became conscious of religious concerns during the Civil

War. Although not baptized formally until 1868, Lee dated his belief in God to the Battle of Second Manassas, when Union troops charged his artillery guns. He was struck by the blunt fact that strong, robust men in good health one moment were struck down, torn apart and killed in the next. He thought the situation ghastly, and it was horrifying to even see his enemies torn apart in similar fashion. Lee concluded that "nothing but some unseen and superintending power" could tell him how all the carnage of battle would end.[50]

Lincoln, Abraham. There are many differences of opinion about what Lincoln believed and was influenced by in his faith and religion. Certainly he didn't worship publicly or formally in any denomination, and it is unclear whether he ever "accepted" Christianity for himself. One author writes that "Lincoln may have come to Christ late in his presidency, in 1863-1864, but evidence remains unclear."[51] He was never a man devoted to any formal religiosity, but was clearly one who nonetheless had deep faith, and had studied the Scriptures well. White says "there is widespread evidence that he was embracing a faith that would sustain him in times of stress and grief. The bulk of his reflection on the meaning of God and faith evolved in the context of the political questions and issues of the Civil War. Sometimes this was done in private . . . most often it was worked out in public addresses and comments."

Despite his lack of formal religiosity, few other leaders in history have developed so many religious themes so explicitly and yet with such complexity. His Second Inaugural is perhaps the best existing single statement of the role of religion and faith in the Civil War, and reveals his own religious beliefs as well. Lincoln's "theology" there is based upon an opposition to mere individualistic, isolated private faith; for him, reaching out to others (i.e., communitarian religion) is the essence of true faith. Religion had to be about ethics, and specifically the ethics of Love, not just mere emotion or theological jargon. In a famous quote, Lincoln once said he was ready to join any church that would inscribe above its altar as the sole qualification for membership the Great Commandment of Love (i.e., love of God, neighbor and self).[52]

Logan, John A. Union general, politician and Methodist. During the Atlanta Campaign, Logan stood as godfather for a Confederate widow's child. "Logan entered the shack to see some of his corps doctors aiding a young woman. He ordered soldiers to clean up the place. Then the baptism commenced with Logan holding the baby while the chaplain performed the ceremony. They christened her "Shell-Anna" because she was born amidst raining artillery fire."[53]

Longstreet, James. Lee's famous "Warhorse" became a scapegoat to the majority of the South after the war when he became a Republican and a government employee. Around March 1877 in New Orleans, in the midst of that ostracism, Longstreet converted to Catholicism, which certainly did not help his public image any. Despite writing virtually nothing of his religious beliefs, it was apparently a sincere personal faith decision which he remained devoutly faithful to until death.[54]

Loring, William W. Confederate general, Episcopalian (Wakelyn)

Lowry, Mark Perrin. One of the Confederate "fighting preachers," Lowry was a Baptist minister who frequently preached to his brigade from a rostrum. He was active in the Atlanta Campaign of spring 1864. Other Confederate "fighting parsons" were Isaac Tichenor at Shiloh (17th AL), Andrew Potter (26th TX Cavalry), and Thomas Duke at Chancellorsville (19th MS).[55]

MacArthur, Arthur. Union officer, Episcopalian.[56]

Mahone, William. Confederate general, Episcopalian (Wakelyn)

Mallory, Stephen. This Confederate Cabinet member, the Secretary of the Navy, was a Roman Catholic. He was a friend of Fr. John Bannon (chaplain of the First Missouri CSA Infantry) and was influential in getting Bannon commissioned to Ireland in 1863 to help prevent further Irish immigrants from joining the Northern armies. He married a Hispanic Catholic woman named Angela Moreno. (Jon Wakelyn, however, calls Mallory an Episcopalian.) [57]

Manly, Basil. Prominent Baptist preacher and educator. (Wakelyn)

McClellan, George B. This much maligned Union general was a Presbyterian, and experienced a religious conversion soon after his appointment to the command of the Army of the Potomoc. He subsequently resolved early in the war that his men would not work on the Sabbath if at all possible. In September 1861, "Little Mac" ordered that the "holy cause" the North was involved in required Sabbath observances in camp, and that divine services should be held on every Sunday morning that military necessity did not prevent such worship.[58]

Morgan, John Hunt. Confederate general, Episcopalian[59]

Mott, Lucretia. This well-known mid-nineteenth century feminist and her husband were both Quakers.

Mudd, Samuel. Catholic. While imprisoned at the Dry Tortugas for his supposed role in the Lincoln assassination, Mudd was visited occasionally by the Catholic Bishop of that area, Augustin Verot.

Northrop, Lucius B. Confederate Commissary General, Catholic (Wakelyn)

Ord, Edward O.C. This Maryland-born Union general was a Catholic. He and his less well-known war-time brother (Lt. Colonel Placidus Ord) were the sons of a former Jesuit seminary student named James Ord, who is described as having a mysterious and intriguing background. Supposedly, James Ord was the son of King George IV (1762–1873) and Mrs. Mary Ann Fitzhubert, and had been whisked away to New York shortly after his birth.[60]

Pegram, John. This Confederate general was Episcopalian. On March 13, 1864 (Passion Sunday) Pegram was one of fourteen Confederate generals in the Episcopal congregation of St. Paul's in Richmond. These generals along with the assembled congregation, heard the Rev. Dr. Charles Minnegerode cry aloud in a fiery speech "From lightning and tempest, from plague, pestilence, and famine, from battle, and murder, and from sudden death," and the congregation responded with "Good Lord, deliver us." On the next Sunday (Palm Sunday) Pegram, along with a host of Confederate officers, was confirmed by John Jones, the Bishop of Virginia.[61]

Pelham, John. This young Confederate artillery officer, called "The Gallant Pelham" for his military prowess and courage, was Presbyterian in denomination.[62]

Pemberton, John L. Of Quaker ancestry and upbringing, but whether he was a later-life Quaker in practice is questionable.[63]

Pender, Dorsey. Raised by non-church-going parents, Pender struggled to "find" religion, debating for two years on faith and works. The revivals of 1862–1863 in the Army of Northern Virginia touched him, however, and Pender became progressively more preoccupied with death and the need for personal sanctity and faithfulness. He was baptized in front of his troops, and then confirmed by the Episcopal bishop of Virginia. He seems to have seen being Christian as a matter of mastering his ruling passions—which he did not feel too successful in ("I was baptized . . . [but] I am not a Christian"). His religion, like his faith, seemed to be a romantic one.

Promoted to commander of the Light Division just before Gettysburg, his wife had a prophetic dream of riding in a hearse. Pender was wounded by an artillery shell on Seminary Ridge, and underwent a failed amputation. Robert E. Lee later said "we would have succeeded had General Pender lived." Pender's favorite Scripture verse is written above his head in the North Carolina church near where he is buried. "I have fought the good fight—I have kept the faith."[64]

Pendleton, William Nelson. After graduating from West Point (1830) and finishing three years of service, Pendleton left the army for a career as an Episcopal priest. He was Rector at Grace Church in Lexington, Virginia when the war broke out, becoming then a captain of the Rockbridge Artillery, and later a brigadier general and chief of artillery for Joseph Johnston and later Robert E. Lee. It is said that Pendleton once named his four six-pounder brass smoothbore cannon "Matthew, Mark, Luke and John." Soldiers under him later swore that when a cannon was aimed to his liking, he bowed his head & prayed "While we kill their bodies, may the Lord have mercy on their sinful souls—FIRE!"

Pendleton later became rector of Grace Episcopal Church in Lexington, Virginia where Robert E. Lee was a vestryman, but never quite made his "personal peace" with the North. Arrested for refusing to reinstate the prayer for the President, Pendleton remained angry at Southern defeat, strongly resisting Northern "occupation" of the South, and believing that the South suffered under "foreign domination" and persecution in ways comparable to first century Christians by the Romans.[65]

Pettigrew, James. Confederate General, Episcopalian (Wakelyn)

Polk, Leonidas. Born in Raleigh, NC, Polk was a 1827 West Point graduate (along with Albert Sidney Johnson in 1826 and Jefferson Davis in 1828), but resigned six months after graduation, was only briefly a Second Lieutenant, and (according to friends) never read a book on military affairs at all before the war. Supposedly Polk was converted by West Point chaplain Dr. Charles Pettit McIlwane (later an Episcopal bishop himself), and feeling called to a religious career, was ordained an Episcopalian priest, doing missionary work and eventually being appointed to the prestigious post of antebellum Senior Bishop of the Protestant Episcopal Church Southwest, working out of Louisiana. When the war broke out, Polk volunteered his services to his old friend Jefferson Davis, who made him a Major General.

This portly, dignified bishop (whose military skills were questionable) fought at Columbus (KY), Shiloh, Perryville, Stones River and Chickamauga before going to Georgia, and dying from a Union artillery barrage on June 14, 1864 at Pine Mountain. Two bloodied religious tracts were found in his pocket at his death, personally addressed to two of his latest converts—John Bell Hood and Joseph Johnston. The two generals took these tracts and kept them as mementoes after the war.[66]

Price, Sterling. Confederate General, Presbyterian (Wakelyn)

Ramseur, Stephen D. Confederate General, Presbyterian (Wakelyn)

Rhodes, Elisha Hunt. A strong Rhode Island Baptist, who after the war became a deacon and superintendent of the Sunday School at his church in Providence. Rhodes' memoirs *All for the Union* are full of references to his strong faith and deeply held-beliefs. He attended church regularly throughout the war whenever possible—even if it meant attending other denominations. At war's end, Rhodes was proud to say that no liquor had ever touched his mouth, and he had been graced to remain faithful while others had not.

Rosecrans, William S. This Union General was a devout Roman Catholic, embracing the faith while at West Point over the objections of his staunchly Methodist parents. He had a priest with him on campaigns (Fr. Jeremiah P. Trecy), and a brother Sylvester who was a priest and later auxiliary bishop of Cincinnati. Rosecrans made it a policy never to fight on Sundays, and followed that dictum scrupulously, even though it may have been detrimental to his military success. After the battle of Stone's River, despite a desperate all-day Saturday fight, he rested his army on Sunday before re-engaging the Confederates on Monday. God evidently honored his faithfulness, as the Confederate army retreated. His motto was "God never fails those who trust." Though known for drinking and swearing heavily, "old Rosy" increased the numbers of chaplains in his army. He and his staff often engaged in religious discussions, and at one point he kept them up until 4:00am for ten nights in a row doing this! He attended Mass daily.

Rosecrans could not escape the prejudices of the time about his Catholics. Charles Dana said this about him at Chickamauga, "I knew we were in trouble when I saw him cross himself." Dana did not care for Rosecrans, who later came under criticism by Protestants who feared that his religious concerns amounted to little more than pessimistic fatalism.[67]

Schofield, John M. This Union general, formerly a Baptist, was a convert to the Episcopalians.[68]

Semmes, Raphael. The Semmes family, with connections both in Maryland and Louisiana, was a strong Roman Catholic family. Raphael Semmes was a Confederate Admiral, his brother Thomas J. Semmes was Attorney General of Louisiana and state representative to the Confederate Congress, and his other brother Alexander J. Semmes became a priest after having been married and given up a brilliant medical career.[69]

Shaw, Robert Gould. Union Colonel of the famed 54th Massachusetts Infantry, Unitarian. Shaw's parents were Unitarians and freely associated with ministers William Channing and Theodore Parker at Brook Farm. Shaw attended Catholic school but protested against his mother's urging him to declare his Unitarianism to his classmates. "I'm sure I wouldn't be afraid of saying we were Unitarians if there could be any kind of use in it, but, as it is, it would bring up discussions and conversations which would be very tiresome, and as I don't want to become a reformer, apostle or anything of that kind, there is no use doing disagreeable things for nothing."[70]

Sheridan, Phillip. Roman Catholic. Born in Ireland, though he spoke later in life at having "been born in Albany, New York"—most likely because, as a foreign-born Irishman, he wouldn't have been eligible for the Presidency![71]

Sherman, William T. As one biographer aptly phrases it, "Sherman's religious leanings were and still are a matter of conjecture."[72] Though baptized as "William" by his strongly religious Catholic mother, Sherman later described himself as "not scrupulous in matters of religion." His wife Ellen was the strongest religious influence in his life. While courting her in 1843, he promised he would examine the doctrines of the Catholic faith "with an honest heart and a wish to believe, if possible", and during their marriage he always supported his wife's beliefs and his children being raised Catholic—but he never showed any serious interest in issues of religion or faith. He probably was, in fact, the source of Ellen's 1854 journal comment, "Prayed for the conversion, etc."

Still, during the War Sherman attended church services from time to time— as in 1864 in Savannah when he attended an Episcopalian service. But in May 1878, Sherman grew quite angry at the Catholic Church when his twenty-one-year old son Tom abandoned the legal career Sherman had laid out for him, deciding instead to become a Jesuit priest, and studying in a European seminary. Sherman wrote "he is absolutely lost to me," and called his son a "deserter" to their family in its time of need. Still, despite his irreligiosity, he received the Catholic sacrament of Extreme Unction on his deathbed in February 1891.[73]

Shields, James. This Irish foreign-born Union general and senator of three different states at different times, was a Catholic.[74]

Shoup, Francis Asbury. This Episcopalian Confederate general was Hood's Chief of Staff in 1864 and became an ordained priest after the war. He later married a daughter of Episcopal bishop Stephen Eliot, received a doctorate in divinity, taught mathematics and was acting chaplain at the University of the South in Sewanee, Georgia.[75]

Smith, Edmund Kirby. This Confederate general was a devout Episcopalian. Quintard describes him in his journal: "He was kindly, big-hearted, and no man was a better friend. During the war, whenever opportunity offered, he held services and officiated as lay-reader. He entered upon his duties in the University of the South in 1875, as a Professor of Mathematics and gave a great deal of attention to botany and natural science. He died as he lived—bright, strong in his Christian faith and hope. One of his last connected utterances was on the fourth verse from the twenty-third Psalm."

This Confederate general believed that God had spread confusion among the Northern host at the moment when victory at First Manassas had seemed certain for them. This was a proof for him that the Confederacy could not win the war by force of arms alone, but only through divine intervention of its behalf. He also was upset at the heavy drinking in the army, because it would arouse divine displeasure and cause the downfall of the Confederate nation.[76]

Smith, Gustavus W. Confederate general, Baptist[77]

Sojourner Truth. Member of the historic African Methodist Episcopal Zion Church. Raised in Ulster County, New York with the given name of Isabella Van Wagener, she escaped slavery in 1827. Isabella was an early adherent of Methodism, but her mystic personality led her to fall into the allurements of various religious charlatans, and she spent several early years attached to the cultic ministries of New York based Elijah Pierson ("the Tishbite") and Robert Matthews ("Matthias"). In 1843 she took the name Sojourner Truth and began traveling east, spreading a simple Gospel message of a loving God.

Her deep-toned speech, marked by a Dutch accent, challenged and captivated anti-slavery audiences for many years. Truth had a tall frame and somewhat masculine features, and this led to occasional rumors and at least one amusing incident. At an Indiana women's right convention, when charged with merely masquerading as a woman, she bared her breasts before a stunned crowd to prove her God-given femininity. She died in 1883 in Battle Creek, MI, and her funeral there was said to have been the biggest ever seen in that area.[78]

Stanley, David Sloane. This Ohio-born Union general was a Catholic.[79]

Stanton, Edwin M. Union Secretary of War, Methodist[80]

Stephens, Alexander. Confederate Vice-President, Presbyterian[81]

Stewart, Alexander P. Although this Confederate general was named a Methodist by Wakelyn, according to other probably more reliable sources, he was Presbyterian. John Brinsfield, Jr. mentions that Stewart was a Presbyterian elder who assisted at the administration of the Lord's Supper for Confederate troops. While still a plebe at West Point, Stewart wrote to his sister Catherine, "But we must submit to the decrees of Heaven and learn to bless the hand that afflicts us, for it is for our own benefit; at least I suppose so: and I hope the consideration of that religion you profess will in a great measure alleviate your grief."[82]

Stowe, Harriet Beecher Stowe. Daughter of Lyman Beecher, she married Calvin Stowe, a student at her father's Lane Theological Seminary (Cincinnati). After her husband got a teaching job at Bowdoin College in Maine, she moved there, becoming a writer. Her classic 1854 *Uncle Tom's Cabin* led Abraham Lincoln to remark upon meeting her, "so here is the woman whose little book helped start this great war."

Strong, George Templeton. Prominent diarist and treasurer of the U.S. Sanitary Commission, Strong was a devout Episcopalian.[83]

Stringfellow, Thorton. This Baptist minister from Culpepper Country, Virginia published in 1856 one of the most influential and widely distributed theological articles in support of slavery (*Slavery—A Theological View*). In it, Stringfellow said "I affirm then, first (and no man denies), that Jesus Christ has not abolished slavery by a prohibitory command." [84]

Stuart, James E.B. According to Gordon Shattuck, Stuart was "celebrated for his outstanding piety." In the words of Tony Horowitz in *Confederates in the Attic*, Stuart was a teetotaler and a devout Christian, though he cultivated the image of a wanton Cavalier, with his extravagantly coiffed beard, silken yellow sash, crimson-lined cape and ostrich plume poking from his slouch hat.[85]

Sweeney, Thomas F. This Union general, 2nd Division commander in McPherson's 16th Corps, was a strong Catholic. Sweeney had the 2nd and 6th IA under him during the Atlanta Campaign, and fought at Lay's Ferry on the Oostanaula River.[86]

Taliaferro, William B. Confederate general, Episcopalian (Wakelyn)

Taney, Roger Brooke. President Andrew Jackson's Secretary of the Treasury (1833-1835), and later Chief Justice of the Supreme Court from 1836-1864. A Roman Catholic, he attempted to steer a middle course on state's rights issues, and was Chief Justice when the infamous Dred Scott decision was decided in 1857.[87]

Taylor, Richard. Confederate general, Episcopalian (Wakelyn)

Thomas, George. With his Episcopalian father and his Huguenot mother, this Virginian-turned-Union general was most likely baptized in, and later professed himself to be an Episcopalian. He married an Episcopalian woman in a religious service in St. Paul's Episcopal Church in Troy, New York. However it seems Thomas was not a regular, faithful churchgoer, except for holydays such as Christmas and Easter.

Thornwell, James Henley. South Carolina's leading theologian, Thornwell was a key pre-war proslavery author, and a Presbyterian minister. He published many works in the influential *Southern Presbyterian Review*, and also helped set up the separate southern wing of the Presbyterian Church.

Toombs, Robert A. Confederate Secretary of State, Episcopalian (Wakelyn)

Tubman, Harriet. This deeply religious woman, a member of the African Methodist Episcopal Zion Church, helped more than 300 runaway slaves escape to freedom through the "underground railroad", including her own parents and siblings. She was fierce in her determination to bring them to freedom, doing whatever she had to do in this process, including carrying a gun and the drug laudanum while helping slaves escape!

Turner, Nat. Born into slavery on a Virginia plantation, his master Benjamin Turner was a committed Methodist, eager to have his slaves become Christian. Thus, Nat was taught to read and write in order to understand the Christian Biblical message. After Benjamin Turner died, Nat belonged to four different masters before he was twenty-five years of age. He studied the Bible faithfully, fasted and prayed, and was "gifted" with strong visionary tendencies.

Turner began preaching in local "black praise" meetings (allowed by his owners), becoming known as "The Prophet." In 1825, he believed that God had given him a vision of impending end of the world, and he awaited a sign of its coming. On August 13, 1831, there was an atmospheric disturbance in which the sun appeared to change colors. It was the sign Turner had awaited, and on August 21, he and six others began a short-loved (forty-eight hour) slave uprising. Though he avoided capture for two months, Turner was eventually caught, convicted and hung on November 11, 1831.[88]

Van Dorn, Earl. This Confederate general (killed by a jealous husband) is called a Presbyterian by one author (Wakelyn) but Episcopalian by another.[89]

Watie, Stand. Confederate general, Cherokee chief and Moravian [90]

Welles, Gideon. Union Secretary of the Navy, Episcopalian [91]

Wheeler, Joseph. Confederate general, Episcopalian [92]

Whiting, William H.C. A pre-war captain in the Army Corps of Engineers, Whiting became a Confederate general, and was a Roman Catholic. (Wakelyn)

Willard, Frances. The Civil War temperance cause never had a bigger advocate than Frances Willard, an active member of the Methodists. Born in New York and raised in Wisconsin, Willard cut her hair short, preferred to be called "Frank," and grew into a self-assured speaker and leader on the "new" social issue of drinking and liquor. In 1874, professedly emboldened by the Holy Spirit's movement during a winter campaign across NY and OH, she became instrumental in creating the *Women's Christian Temperance Movement*, becoming its first President in 1879. Capitalizing on the Victorian assumption that a woman's place was the home, Willard rallied great support not only around temperance but also women's suffrage. Even after her 1898 death, she continued to receive adulation, including the placing of her statue in Washington in 1905.[93]

Wood, S.A.M. Confederate general, Catholic.[94]

Notes

1. Robert Joseph Murphy, "The Catholic Church in the United States during the Civil War Period," *Records of the American Catholic Historical Society,* vol. 39, no. 4, (December 1928). Cf. also Charles Quintard, *Doctor Quintard, Chaplain CSA and Second Bishop of Tennessee,* Sam Davis Elliot, editor (Baton Rouge, LA: Louisiana State University Press, 2003), 101.

2. Alexander, Edward Porter, *Fighting for the Confederacy—The Personal Recollections of General Edward Porter Alexander,* Gary Gallagher, editor (Chapel Hill: University of North Carolina Press, 1989), 59.

3. Jon L. Wakelyn, *Biographical Dictionary of the Confederacy* (Westport, CT: Greenwood Press, 1977), 529–533. Cf. also Thomas M. Owen, "Alabama," *The Catholic Encyclopedia, Volume I,* http://www.newadvent.org/cathen/01240a.htm (2006); and Murphy, *op. cit.*

4. James G. Hollandsworth, Jr., *Pretense of Glory: The Life of General Nathaniel P. Banks* (Baton Rouge: Louisiana State University Press, 1998).

5. Bell I. Wiley, *The Life of Johnny Reb* (Baton Rouge: Louisiana State University Press, 1943); Michael Perko, *Catholic and American—A Popular History* (Huntington, IN: Our Sunday Visitor Publishing, 1989), and Murphy, *op. cit.*

6. Sidney Ahlstrom, *Religious History of the American People* (New Haven, Conn.: Yale University Press, 1972), 421–422.

7. Nina Brown Baker, *Cyclone in Calico* (Boston: Brown and Co., 1952).

8. Quintard, *op. cit.,* 69–70; Gardiner Shattuck, Jr., *A Shield and Hiding Place: The Religious Life of the Civil War Armies* (Macon, GA: Mercer University Press, 1987).

9. Murphy, *op. cit.*

10. William C. Davis, *Breckinridge, Statesman, Soldier, Symbol* (Baton Rouge: Louisiana State University Press, 1974).

11. Mark A. Noll, Nathan Hatch, George Marsden, David Wells and John Woodbridge, eds., *Eerdmans' Handbook to Christianity in America* (Grand Rapids, MI: Eerdman's Publishing Company, 1983); Mark Galli, "Firebrands and Visionaries," *Christian History;* vol. 11, no. 1 (1992).

12. Dick Nolan, *Benjamin Franklin Butler, the Damnedest Yankee* (Novato CA: Presidio Press, 1991).

13. Henry Clay letter to William A. Booth, 7 April 1845, in *The Works of Henry Clay*, ed. Calvin Colvin, 6 vols. (New York, 1857), as cited in C. C. Goen, *Broken Churches, Broken Nation—Denominational Schisms and the Coming of the Civil War* (Macon, GA: Mercer University Press, 1985), 101 and 105–6.

14. Murphy, *op. cit.*, 101.

15. D. A. Kinsley, *Custer: Favor the Bold* (New York: Promontory Press, 1988). Cf. also Paul Kensey, *George Armstrong Custer—American Hero or Just a Fool*, Civil War Roundtable of Australia, http://www.americancivilwar.asn.au/meet/2004_04_Custer.pdf (April 2004).

16. Wallace Hettle, "The Minister, the Martyr and the Maxim," *Civil War History* 49, no. 4 (December 2003), 353; and Shattuck, *op. cit.*, 117. For a fascinating story about Dabney, read pages 38–39 of Steven Woodworth, *While God is Marching On—The Religious Life of Civil War Soldiers* (Lawrence: University Press of Kansas, 2001), 38–39.

17. Randall M. Miller, Harry S. Stout, and Charles R. Wilson, eds., *Religion and the American Civil War* (New York: Oxford Press, 1998), 24 and 409; Shattuck, *op. cit.*, 107; and Wakelyn, *op.cit.*

18. Louis Hippolyte Gache, *A Frenchman, a Chaplain, a Rebel—the Civil War Letters of Pere Louis Hippolyte Gache, SJ*, edited by Cornelius Buckley (Chicago: Loyola University Press, 1981), 179–80 and 186. Cf. also Wakelyn, *op. cit.*

19. Gerard Patterson, *Debris of Battle* (Mechanicsburg, PA: Stackpole Books, 1997), 100–105.

20. Paul Finkelman, ed., *Encyclopedia of African American History 1619–1895*, vol. 1: A–E (New York: Oxford University Press, 2006); and Galli, *op. cit.*

21. Kevin J. Weddle, *Lincoln's Tragic Admiral* (Charlottesville: University of Virginia Press, 2005).

22. Hettle, *op. cit.*, 425; E. M. Boswell, "Rebel Religion," *Civil War Times Illustrated* 11, no. 8 (October 1972). I am also grateful to James McPherson for his personal insights on Ewell's faith.

23. James B. Sheeran, *Confederate Chaplain—A Military Journal*, edited by Joseph T. Durkin (Milwaukee: Bruce Publishing, 1960), 58 and 74–77.

24. Murphy, *op. cit.*, and David and Jeanne Heidler, eds., *Encyclopedia of the American Civil War* (New York: W.W. Norton and Company, 2000).

25. Quintard, *op. cit.*, 53.

26. Quintard, *op. cit.*, 106.

27. Andrew Rolle, *John Charles Fremont* (Norman: University of Oklahoma Press, 1991).

28. John Patrick Daly, "Holy War—Southern Religion and the Road to War and Defeat, 1861–1865," *North and South* 6, no. 6 (September 2003), 34–45.

29. Carter, *op. cit.*

30. Reid Mitchell, *Civil War Soldiers* (New York: Penguin Books, 1988), 113.

31. Shattuck, *op. cit.*, 105, 12; and Wakelyn, *op. cit.*

32. Shattuck, *op. cit.*, 106.

33. Quintard, *op. cit.*, 189.

34. Shattuck, *op. cit.*, 104; and Jeffrey Warren Scot, "Fighters of Faith," *Christian History*, 11, no. 1 (1992), 36–37.

35. Lydia Boyd, *Rose O'Neal Greenhow Papers—As On-Line Archival Collection*, Duke University Special Collections Library, http://scriptorium.lib.duke.edu/greenhow (May 1996); and Wakelyn, *op. cit.*

36. David M. Jordan, *Winfield Scott Hancock: A Soldier's Life* (Bloomington: Indiana University Press, 1988).

37. John W. Brinsfield, Jr., *The Spirit Divided—Memoirs of Civil War Chaplains* (Macon, GA: Mercer University Press, 2006), 191; Perko, *op. cit.*, 199; and Wakelyn, *op. cit.* I am grateful to Bruce Allerdice (Chicago Civil War Round Table) for his insights here.

38. William Woods Hassler, *A. P. Hill—Lee's Forgotten General* (Chapel Hill: University of North Carolina Press, 1957), 172–74.

39. Shattuck, *op. cit.*, 105 and 119, also Wakelyn, *op. cit.*

40. Wakelyn, *op. cit.*, and Shattuck, *op. cit.*, 103.

41. The story of Holmes' Ball's Bluff wound is found at Woodworth's *While God Is Marching On, op. cit.*, 64 (footnote #3, p. 306). Cf. also Miller, *op. cit.*, 36; and James McPherson, *Abraham Lincoln and the Second American Revolution* (New York: Oxford University Press, 1991), 68. Holmes' father, Dr. Oliver Wendell Holmes, was a prominent Unitarian and professor of medicine who, with other Harvard Unitarians (Longfellow, John Quincy Adams, etc.) helped make Harvard a major force in the liberal Unitarian movement (Cf. Ahlstrom, *op. cit.*, 398; Heidler and Heidler, *op. cit.*, 988).

42. Miller, *op. cit.*, 194; Shattuck, *op. cit.*, 76; and Scott, *op. cit.* Again I am grateful to James McPherson for his clarifying insights on Howard's religion.

43. Murphy, *op. cit.*

44. James I. Robertson, *Stonewall Jackson—The Man, The Solider, The Legend* (New York: MacMillian Publishers, 1997), 684; and Scott, *op. cit.*

45. Murphy, *op. cit.*

46. Quintard, *op. cit.*, 63–64.

47. I am grateful to Bruce Allardice of the Chicago Civil War Round Table for his insight on Kershaw.

48. Wakelyn, *op. cit.*; also Wikipedia—The Free Encyclopedia, *James H. Lane* http://en.wikipedia.org/wiki/James_H_Lane_%28general%29 (4 December, 2006).

49. Ted Baehr and Susan Wales, *Faith in God and Generals* (New York: Broadman and Holman, 2003), 84–100. Cf. also Scott, "Fighters of Faith," *op. cit.*

50. Shattuck, *op. cit.*, 98; and "History of the First Baptist Church from 1832–2003," http://www.columbusfbc.org/history/historyframe.htm (2003).

51. Woodworth, *op. cit.*, 268.

52. Ronald C. White, *Lincoln's Greatest Speech* (New York: Simon and Schuster, 2002), 208; cf. also Woodworth, *op. cit.*, 268.

53. Gary Ecelbarger, *Black Jack Logan* (Guilford, CT: The Lyons Press, 2005).

54. Jeffry D. Wert, *General James Longstreet—The Confederacy's Most Controversial Soldier* (New York: Simon and Schuster, 1993), 18. I also am grateful for the personal witness of Dan Paterson, Longstreet's great-grandson, and head of *The Longstreet Society*.

55. John W. Brinsfield, Jr., William C. Davis, Benedict Maryniak, and James I. Robertson, Jr., *Faith in Fight—Civil War Chaplains* (Mechanicsburg, PA: Stackpole Books, 2003), 83–84. Brinsfield's new book, *The Spirit Divided* has more extensive summaries of some of the War's "fighting chaplains." Cf. Brinsfield, *op. cit.*, 98–111.

56. Kenneth R. Young, *The General's General: The Life and Times of Arthur MacArthur* (Boulder, CO: Westview Press, 1994).

57. Cf. William Barnaby Faherty, *Exile from Erin—A Confederate Chaplain's Story, the Life of Fr. John B. Bannon* (St. Louis: Missouri Historical Press, 2000). I am again grateful to Bruce Allardice (Chicago Civil War Round Table) for insights here.

58. Shattuck, *op. cit.*, 76. I am grateful to James McPherson for insights here as well.

59. James A. Ramage, *Rebel Raider: The Life of John Hunt Morgan* (Lexington: University Press of Kentucky, 1986).

60. Gache, *op. cit.*, 228; Wakelyn, *op. cit.*; and Murphy, *op. cit.*

61. Walter S. Griggs, Jr., *General John Pegram, C.S.A.* (Lynchburg, VA: H. E. Howard, Inc., 1993).

62. Charles G. Milham, *Gallant Pelham* (Washington, DC: Public Affairs Press, 1959).

63. Wakelyn, *op. cit.*, I am grateful to Bruce Allardice for his insights here.

64. Dorsey Pender and his wife's deep faith are spoken of in depth in Kent Gramm, *Gettysburg—Meditation on War & Values* (Bloomington: Indiana University Press, 1994), 210–37. Cf. also Shattuck, *op. cit.*, 98.

65. Shattuck, *op. cit.*, 115; Webb Garrison, *Civil War Curiosities—Strange Stories, Oddities, Events and Coincidences* (Nashville, TN: Rutledge Hill Press, 1994), 49; Scott "Fighters of Faith," *op. cit.*; and Kent T. Dollar, *Soldiers of the Cross—Confederate Soldier-Christians and the Impact of War on Their Faith* (Macon, GA: Mercer University Press, 2005).

66. Joseph H. Parks, *General Leonidas Polk, C.S.A.—The Fighting Bishop* (Baton Rouge: Louisiana State University Press, 1962). I am grateful to Bruce Allardice for his insights here as well.

67. Peter Cozzens, *No Better Place to Die* (Chicago: University of Illinois Press, 1991), 18; Shattuck, *op. cit.*, 79; and Scott, "Fighters of Faith," *op. cit.*

68. Donald B. Connelly, *John M. Schofield and the Politics of Generalship* (Chapel Hill: University of North Carolina Press, 2006).

69. Perko, *op. cit.*, 199; Wakelyn, *op. cit.*; Murphy, *op. cit.*; Buckley, *op. cit.*, 113f.

70. Peter Burchard, *One Gallant Rush* (New York: St. Martin's Press, 1965).

71. Perko, *op. cit.*, 199.

72. Lee Kenneth, *Sherman* (New York: Harper Collins, 2001), 6.

73. Kennth, *passim*; Woodworth, *op. cit.*, 249.

74. Murphy, *op. cit.*, and Heidler and Heidler, *op. cit.*

75. Wakelyn, *op. cit.*,and Quintard, *op. cit.*, 88 and 146.

76. Quintard, *op. cit.*, 56–57; Shattuck, *op. cit.*, 106.

77. Leonne M. Hudson, *The Odyssey of a Southerner: The Life and Times of Gustavus Woodson Smith* (Macon, GA: Mercer University Press, 1998).

78. Chris Armstrong, "People Worth Knowing—No Little Women Here," *Christian History and Biography* 81 (January 1, 2004), 43–45.

79. Murphy, *op. cit.*; and Heidler and Heidler, *op. cit.*

80. Benjamin P. Thomas and Harold M. Hyman, *Stanton: The Life and Times of Lincoln's Secretary of War* (New York: Alfred A. Knopf, 1962).

81. Wakelyn, *op. cit.* I am grateful to Bruce Allardice for his insights here as well.

82. Sam Davis Elliott, *General Alexander P. Stewart and the Civil War in the West* (Baton Rouge: Louisiana State University Press, 1999); Brinsfield, *The Spirit Divided, op. cit.*, 190; and Wakelyn, *op. cit.*

83. Heidler and Heidler, *op. cit.*

84. John Patrick Daly, "Holy War—Southern Religion and the Road to War and Defeat, 1861–1865," *North and South* 6, no. 6 (September 2003), 34–45.

85. Tony Horowitz, *Confederates in the Attic* (New York: Vintage Books, 1999), 239; and Shattuck, *op. cit.*, 105.

86. Murphy, *op. cit.*

87. Warren B. Armstrong, *For Courageous Fighting and Confident Dying* (Lawrence: University of Kansas Press, 1998), 117.

88. Mark A. Noll, Nathan Hatch, George Marsden, David Wells, and John Woodbridge, eds., *Eerdman's Handbook to Christianity in America* (Grand Rapids, MI: Eerdman's Publishing Company, 1983), 264.

89. Robert G. Hartje, *Van Dorn: The Life and Times of a Confederate General* (Nashville, TN: Vanderbilt University Press, 1967).

90. Kenny A. Franks, *Stand Watie and the Agony of the Cherokee Nation* (Memphis, TN: Memphis State University Press, 1979).

91. John Niven, *Gideon Welles: Lincoln's Secretary of the Navy* (New York: Oxford University Press, 1979).

92. John P. Dyer, *Fightin' Joe Wheeler* (Baton Rouge: Louisiana State University Press, 1941).

93. Armstrong, *op. cit.* I am grateful to Bruce Allardice for his insights here.

94. Murphy, *op. cit.*; cf. also Thomas M. Owen, "Alabama," *The Catholic Encyclopedia Volume I*, http://www.newadvent.org/cathen/01240a.htm (2006).

Select Bibliography

Aamodt, Terrie D. *Righteous Armies, Holy Causes: Apocalyptic Imagery and the Civil War.* Macon, GA: Mercer University Press, 2002.

Ahlstrom, Sydney. *Religious History of the American People.* New Haven, CT: Yale University Press, 1972.

Armstrong, Warren B. *For Courageous Fighting and Confident Dying.* Lawrence: University of Kansas Press, 1998.

Ayers, Edward, ed. *A House Divided —A Century of Great Civil War Quotations.* New York: John Wiley and Sons, 1997.

Baehr, Ted, and Susan Wales. *Faith in God and Generals.* New York: Broadman and Holman, 2003.

Baker, Liva. "The Burning of Chambersburg." Pp. 165–173 in *The Civil War—The Best of American Heritage,* edited by Stephen Sears. New York: American Heritage Press, 1991.

Baird, Robert. *Religion in America—The Origin, Relation to the State and Present Condi tion of the Evangelical Churches in the United States.* New York: Harper and Brothers, 1856.

Barone, Michael. "A Place Like No Other." *U.S. News and World Report,* June 28, 2004: 38–39.

Bennett, William. *Narrative of the Great Revival in the Southern Armies During the Late Civil War between the States of the Federal Union.* Harrisonburg, VA: Sprinkle Publications, 1989.

Berry, Stephen. "When Metal Meets Mettle—The Hard Realities of Civil War Soldiering." *North and South* 9, no. 4 (August 2006): 12–21.

Billingsley, Andrew. *Mighty Like a River—The Black Church and Social Reform.* New York: Oxford University Press, 1999.

Blied, Benjamin. *Catholics and the Civil War.* Milwaukee: Bruce Publishing Company, 1945.

Blight, David W. *Race and Reunion—The Civil War in American Memory.* Cambridge, MA: Belknap Press, 2001.

Blum, Edward. "Grapes of Wrath." *Books and Culture* (March/April 2006): 15–22.

Bonekemper, Edward H. *How Robert E. Lee Lost the Civil War.* Spotsylvania, VA: Sergeant Kirkland's Press, 1999.

———. *A Victor, Not a Butcher—Ulysses S. Grant's Overlooked Military Genius.* New York: Regnery Publishing Company, 2005.

Boswell, E.M. "Rebel Religion." *Civil War Times Illustrated* 11, no. 8 (October 1972): 26–33.

Brinsfield, John W., William C. Davis, Benedict Maryniak, and James I. Robertson, Jr., *Faith in the Fight—Civil War Chaplains.* Mechanicsburg, PA: Stackpole Books, 2003.

Brinsfield, John Wesley. *The Spirit Divided—Memoirs of Civil War Chaplains, The Confederacy.* Macon, GA: Mercer University Press, 2006.

Burton, William L. *Melting Pot Soldiers—The Union's Ethnic Regiments.* New York: Fordham University Press, 1998.

Carmichael, Peter. "So Far from God, So Close to Stonewall." *Civil War Times* 42, no. 2 (June 2003): 42–77.

Carter, Alden R. *Bright Starry Banner*. New York: Soho Press, 2003.

Carwardine, Richard J. *Evangelicals and Politics in Antebellum America*. New Haven, CT: Yale University Press, 1993.

Chesebrough, David B. *Clergy Dissent in the Old South, 1830-1865*. Carbondale: Southern Illinois University Press, 1996.

Connelly, Thomas L., and Barbara L. Bellows. *God and General Longstreet—The Lost Cause and the Southern Mind*. Baton Rouge, LA: Louisiana State University Press, 1982.

Coppersmith, Andrew S. "Battlelines and Headlines—The Debate over 'Negro Soldiers.'" *North and South* 9, no. 4 (August 2006): 72–82.

Crowther, Edward R. *Southern Evangelicals and the Coming of the Civil War*. Lewiston, NY: Edward Mellen Press, 2000.

Cummings, Kathleen Sprows. "The Real Secrets of Charleston." *American Catholic Studies Newsletter* 28, No. 2 (Fall 2001): 13–15.

Curry, Andrew. "The Better Angels." *U.S. News and World Report*, September 30, 2002: 58–63.

Daly, John Patrick. "Holy War—Southern Religion and the Road to War and Defeat, 1861–1865." *North and South* 6, no. 6 (September 2003): 34–45.

———. *When Slavery Was Called Freedom*. Lexington: University Press of Kentucky, 2002.

Daniel, W. Harrison. "The Southern Baptists in the Confederacy." *Civil War History* 6, no. 4 (1960): 389–401.

———. "The Effects of the Civil War on Southern Protestantism." *Maryland Historical Magazine* 69 (1974): 47–48.

Davis, Allen F., and Harold D. Woodman, eds. *Conflict and Consensus in Early American History*. Washington, DC: Heath and Company, 1988.

Davis, Cyprian. *The History of Black Catholics in the United States*. New York: Crossroad Publishing Company, 2000.

———. "The Black Catholic Experience." *U.S. Catholic Historian* 5, no. 1 (1986): 1–17.

Davis, Kenneth C. *Don't Know Much About the Civil War*. New York: Perennial Books, 2001.

Dollar, Kent T. *Soldiers of the Cross—Confederate Soldier-Christians and the Impact of War on Their Faith*. Macon, GA: Mercer University Press, 2005.

Dyer, Gwynne. *War*. New York: Crown Publishers, 1985.

Ellis, John Tracy. *Documents of American Catholic History*. Milwaukee: Bruce Publishing Company, 1956.

Escott, Paul, Lawrence Powell, James I. Robertson, Jr. and Emory Thomas, eds. *Encyclopedia of the Confederacy*, vol. 4. New York: Simon and Schuster, 2002.

Ethier, Eric. "Who Was the Common Soldier of the Civil War?" *Civil War Times* 42, no. 5 (December 2003): 52–53.

Faust, Drew Gilpin. "Christian Soldiers: The Meaning of Revivalism in the Confederate Army." *Journal of Southern History* 53, No. 1 (February 1987): 63–90.

———. "The Civil War Soldier and the Art of Dying." *The Journal of Southern History* 67, no. 1 (February 2001): 3–38.

Finkelman, Paul, ed. *Encyclopedia of African American History 1619–1895*, vol. 1 (A-E). New York: Oxford University Press, 2006.

Fordham, Monroe. *Major Themes in Northern Black Religious Thought, 1800–1860.* Hicksville, NY: Exposition Press, 1975.

Garrison, Webb. *Civil War Curiosities—Strange Stories, Oddities, Events and Coincidences.* Nashville, TN: Rutledge Hill Press, 1994.

Genovese, Eugene. *Roll, Jordan, Roll—The World the Slaves Made.* New York: Vintage Books, 1974.

Genovese, Eugene and Fox-Genovese, Elizabeth. *The Mind of the Master Class—History and Faith in the Southern Slaveholders' Worldview.* New York: Cambridge University Press, 2005.

———. "The Religious Ideals of Southern Slave Society." *Georgia Historical Quarterly* 70, no. 1 (Spring 1986): 1–16.

Germain, Aidan. *Catholic Military and Naval Chaplains—1776-1917.* Washington, DC: Catholic University of America, 1929.

Gleason, Edward. *Erin Go Gray!* Carmel, IN: Guild Press of Indiana, 1997.

———. *Rebel Sons of Erin—A Civil War Unit History of the 10th TN Irish Infantry CSA Volunteers.* Carmel, IN: Guild Press of Indiana, 1993.

Goen C.C. *Broken Churches, Broken Nation - Denominational Schisms and the Coming of the Civil War.* Macon, GA: Mercer University Press, 1985.

Gorley, Bruce T. "Recent Historiography on Religion and the Civil War." Christian History Institute. http:www.gospelcom.net/chi/HERITAGF/Issuenos/ch11033.shtml (1999).

Gramm, Kent. *Gettysburg—Meditation on War & Values.* Bloomington, IN: Indiana University Press, 1994.

Grant, Susan-Mary. "Landscapes of Memory." *History Today* 56, no. 3 (March 2006): 18–20.

Guelzo, Allen C. "Free to Do What?" *Books and Culture* 9, No. 4 (July/August 2003): 30–32.

Hackett, Horatio. *Christian Memorials of the War.* Concord VA: RMJC Publications, 2002.

Hattaway, Herman and Lloyd Hunter. "The War Inside the Church." *Civil War Times Illustrated* 26 (January 1988): 28–33.

Hayes, Frederic H. *Michigan Catholics in the Era of the Civil War.* Lansing, MI: The Michigan Civil War Centennial Observance Commission, 1965.

Heidler, David, and Jeanne Heidler, eds. *Encyclopedia of the American Civil War.* New York: W.W. Norton and Company, 2000.

Hennessey, James. *American Catholics—A History of the Roman Catholic Community in the United States.* New York: Oxford University Press, 1981.

Henry. James O. "The United States Christian Commission in the Civil War." *Civil War History* 6, no. 4 (1960): 374–388.

Hill, Samuel S. *The South and the North in American Religion.* Athens, GA: University of Georgia Press, 1980.

———. *Southern Churches in Crisis Revisited.* Tuscaloosa, AL: University of Alabama, 1999.

Hill, Samuel S., and Charles H. Lippy. *Encyclopedia of Religion in the South.* Macon, GA: Mercer University Press, 2005.

Honeywell, Roy J. *Chaplains of the United States Army.* Washington, DC: Office of the Chief of Chaplains, Department of the Army, 1958.

Horowitz, Tony. *Confederates in the Attic.* New York: Vintage Books, 1999.

Huggins, Nathan Irvin. *Black Odyssey—The African-American Ordeal in Slavery.* New York: Vintage Books, 1990.

Humence, Belinda, ed. *My Folks Don't Want Me to Talk About Slavery.* Winston-Salem, NC: John H. Blair Publishers, 1984.

Johnson, Curtis D. *Redeeming America—Evangelicals and the Road to the Civil War.* Chicago: Ivan R. Dee, 1993.

Johnson, Paul E., ed. *African-American Christianity—Essays in History.* Berkeley: University of California Press, 1994.

Jones, John William. *Christ in Camp—The True Story of the Great Revival during the War Between the States.* Harrisonburg, VA: Sprinkle Publications, 1986.

Jones, Preston. "Planet Dixie." *Books and Culture* 9, no. 4 (July/August 2003): 28–29.

Katcher, Philip. *Civil War Source Book.* New York: Facts on File Publishers, 1992.

Kirkham, E. Kay. *A Survey of American Church Records.* Salt Lake City: Deseret Book Company, 1959.

Korn, Bertram M. *American Jewry and the Civil War.* Philadelphia, PA: Jewish Publication Society, 1951.

Levene, Helene H. "Illinois Catholics in the Civil War." *Illinois Civil War Sketches,* Number 2 (June 1963).

Levine, Alan J. *Race Relation with Western Expansion.* Westport, CT: Praeger Press, 1996.

Linderman, Gerald. *Embattled Courage: The Experience of Combat in the American Civil War.* New York: Simon and Schuster, 1987.

Lonn, Ella. *Foreigners in the Union Army and Navy.* Baton Rouge, LA: Louisiana State University Press, 1951.

Mays, Benjamin and Joseph William Nicholson. *The Negro's Church.* New York: Arno Press and New York Times, 1969.

McBrien, Richard. *Catholicism.* Minneapolis: Winston Press, 1980.

McKenzie, Steven L. *All God's Children—A Biblical Critique of Racism.* Louisville: Westminster Press, 1997.

McKim, Randolph. *A Soldiers Recollections—Leaves from the Diary of a Young Confederate.* New York: privately published, 1910.

McPherson, James M. *Abraham Lincoln and the Second American Revolution.* New York: Oxford University Press, 1991.

———. *For Cause and Comrades—Why Men Fought in the Civil War.* New York: Oxford University Press, 1997.

———. *The Negroes Civil War.* New York: Ballantine Books, 1991.

Mead, Frank, and Samuel S. Hill. *Handbook of Denominations in the United States (11th Edition).* Nashville, TN: Abingdon Press, 2001.

Middleton, J. Richard. *The Liberating Image—The 'Imago Dei' in Genesis 1.* Grand Rapids, MI: Brazos Press, 2005.

Miller, Randall M., Harry S. Stout, and Charles R. Wilson, eds. *Religion and the American Civil War.* New York: Oxford Press, 1998.

Miller, Randall M. and Jon L. Wakelyn. *Catholics in the Old South.* Macon, GA: Mercer University Press, 1983.

Mitchell, Laura L. "Original Sin." *Books and Culture* 9, no. 4 (July/August 2003): 28–29.

Mitchell, Reid. *Civil War Soldiers.* New York: Penguin Books, 1988.

Monroe, Haskell. "Southern Presbyterians and the Secession Crisis." *Civil War History* 6, no.4 (1960): 351–360.

Montgomery, William H. *Under Their Own Vine and Fig Tree—African-American Churches in the South, 1865–1900.* Baton Rouge, LA: Louisiana State University Press, 1992.

Moorhead, James Howell. *American Apocalypse—Yankee Protestants and the Civil War, 1860–1869.* New Haven, CT: Yale University Press, 1978.

———. "The Role of Religion in the American Civil War: The Northern Side." http://nhc.rtp.nc.us:8080/tserve/nineteen/nkeyinfo/cwnorth.htm, National Humanities Center, October 2000.

Morgan, Edmund S. *Colonial America—Essays in Politics and Social Development.* New York: McGraw-Hill, 1993.

Murphy, Robert Joseph. "The Catholic Church in the United States during the Civil War Period." *Records of the American Catholic Historical Society;* vol. 39, no. 4 (December 1928): 350–375.

Niebuhr, Reinhold. "The Religion of Abraham Lincoln." *The Christian Century* 82 (February 10, 1965): 172–175.

Noll, Mark A. *America's God—from Jonathan Edwards to Abraham Lincoln.* New York: Oxford University Press, 2002.

———. *The Civil War as a Theological Crisis.* Chapel Hill: University of North Carolina Press, 2006.

———. "Getting It Half-Right." *Books and Culture* 9, no. 4 (July/August 2003): 18–19.

Noll, Mark A., Nathan Hatch, George Marsden, David Wells, and John Woodbridge, eds. *Eerdmans' Handbook to Christianity in America.* Grand Rapids, MI: Eerdman's Publishing Company, 1983.

Norton, Herman. "Revivalism in the Confederate Armies." *Civil War History* 6, no.4 (1960): 410–424.

Owen, Thomas, M. "Alabama—History and Culture." *The Catholic Encyclopedia, Volume I.* http://www.newadvent.org/cathen/01240a.htm (2006).

Paludan, Phillip Shaw. *A People's Contest—The Union and the Civil War, 1861–1865.* New York: Harper and Row, 1988.

Patterson, Gerard. *Debris of Battle.* Mechanicsburg, PA: Stackpole Books, 1997.

Perko, F. Michael. *Catholic and American—A Popular History.* Huntington, IN: Our Sunday Visitor Publishing, 1989.

Pierro, Joseph. "Praying with Robert E. Lee." *Civil War Times* 45, no. 1 (February 2006): 40–43.

Pitts, Charles F. *Chaplains in Gray—The Confederate Chaplains' Story.* Concord, VA: R.M.J.C. Publications, 2003.

Ransom, Roger L. *Conflict and Compromise—The Political Economy of Slavery, Emancipation, and the American Civil War.* Cambridge MA: Cambridge University Press, 1989.

Regan, Richard J. *Just War—Principles and Cases.* Washington, DC: Catholic University Press, 1996.

Richey, Russell and Donald G. Jones, eds. *American Civil Religion.* New York: Harper Forum Books, 1974.

Robertson, James I. *Soldiers Blue and Gray*. Columbia: University of South Carolina Press, 1988.

———. "The War in Words." *Civil War Times* 23, no. 6 (October 1983): 38–43.

———. "Tests of Honor." Pp. 7–13 in *Tenting Tonight, A Soldiers Life*. Alexandria, VA: Time Life Books, 1984.

Rolfs, David. "When Thou Goest Out to Battle." *Books and Culture* 9, no. 4 (July/August 2003): 19.

Romero, Sidney J. *Religion in the Rebel Ranks*. Lanham, MD: University Press of America, 1983.

Rosen, Robert H. *Jewish Confederates*. Columbia: University of South Carolina Press, 2003.

Schmier, Louis. "An Act Unbecoming." *Civil War Times Illustrated* 23, no. 6 (October 1984): 21–15.

Shattuck Jr., Gardiner. *A Shield and Hiding Place: The Religious Life of the Civil War Armies*. Macon GA: Mercer University Press, 1987.

Silver, James W. *Confederate Morale and Church Propaganda*. Tuscaloosa, AL: The Confederate Publishing Company, 1957.

Simon, John. "That Obnoxious Order." *Civil War Times Illustrated* 23, no. 6 (October 1984): 14–17.

Smith, Edward P. *Incidents of the Christian Commission*. Concord, VA: R.M.J.C. Publications, 2003.

Smith, H. Shelton. *In His Image, But . . . Racism in Southern Religion, 1780–1910*. Durham, NC: Duke University Press, 1972.

Smith, Page. *Trial by Fire—A People's History of the Civil War and Reconstruction*. New York: Penguin Books, 1982.

Snay, Mitchell. "Civil War Religion—Needs and Opportunities." *Civil War History* 49, no. 4 (December 2003): 388–394.

Stafford, Tim. "Still Writing the Civil War." *Books and Culture* 9, no. 4 (July/August 2003): 27.

Stampp, Kenneth M. *The Peculiar Institution—Religion in the Antebellum South*. New York: Vintage Books, 1956.

Stout, Harry S. "Baptism in Blood." *Books and Culture* 9, no. 4 (July/August 2003): 16–17, 33–35.

———. *Upon the Altar of the Nation—A Moral History of the Civil War*. New York: Viking/Penguin, 2006.

Stowell, Daniel W. "Crossing Jordan—The Black Quest for Religious Autonomy." Paper presented at the annual meeting of the American Society of Church History, Atlanta, GA, January 1996.

Stravinskas, Peter, ed. *Our Sunday Visitor's Catholic Encyclopedia*. Huntington IN: Our Sunday Visitor, 1991.

Sweet, William. "Lincoln and the Preachers." *The Mississippi Valley Historical Review* 36, no. 1 (June 1949): 145–46.

Talbott, John. "Combat Trauma in the American Civil War." *History Today* 46, no. 3 (March 1996): 41–47.

Thomas, Hugh. *The Slave Trade: The Story of the Atlantic Slave Trade, 1440–1870*. New York: Simon and Schuster, 1997.

Tolson, Jay. "The Faith of our Fathers." *U.S. News and World Report*, June 28/July 5, 2004: 54–57.

———. "Forget Politics. It's About the Music." *U.S. News and World Report*, April 19, 2004, 43–45.

Wacker, Grant. "Telling Lincoln." *Books and Culture* 9, no. 4 (July/August 2003): 20–21.

Wagner, Margaret, Gary Gallagher, and Paul Finkelman, eds. *Library of Congress Civil War Desk Reference*. New York: Simon and Schuster, 2002.

Wakelyn, Jon L. *Biographical Dictionary of the Confederacy*. Westport, CT: Greenwood Press, 1977.

Walters, Ronald G. *American Reformers 1815–1860*. New York: Hill and Wang, 1978.

Warren, Robert Penn. *The Legacy of the Civil War*. Lincoln, NE: University of Nebraska Press; 1961.

Wax, Bernard. "Illinois Jews in the Civil War." *Illinois Civil War Sketches,* no. 3 (June 1963).

West, John. "Going Back to Uncle Tom's Cabin." *Books and Culture* 9, no. 4 (July/August 2003): 27–29.

White, Ronald G. *Lincoln's Greatest Speech*. New York: Simon and Schuster, 2002.

Wight, Willard E. "The Churches and the Confederate Cause." *Civil War History* 6, no. 4 (September 1960): 361–373.

Wiley, Bell I. *Embattled Confederates—An Illustrated History of Southerners at War*. New York: Bonanza Books, 1950.

———. *The Life of Billy Yank*. Baton Rouge: Louisiana State University Press, 1952.

———. *The Life of Johnny Reb*. Baton Rouge: Louisiana State University Press, 1943.

Wilson, Charles Reagan. *Baptized in Blood—The Religion of the Lost Cause*. Athens, GA: University of Georgia Press, 1980.

Woodworth, Steven E. *While God is Marching On—The Religious Life of Civil War Soldiers*. Lawrence: University Press of Kansas, 2001.

———. "The Meaning of Life in the Valley of Death." *Civil War Times* 42, no. 5 (December 2003): 55–88.

Yoder, John Howard. *When War is Unjust*. New York: Orbis Books, 1996.

Diaries, Journals, and Biographies

Alexander, Edward Porter. *Fighting for the Confederacy—The Personal Recollections of General Edward Porter Alexander*. Gary Gallagher, ed. Chapel Hill: University of North Carolina Press, 1989.

Allardice, Bruce. *More Confederate Generals in Gray*. Baton Rouge: Louisiana State University Press, 1995.

Andrews, Rena Mazyck. *Archbishop Hughes and the Civil War*. Chicago: University of Chicago, 1935.

Armstrong, Chris. "People Worth Knowing—No Little Women Here." *Christian History and Biography*, Issue 81 (January 1, 2004): 43–45.

Baker, Nina Brown. *Cyclone in Calico*. Boston: Little Brown and Co., 1952.

Barton, George. "History of the Labors of Catholic Sisters in the Civil War." *Christian History Institute.* http:www.gospelcom.net/chi/HERITAGF/Issuenos/ch11033.shtml Fall 1999.

Beaudry, Louis N. *War Journal of Louis N. Beaudry, Fifth New York Cavalry.* Richard E. Beaudry, ed. Jefferson, NC: McFarland and Company Publishers, 1996.

Betts, A.D. "The Experiences of a Confederate Chaplain." W.A. Betts, ed. http:www.docsouth.unc.edu/betts/betts.html. 2000.

Buckley, Janet. "The Seton Family at War." *Surgeon's Call* (Summer 2004): 13–14.

Burchard, Peter. *One Gallant Rush.* New York: St. Martin's Press, 1965.

Carwardine, Richard. "The Wisest Radical of Them All." *Books and Culture* 9, no. 4 (July/August 2003): 20–21, 36.

"Chaplains During the Civil War of 1861." *Woodstock Letters* 14 (1885): 375–380.

Connelly, Donald B. *John M. Scofield and the Politics of Generalship.* Chapel Hill: University of North Carolina Press, 2006.

Corby, William. *Memoirs of Chaplain Life—Three Years with the Irish brigade in the Army of the Potomac.* Lawrence Frederick Kohl, ed. New York: Fordham University Press, 1992.

Davis, William C. *Breckinridge, Statesman, Soldier, Symbol.* Baton Rouge: Louisiana State University Press, 1974.

Dyer, John P. *"Fightin" Joe Wheeler.* Baton Rouge: Louisiana State University Press, 1941.

Ecelbarger, Gary. *Black Jack Logan.* Guilford, CT: The Lyons Press, 2005.

Elliott, Sam Davis. *General Alexander P. Stephens and the Civil War in the West.* Baton Rouge: Louisiana State University Press, 1999.

Elmore, Tom. "The Cavalier of Carolina." *Civil War Times* 43, no. 5 (December 2004): 55–79.

Faherty, William Barnaby. *Exile from Erin—A Confederate Chaplain's Story, the Life of Fr. John B. Bannon.* St. Louis: Missouri Historical Press, 2000.

Ferris, Marc. "Aunt Harriet's Home." *American Legacy* (Summer 2004): 63–68.

Fielder, Alfred. *The Civil War Diaries of Capt. Alfred Fielder, 12th TN Regiment Infantry, Company B, 1861–1865.* Ann York Franklin, ed. Louisville, KY: privately published, 1996.

Fisk, Wilbur. *Hard Marching Every Day: The Civil War Letters of Pvt. Wilbur Fisk 1861–65.* Emil Rosenblatt and Ruth Rosenblatt, eds. Lawrence: University of Kansas Press, 1992.

Fitzpatrick, Michael E. "The Mercy Brigade—Roman Catholic Nuns in the Civil War." *Civil War Times Illustrated* 36, no. 5 (October 1997): 34–40.

Franks, Kenny A. *Stand Watie and the Agony of the Cherokee Nation.* Memphis, TN: Me,mphis State University Press, 1979.

Fuller, James A. *Chaplain to the Confederacy: Basil Manly and Baptist Life in the Old South.* Baton Rouge: Louisiana State University Press, 2000.

Gache, Louis Hippolyte. *A Frenchman, a Chaplain, a Rebel—the Civil War Letters of Pere Louis Hippolyte Gache, SJ.* Cornelius Buckley, ed. Chicago: Loyola University Press, 1981.

Galli, Mark. "Firebrands and Visionaries." *Christian History;* vol. 11, no. 1 (1992): 33–35.

Gannon, Michael V. *Rebel Bishop—The Life and Era of Augustin Verot.* Milwaukee: Bruce Publishing Company, 1964.

Gerdes, Sr. M. Regina. "To Educate and Evangelize—Black Catholic Schools of Oblate Sisters of Providence (1828–1880)." *U.S. Catholic Historian* 7, no. 2/3 (1988): 183–199.

Griggs Jr., Walter S. *General John Pegram, C.S.A.* Lynchburg, VA: H. E. Howard, 1993.

Haney, Milton. *The Story of My Life.* Normal, IL: privately published, 1904.

Hassler, William Woods. *A.P. Hill—Lee's Forgotten General.* Chapel Hill: University of North Carolina Press, 1957.

Hartje, Robert G. *Van Dorn: The Life and Times of a Confederate General.* Nashville, TN: Vanderbilt University Press, 1967.

Hettle, Wallace. "The Minister, the Martyr and the Maxim—Robert Lewis Dabney and Stonewall Jackson." *Civil War History* 49, no. 4 (December 2003): 353–369.

Higginson, Thomas Wentworth. *Army Life in a Black Regiment and Other Writings.* New York: Penguin Books, 1997.

Hollandsworth Jr., James G. *Pretense of Glory: The Life of General Nathaniel P. Banks.* Baton Rouge: Louisiana State University Press, 1998.

Holmes Jr., Oliver Wendell. *Touched by Fire—Civil War Letters and Diary of Oliver Wendell Holmes Jr. 1861–1864.* Mark de Wolfe Howe, ed. Cambridge, MA: Howard University Press; 1946.

Honeywell, Roy. "Men of God in Uniform." *Civil War Times Illustrated* 6 (August 1967): 31–36.

Hudson, Leonne M. *The Odyssey of a Southerner: The Life and Times of Gustavus Woodson Smith.* Macon, GA: Mercer University Press, 1998.

Jordan, David M. *Winfield Scott Hancock: A Soldier's Life.* Bloomington: Indiana University Press, 1988.

Kenneth, Lee. *Sherman.* New York: Harper Collins, 2001.

King, T.S. "Letters of Civil War Chaplains—Peter Tissot S.J." *Woodstock Letters* 43 (1914): 169–180.

Kinsley, D.A. *Custer: Favor the Bold.* New York: Promontory Press, 1988.

Longacre, Edward G. *Joshua Chamberlain: The Soldier and the Man.* Conshohocken, PA: Combined Publishers, 1999.

Lucey, William L. "The Diary of Joseph B. O'Hagan, S.J., Chaplain of the Excelsior Brigade" *Civil War History* 6, no.4 (1960): 402–409.

Marzalek, John. "The Inventor of Total Warfare." *Notre Dame Magazine* 18, no. 2 (Summer 1989): 28–30.

———. *Sherman—A Soldier's Passion for Order.* New York: Vintage Civil War Library, 1993.

Meaney, Peter J. "Valiant Chaplain of the Bloody Tenth." *Tennessee Historical Quarterly* 41, no. 1 (Spring 1982): 37–47.

Milham, Charles G. *Gallant Pelham.* Washington, DC: Public Affairs Press, 1959.

Niven, John. *Gideon Welles: Lincoln's Secretary of the Navy.* New York: Oxford University Press, 1973.

Nolan, Richard. *Benjamin Franklin Butler, the Damndest Yankee.* Novato, CA: Presidio Press, 1991.

"Obituary of Father Joseph O'Hagan." *Woodstock Letters* 8, (1879): 173–183.

Ochs, Stephen J. *A Black Patriot and A White Priest—Andre Cailloux and Claude Paschal Maistre in Civil War New Orleans.* Baton Rouge, LA: Louisiana State University Press, 2000.

Parks, Joseph H. *General Leonidas Polk, C.S.A.—The Fighting Bishop.* Baton Rouge: Louisiana State University Press, 1962.

Partin, Robert. "The Sustaining Faith of an Alabama Soldier." *Civil War History* 6, no.4 (1960): 425–438.

Quintard, Charles. *Doctor Quintard, Chaplain CSA and Second Bishop of Tennessee.* Sam Davis Elliot, ed. Baton Rouge: Louisiana State University Press, 2003.

Rafuse, Ethan S. "He Started the Civil War." *Civil War Times* 41, no, 5 (October 2002): 24–30.

Ramage, James A. *Rebel Raider: The Life of John Hunt Morgan.* Lexington: University Press of Kentucky, 1986.

Rhodes, Elisha Hunt. *All for the Union—The Civil War Diary and Letters of Elisha Hunt Rhodes.* Robert H. Rhodes, ed. New York: Orion Books, 1985.

Rissler, Elizabeth. "The Preacher's Regiment." *Illinois Civil War Sketches* no. 1 (June 1963).

Robertson, James I. *Stonewall Jackson—The Man, The Soldier, The Legend.* New York: MacMillan Publishers, 1997.

Rolle, Andrew. *John Charles Fremont.* Norman: University of Oklahoma Press, 1991.

Scott, Jeffrey Warren. "Fighters of Faith." *Christian History* vol. 11, no. 1 (1992): 18–22.

Sheeran, James B. *Confederate Chaplain—A Military Journal.* Joseph T. Durkin, ed. Milwaukee: Bruce Publishing, 1960.

Springer, Francis. *The Preachers Tale—The Civil War Journal of Rev. Francis Springer, Chaplain, U.S. Army of the Frontier.* William Furry, ed. Fayetteville: University of Alabama Press, 2001.

Stuckenberg, John Henry. *I'm Surrounded by Methodists—Diary of John H.W. Stuckenberg, Chaplain of the 145th Pennsylvania Volunteer Infantry.* David T. Hedrick and Gordon Barry Davis, Jr., eds. Gettysburg, PA: Thomas Publications, 1995.

Taaffe, Thomas Gaffney. "Rev. Peter Tissot—A Year with the Army of the Potomac." *Historical Records and Studies* 3, no. 1 (January 1903): 38–85.

Thomas, Benjamin P., and Harold M. Hyman. *Stanton: The Life and Times of Lincoln's Secretary of War.* New York: Alfred A. Knopf, 1962.

Tucker, Philip T. *The Confederate Fighting Chaplain—Father John B. Bannon.* Tuscaloosa, AL: University of Alabama Press, 1992.

Wakelyn, Jon L. *Biographical Dictionary of the Confederacy.* Westport, CT: Greenwood Press, 1977.

Weddle, Kevin J. *Lincoln's Tragic Admiral.* Charlottesville: University of Virginia Press, 2005.

Wiatt, William Edward. *Confederate Chaplain William Edward Wiatt—An Annotated Diary.* Alex L. Wiatt, ed. Lynchburg, VA: The Virginia Civil War Battles & Leaders Series, 1994.

Wight, Willard E. "The Bishop of Natchez and the Confederate Chaplaincy." *Mid-America—An Historical Review* 39, no. 2 (April 1957): 67–71.

Young, Kenneth R. *The General's General: The Life and Times of Arthur MacArthur.* Boulder, CO: Westview Press, 1994.

Index

About the Author

Robert J. Miller is a Roman Catholic priest, presently ministering as pastor of a south-side Chicago African-American congregation. For more than a decade, he has taught Church History (Ecclesiology) in the Archdiocese of Chicago's deacon formation program, and spoken frequently on the topic of Civil War religion and church history. From 2003–2006, he held official positions in the *Civil War Round Table of Chicago*, helping lead two battlefield tours, and becoming President of that group in 2005–2006. This book (*Both Prayed to the Same God*) is the result of a long study of the topic of Civil War religion, and research done a 6-month sabbatical at Notre Dame University in early 2006.

In 1996 he was the founder of *Genesis Housing Development Corporation,* a faith-based group building affordable housing on Chicago's south-side—a group that he continues to be active Chair of to this day. Ordained in 1976, he has traveled extensively around the country in the teaching and preaching of missions, retreats and spiritual renewal events. He holds a B.A. in Philosophy, and M.A. degrees in Religious Education and Divinity. He has authored five previous books (as well as numerous articles), including *Finding Your Place in the Universe* (Abbey Press, 1995), *GriefQuest—Reflections and Stories for Men Coping with Loss* (Abbey Press, 1996), *Falling into Faith* (Sheed & Ward, 2000), *Fire in the Deep* (2001) and *Surprised by Love* (2002). His hobbies are walking, piano-playing, Civil War history, and computer games.